ON PATHS
OF ASH

Robert Holman
edited by Peter Thomson

ON PATHS OF ASH

The extraordinary story of an Australian prisoner of war

Contents

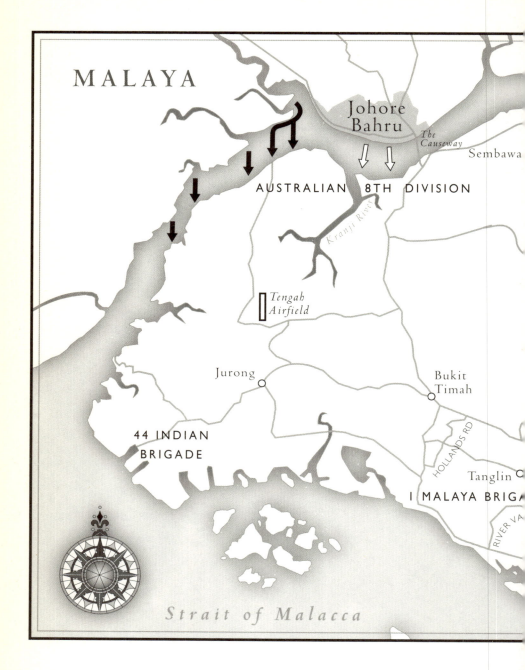

MALAYA

Johore
Bahru

*The
Causeway*

Sembawa

AUSTRALIAN   8TH   DIVISION

Kranji River

Tengah
Airfield

Jurong ○

Bukit
Timah ○

44 INDIAN
BRIGADE

HOLLANDS RD

Tanglin ○

I MALAYA BRIGA

RIVER VA

Strait of Malacca

Source: Lionel Wigmore, *Australia in the War of 1939–1945: Series One, Army, Vol. IV – The Japanese Thurst*, Canberra, 1957

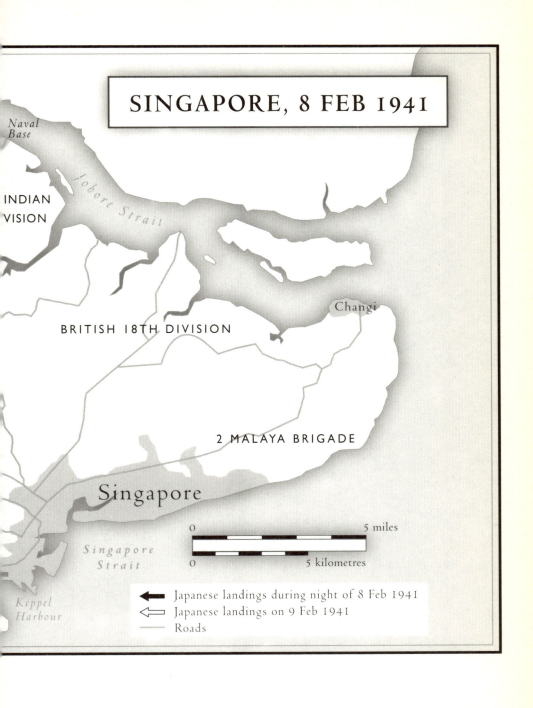

SINGAPORE, 8 FEB 1941

Naval Base

INDIAN VISION

Johore Strait

Changi

BRITISH 18TH DIVISION

2 MALAYA BRIGADE

Singapore

Singapore Strait

Keppel Harbour

0   5 miles

0   5 kilometres

Japanese landings during night of 8 Feb 1941
Japanese landings on 9 Feb 1941
Roads

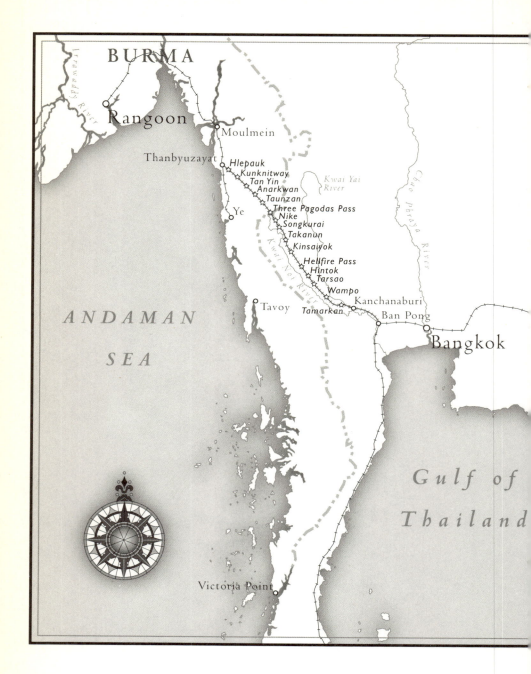

Sources: Rowley Richards, *A Doctor's War*, HarperCollins, Sydney, 2006, and
Brian MacArthur, *Surviving the Sword*, Random House, New York, 2005

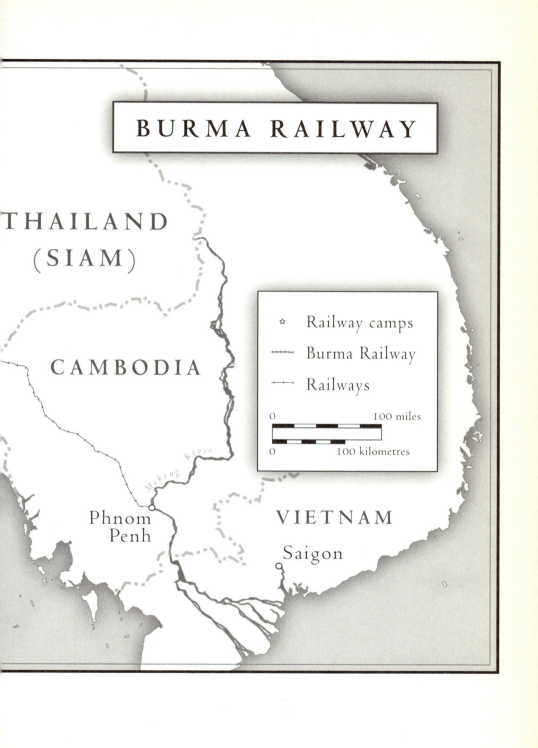

BURMA RAILWAY

THAILAND
(SIAM)

CAMBODIA

Mekong River

Phnom
Penh

VIETNAM

Saigon

☆ Railway camps

╫╫╫ Burma Railway

┼┼┼ Railways

0   100 miles

0   100 kilometres

KYUSHU ISLAND, JAPAN

HONSHU

Moji

Kokura

Shimonoseki Strait

Fukuoka

Omuta
△ FUKUOKA BRANCH
CAMP NO. 17

Nagasaki

KYUSHU

Miyazaki

Sendai

EAST

CHINA

SEA

0   50 miles

0   50 kilometres

⇦ Planned invasion US Forces
Operation Olympic, Nov 1945

Editor's Introduction

Bright sunlight, the year 2006, and I was reading the morning papers over breakfast in my Darlinghurst courtyard. On the obituaries page of the *Sydney Morning Herald*, I noted the passing of Jack Holman on 8 September and read for the first time of the way fate cruelled Jack and his brother Robert in World War II. Robert, I read, had passed away the year before. I was deeply moved by their story and it stayed with me for a long while after. I found myself reflecting – not for the first time – on the wartime adversity of their generation, and how they gave us the peace and plenty of our times.

Eight months later, the publisher rang to ask if I'd be prepared to work on a book about two brothers who'd been POWs on the Burma Railway. They said the brothers had subsequently gone to Japan to toil as slave labourers in a coal mine and one of them had witnessed the Nagasaki atomic explosion. One of the brothers had left a memoir of his wartime experiences. With a growing sense that fate was delivering a coalescent moment, I asked if they were perhaps referring to the Holman brothers.

That was the beginning of a long journey for me. I read Robert Holman's memoir and found further works he'd deposited in the archives of the University of Wollongong. In books, web pages and unpublished memoirs, I examined myriad POW records. I saw how all the words the surviving POWs wrote were first and foremost in honour of their dead mates, and that however painful the task of holding to those memories, there was a vigilance about them in bearing witness to the atrocities they had endured. As I delved further, reading their words, I wept many tears of bitter sorrow. But there were tears of joy as well, for their accounts tell of the spirit of compassion among the dying, of acts of selfless kindness, delight in small things, and of an end to unimaginable suffering.

In the course of my research, I spent an afternoon at the home of Dr Rowley Richards in Sydney. It was one of the treasured days of my life: I felt as if I had stepped through a time portal with a very special guide, for this great man had spent his war years saving countless lives. Richards was the same man who had stood on the wretched deck of an oil tanker in Hainan, under a punishing sun, after the sinking of the Japanese vessels *Rakuyo Maru* and *Kachidoki Maru* with their cargo of Allied POWs. Over 500 anguished POWs coated in oil sizzled on the hot metal before him. For twenty-four hours this human flotsam had swum in the thick oil slicks of their sunken ship and, in the words of Dr Richards, were now the living dead. With no medical supplies or instruments of any sort – for their captors would give no assistance but a bucket to collect seawater – Dr Richards had set to, tending to the burnt flesh, blinded eyes and broken limbs.

We talked of how the survivors of the Burma Railway had clad themselves in their own choice of personal armour, with duty, loyalty, humour, faith, hope and mateship all on the list. We talked of the damage they carried with them, of the destruction of sensitivity, of the sometimes precarious nature of the will to live, and of the hard-won wisdom of discerning what we can and cannot control.

Jack and Robert Holman having both passed on, it was in my meeting with Dr Richards that I first shook hands with a representative of Anderson Force. This was the group of POWs that Robert Holman was part of, the first force to be sent to labour on what became known as the Railway of Death. Through the clarity of the good doctor's thoughts, his record-keeping and the obvious strength of his will, I was able to gain some understanding of the consequences of the railway and the POW experience. And though I could never sup from the same bitter cup, I got hints of its taste as I listened to one who'd supped so deeply.

During the process of editing and notating Robert Holman's memoir, I discovered in some of his other writing how deeply troubled he was by thoughts of the suffering of women and children held in Japan's POW camps around Asia. He was right to be troubled, as I can attest as a personal witness to the long-term effects of such suffering. In the course of my working on this book, my wife's mother, Loelie Wynberg, passed away. She spent three and a half years of her youth in the POW camps of Java, while her father, a doctor, rotted in a jungle camp on the island of Sumatra and her older brother was detained in a boys' camp. The horrors of what Loelie, her siblings and her mother endured in those camps belong to another story. After liberation, Loelie Wynberg battled on and grew to be a woman known for staunch resilience and keen intelligence, and she bore and raised seven beautiful children. But like most who went through those camps, she suffered the consequences, her existence forever scarred by the Imperial Japanese Army's peculiar cruelties. When we stood by the coffin at Loelie's funeral, her younger brother told me that when you pared it all down, ever since those camps in Java she'd spent most of her life afraid. My work on this book is dedicated to her memory, saying now what I wish I'd said to her in life: 'Fear no more, Loelie, fear no more.'

What follows in these pages is the story of a fettler and a carpenter. Robert and Jack Holman, two brothers from a working-class Sydney family, were born into hard times. For them, family was everything, and when the Depression came down and hard times got harder, the story tells how the power of family love carried them through. Jack and Robert were the kind of men you pass by every day, doing their daily work, attending to their responsibilities, hoping only to live in a world of decency. But just two decades after the war to end all wars, belligerent militarism was back, and Jack and Robert were of the age that armies require.

So the Holman brothers stepped forward to slog it out as foot soldiers for Australia. Their destinies were not heroic, but they battled manfully at the front and they were diggers who always did their duty. The war took them to South-east Asia and the battles that lost Malaya and then Singapore. In 1942 they marched into Changi as prisoners of war and were soon in the holds of ships bound for Burma. There they laboured on the Burma Railway – the Railway of Death – at the pleasure of the Emperor of Japan. Reduced to emaciation by institutionalised brutality, starvation and disease, the Holmans survived that atrocity, only to be taken on a box-wagon odyssey to Saigon and Singapore, for eventual shipment as slaves to the coal mines of Japan.

Robert and Jack Holman had done what their country asked of them, going to the defence of their homeland against a militaristic aggressor, and it could never be said of them that they took their birthright for granted. They were to experience in full the ignominy of Singapore's fall and they fought bravely to the end, alongside many an Allied soldier who did the same. After three and half years of intense suffering, when the prison gates were finally thrown open Jack and Robert Holman were in the mob of damaged survivors who emerged to set off on the long road home.

And when they got home, their heads were not held high in pride; they'd seen too much, and carried too much with them, to hold themselves that way. They were men who came home bearing reports of dead mates and the outrages inflicted upon them. They received no medals for their sacrifice, nor asked for them, but they would always be men who'd performed their duty. No one could take that away from them. And if their spirits were always to bear the weight of the injustices laid on them, their consciences were clear, for they'd done the right thing by Australia and their fellow men. They'd returned home with integrity intact.

By the time of World War II, the Japanese Empire had been in an expansion mode for fifty years. As a result, the rising sun banner was fluttering over the Ryuku Islands, Taiwan and the Pescadores, the Korean Peninsula, most of Micronesia, Manchuria, Inner Mongolia and increasingly large chunks of China. The advent of Emperor Hirohito's reign in 1926 had carried the institution of emperor-worship and militaristic nationalism to a point where it had quite overcome Japan, with civilian government effectively unable to control the imperial-military cult from 1932 onwards.

In 1940, Tokyo signed up to the Tripartite Pact, putting itself into Axis league with the fascist states of Europe. With the German occupation of the majority of Europe already a *fait accompli*, Tokyo's imperial ambitions turned to areas of opportunity in Asia, where the rich prize would be the natural resources of the Dutch East Indies, with Malaya and Singapore to be taken along the way. In Europe, the Nazis had the Dutch firmly under their jackboot and had backed the British into their bomb-battered island home. There was no better time for a rival power to seize Malaya, Singapore and the Indies, and that is exactly what imperial Japan did.

The awful excesses of the IJA, the Imperial Japanese Army, before and during World War II were recorded and revealed to the world. Thus at war's end, for its crimes against humanity the IJA was consigned to its rightful place: oblivion. At the same time, Emperor Hirohito's fate hung with the head of the Allied occupation force in Japan, General Douglas MacArthur. He chose to work with Hirohito, and in balance he chose wisely; for, as he predicted, by reinventing the tarnished emperor as a man of peace dedicated to constitutional monarchy, Japan's resuscitation as a stable democracy was greatly facilitated.

Sufficient years have now passed for the pragmatism of MacArthur's choice to have been demonstrated to a grateful world. In Japan itself, respect for democracy and the full measure of human rights has become entrenched. Nonetheless, when I lived in Tokyo in the 1980s, most days in the streets of inner Tokyo right-wing extremists drove around in ex-military vehicles with loudspeakers blaring propaganda and marching music from the bad old days of the IJA. My Japanese friends explained the murky links between these noisy extremists, the imperial-militaristic cult of old and the influence of the *yakuza* underworld.

These same friends were appalled that as a diplomat I was sometimes rubbing shoulders with people they regarded as notorious: certain politicians and grand businessmen known in Japanese society to have had highly questionable war records. They also cautioned me about being too candid in my questions pertaining to World War II and the imperial-militaristic regime, saying it was still taboo to talk about the Emperor's involvement in the war. This advice rang in my ears when I read about Hitoshi Motoshima, the mayor of Nagasaki. In January 1990, Mayor Motoshima answered a question at a city council meeting with some moderate words on Emperor Hirohito's war responsibility. As a result, Motoshima was subjected to a barrage of threats and before the day was out, had been shot in the chest by an ultranationalist.

There is little excuse not to know today of the Imperial Japanese Army's unconscionable conduct in World War II. We live in an age of easy access to information and enough time has passed for declassifications and oral histories to have overcome the expedient obfuscations thrown up by General MacArthur's fixers. Indeed, to obtain information on even the most obscure of subjects, all we need today is a computer screen and access to the internet. The websites that pop up in the main give dispassionate summary reports, but therein the IJA's heinous deeds are laid bare: the Sandakan Death Marches, the Sook Ching Massacre, the Rape of Nanking, Unit 731 of Pingfan, the hellship *Oryoku Maru*, the Banka Island Massacre, the suffering of the 'Comfort Women' – the list is long, and infamous.

Robert Holman was vigilant in his post-war stand whenever he encountered revisionism. Apologists for Japan's excesses in World War II like to say that at the very least, the Japanese freed Asia of its European colonial rulers. Hirohito's capitulation speech at the end of the war more than hinted at this lie. It is true that the age of empires, an age that had dominated global geography for the preceding 500 years, came to an end not long after 1945. But it is equally true that no political credit for that fact lies with Japan.

The termination of the age of empires was due to moral force emanating from many quarters, particularly from enlightened movements for national independence and the leadership of people of the stature of Mahatma Gandhi. Moreover, it insults the historic achievements of such people, begun long before World War II, to have them associated, however tenuously, with the imposed economic order the Japanese dubbed the Greater East Asia Co-Prosperity Sphere. As was made morbidly clear to the press-ganged Asian labourers on the Railway of Death, the Co-Prosperity Sphere was in essence a Japanese resource-grab, and rather than ridding Asia of imperialism, the Sphere was a last desperate bid at prolonging it, with Hirohito at its Asian pinnacle.

In the course of the imposition of the Co-Prosperity Sphere, over 10 million people in the Asia-Pacific region met their deaths at the hands of imperial Japan's aggression, largely through its organ of relentless brutality and control, the Imperial Japanese Army. Driven by brutal discipline, cultish certainty, racial hatred and supposedly divine leadership, the IJA managed to pull off the Asian Holocaust, one of the great democides of modern history.

For POWs like Robert and Jack Holman, the story of the twentieth century will not be properly told unless the acronym IJA carries the weight of a reputation as heinous as Hitler's SS, or unless the words *Kempei Tai* are classed in the same appalling company as *Gestapo*. The *Kempei Tai*, the military police of the IJA, had special responsibilities for the IJA's 'Comfort Women' brothels and regulated the camps for forced labour and POWs. More will be learnt of them in the course of Robert Holman's memoir.

'Forgive, but do not forget' is the POW mantra, with the onus on those who respect the terrible sacrifices made to keep the record true. It is not often the Nazis get a tick, but the record shows it was seven times more lethal for Allied prisoners to be incarcerated in IJA camps than it was to be held in German POW camps during World War II.

The manuscript of Robert Holman's original memoir, written in his meticulous hand, is contained in a collection of exercise books in the archives of the University of Wollongong, New South Wales. Before they were deposited in the archives in 1988, Robert lent the books to the schools of the southern Illawarra area, in the hope they would give students a greater understanding of their heritage. It was his wish that one day his memoir would be published for the furtherance of this purpose.

Robert's niece, Robyn Moss, typed up a manuscript incorporating Robert's main memoir and some of the short tales he had appended in his exercise books. It was this typed manuscript that was used as the working document for *On Paths of Ash*. Robert had written his memoir as a continuous narrative, but in the editing process of this work, for the sake of readers, it was divided into chapters. Also, where relevant to the story, a few of his short tales have been incorporated into the narrative.

It should be noted that Robert did not keep a journal during his war experiences and that his memoir was written some decades after the events described. It was thus an important part of the editing process to double-check Robert's facts and assertions, where possible performing multiple checks. The checking process was greatly assisted by three books – *Slaves of the Son of Heaven* by Roy Whitecross, *A Doctor's War* by Dr Rowley Richards, and *The Japanese Thrust* by Lionel Wigmore. Roy Whitecross and Dr Richards were both members of Anderson Force and thus followed the same tracks as Robert Holman from Changi to the end of the Railway of Death. Roy Whitecross subsequently made the same odyssey as the Holman brothers to Saigon, Singapore and Kyushu. Lionel Wigmore's book is the Australian official war history of the Japanese invasion of Malaya and Singapore, incorporating a section on the experiences of Australian prisoners of war in Asia.

Memoirs of recollection are subject to tricks of memory and there are some simple errors of fact in Robert's original manuscript. These were corrected during the editing process – for example, the Omuta mine in Kyushu belonged not to Mitsubishi, as recollected by Robert, but to Mitsui. Where a contentious assertion in the manuscript was not able to be verified, it was omitted – a measure taken for the sake of both the reader and the publisher, in the knowledge that the original manuscript is extant at the archives of the University of Wollongong.

No attempt has been made to edit out contentious assertions that were unverifiable or subjective, such as Robert's expression of prejudices of the time. Readers will come across racially charged comments in the memoir that they may find quite unacceptable, with Robert Holman giving vent to his prejudices, not just against Japanese oppressors, but his allies the Dutch and English as well. As trying as it may be to today's readers, leaving such commentary within the published text allows the memoir to stay true to its times, for a wider reading of POW accounts demonstrates Robert Holman was by no means alone in holding these views.

Robert and Jack Holman were indeed men of their time, and it was the toughest of times. Fate had them enter a realm of great injustice after Singapore fell, when they became prisoners of the Imperial Japanese Army. For as subjects of the IJA camps on the Railway of Death, they came to a place beyond the perimeters of human decency, a place governed by the darkness of bestial guards, killer diseases and an imperial-militaristic cult that was increasingly desperate for survival. The prisoners' light shone on in that darkness; a light distilled from the spirit of mateship, from compassion and a faith that one day justice would prevail. Some men died awful deaths and some lived on through the ordeal, with the survivors taking on the burden of testimony for the living and the dead. That these men were damaged by their wartime experience is beyond question, and Robert Holman wrote that he, and many others like him, never did fit back into civilian society. But they had seen that light in the darkness and it had meant everything to them. This is Robert Holman's story of those times; a story that fulfils his commitment to let that light shine on.

Peter Thomson, Sydney, September 2008

Sydney

Now that I am retired I thought I might write down a rough summary of my life up till just after World War II. I can sit down now and contemplate, as reliably as memory will allow me, the many interesting things that have happened to me over the years, and feel a genuine sympathy for those unfortunate people whose lives have just been one monotonous day after another. With whatever time I have left to live I can sit in the warm sun and re-live the past, or sit by my fire on a cold winter's night and, looking into the flames, let memory take me back through those wonderful days. Once again I can hear the thunder of the guns, the roar of bombers overhead, the sight of monstrous green waves and the screaming of a gale wind through the rigging of a ship; the sounds of the jungle and the sight of rough, rugged men transformed into gentle ministering angels. Most of all I treasure the knowledge of having rubbed shoulders with some of the bravest, greatest men who ever trod this earth.

I, Robert Holman, was born early in the morning of the twelfth day of February, 1919, the youngest of a family of six children: two girls and four boys. A kindly Irish midwife assisted with the birth. I don't know if there is such a thing as reincarnation, but I realise that on that morning I was fortunate to have been born into such a kind, considerate family. My parents were simple working-class Australians of British origin. My mother was of Welsh descent and my father's forebears came from Sussex. Our house was a simple weatherboard dwelling of the period, situated at 88 Greenhills Street in the Sydney suburb of Croydon. My father was a glazier by trade and worked hard, long hours for little money, and only for the fact that my mother was a good manager, we would have gone hungry like many people during those early years.

As well as the members of my family I became accustomed to the company of a friend of the family known to us children as Uncle Bert, who was a friend of my parents. Uncle Bert was a returned soldier of the Great War which had just ended, and he was suffering from war neurosis. It seems he felt more relaxed and happy in the company of children, and fortunately he didn't mind nursing me. I was a frail, sickly child and prone to cry a lot, and my mother was only too glad to hand me over to Uncle Bert to nurse. He would rock me gently in his arms whilst singing the popular World War I song 'Smile Awhile', and within minutes I would be sound asleep.

Although the war had officially ended in 1918, troops were still returning during 1919 and they brought back with them the deadly influenza virus, which had swept through Europe with devastating results. Unfortunately, the Holman family were also among its victims. I remember my mother saying that both she and I had hovered between life and death, and that the local Methodist minister went down on his knees and prayed I would live, knowing that if I died my mother would probably die too. My mother said I just looked like a little wrinkled Chinaman. My old, wrinkled, stoop-backed grandfather was the hero of the day, doing all the odd jobs about the place and running messages. Mum said he smoked a dirty old pipe and had claimed that the nicotine in his bloodstream had protected him. Everyone had finally recovered and then down went Granddad, but he wasn't down for long due to the nicotine killing off the virus, so he boasted.[1]

From what my mother told me, my very early childhood was bound up with a series of pets, and I think my mother learned very early that I wasn't really interested in what humans did, but I was interested in animals and birds. My brother Jim was older and learned things quicker, and passed them down to me, so that if my older brothers read books by James Fenimore Cooper about Indian savages raiding and scalping in America, all these exciting stories would eventually reach me. I do faintly remember sailing a wooden canoe filled with tiny Indians I had made with clay in a tub of water, and I used to dream about America.

Visits to the zoo were like visits to Paradise. The trip on the ferry was a real adventure and as we crossed the harbour, Dad would point out objects of interest, and Jim would pass the information back to me. The sights of the harbour, the salt water, the screaming seagulls, the huge battleships moored at anchor, the hooting and tooting of the busy tugs and colliers with their tall smoking stacks – it was all very intoxicating to me. Sometimes Dad would take Jim and me out to Gladesville, where he would hire a rowboat and row us around the cargo steamers anchored in the Parramatta River.

There was a lonely little girl who lived next door to us in Croydon and my mother used to order me to play with her. I remember getting upset about this one day, and Jim defended me. 'You can't expect him to play with that snotty-nosed little brat,' he said. 'She's always getting worms, and besides, she has candles hanging out her nose.' Little did

13

Jim know that he would later marry this snotty-nosed little brat. And when he led me out onto the street to watch the early biplanes slowly droning across the sky, he couldn't foresee that one day he would be in the ground-crew of an Australian Air Force bomber.

My main trouble in those days was the clash of wills between my mother and myself over taking castor oil, or playing with the girl Marjorie next door. When we did play it was mostly the morbid game of burial. We would discover a dead bird or mouse, or some small creature, and after placing the tiny corpse in a matchbox or tobacco tin, we would bury it. I would construct a wooden cross and place it at the head of the grave and cover the grave with white gravel. Then Marj would make a wreath of flowers and place it on the grave. I asked Marjorie what happened when you died and were put in a coffin and buried, and she said you went up to heaven and lived with God. Remembering a swallow which we had placed in a tobacco tin and buried near the fence months before, I decided to dig it up to see if the tin was empty. All I found was a stinking, oily-looking mess and a few decayed feathers. From then on I decided to be wary of believing all Marjorie's beautiful stories.

The old weatherboard houses of the period used to have an outlet pipe known as a stink pipe, which was bracketed to the wall of the house and extended several feet above the guttering. I had watched my brothers climb up this pipe and I knew I could climb it too, but I was also afraid of heights and this had deterred me from attempting to copy them. Then one morning, Mum suggested I needed a dose of castor oil and up that pipe I went like a monkey, refusing to come down till she promised not to give me castor oil again. But from then on I received vile senna tea instead, whenever Mum thought I needed medicine. I didn't win every battle, as I found out when I threatened to run away from home and never come back again. This threat was greeted by a casual wave of the hand from my mother, accompanied by the words,

'All right, away you go. Ta ta.' Whereupon I would wander up to the local carrier's house and watch the solid rubber-tyred Dennis trucks and Stanley steam trucks coming and going from their sheds at the rear of the house. The Stanley Steamer, with its tall funnel belching smoke and high shrieking whistle, was a real spectacle. Our neighbour used to ask Mum, 'Aren't you afraid, Mrs Holman, that Bob will really clear off somewhere one day?' And Mum would reply, 'No, I know he'll come back when he starts to get hungry.' This battle with my mother and my stomach I always lost.

My mother was a practising Christian and was always ready to be the good Samaritan, so I wasn't afraid to bring in a poor little stray puppy I found on the street. I asked Mum why he walked in a wobbly fashion and she explained that he was suffering from malnutrition and had what was known as rickets. He was christened Mac and was given a warm bed and warm soup, but still walked with a wobbly gait for quite a while before he recovered. Our baker, when seeing him for the first time, called out, 'Hello, Staggers.' Mac took instant affront and barked angrily at him every time he called after that. Then came the terrible day when Mum alighted from a tram up at the corner and little Mac, wagging his tail happily, ran forward to meet her. A large vicious dog rushed out of a house and seizing poor little inoffensive Mac in his large jaws, crushed the life out of him. I was sick with shock and horror as Mum tenderly carried Mac's broken body inside the gate. I had learned a lesson in life – it is the large animal who will crush the smaller and weaker animal. I would never forget this lesson as I was to see it dramatised many more times in the following years. That was a sad day in my life.

The baker's horse was one of my adopted pets and used to be given a loving pat and handfuls of grass every time he pulled up in front of our house. However, one day the baker leapt onto his cart and, seizing his whip, he whipped the horse across the flanks. Flushed with sudden anger, I rushed after the cart, gathering handfuls of loose metal off the roadside and pelting the baker with it. He returned and protested to my mother, who had to explain to him my intense love for animals and that to me he was doing something very cruel. It took the baker a while to forgive me, but he never ever struck his horse in front of me again.

It was a sad day for me when I had to go to school and mix with other boys. I soon learned one thing: I was the proverbial square peg that wouldn't fit in the round hole. In class I was always in trouble for not paying attention. The teachers complained that I wasn't a bit interested in what they were trying to teach me, but that I was more interested in such things as a bird building a nest in a tree outside the schoolroom, or the shape and colour of passing clouds. In essence, I appeared to be a dreamer, not a scholar, and was living in a world of my own.

To make matters worse, I wasn't an aggressive type of boy and the other boys learned that I avoided fights with anyone, so it wasn't long before the word was passed around that I was a real punching bag and that was what I became – a punching bag for any boy who wished to assert his masculinity. I appealed to my brother Jim for assistance, but he just told me to learn to solve my own problems. My solution was to hide outside the school till the bell rang, and then run into the school and line up with my class. I would then hear the bullies grumbling, 'Where have you been all this time, Holman?'

An event occurred during this early school period which would increase my growing distrust of my fellow man. A parcel was thrown over the school playground fence, landing very close to where my brother Jim and some other boys were playing. When they looked towards the parcel they noticed that the paper around it had burst on impact and a tiny baby hand was exposed to view. The teacher was summoned and soon children were being kept away from the area. I questioned Jim about it and he told me the parcel contained the body of a baby all cut up in little pieces. I was horrified and could not understand why any man or woman could kill a helpless, innocent baby.

One day, coming home from school I noticed some boys standing beneath a tall black pine tree, looking upward. Arriving at the spot, I too looked up, and there right in the topmost branches of this tree, which was all of fifty feet in height, was a dove caught up by the leg in a snare. It had evidently broken a ground snare made of fishing line and had flown to the top of the tree with some of the fishing line still dangling from its foot, and now the line was caught in a small branch and the bird hung, beak downwards. My brother Jim had inspected this tree and had formed the opinion, which had been passed on to me, that the tree could easily be climbed because the branches were all close together. All I can remember of the climbing of that tree was that I was terrified all the way up and all the way down. I just kept my mind on saving that dove and slowly but surely I made my way up, broke off the branch, and with the dove safely tucked inside my shirt, climbed down again. At no point, either on the way up or down was I going to look downwards or I would have frozen to the branch with fear. If I were asked to climb that tree today I wouldn't be game to attempt it and yet I was only seven years old and a nervous little boy at that when I performed my act of mercy.

My father had injured his right thumb several times at work, bruising the same area each time. At first he complained of a nagging pain in his thumb and then his hand and he was finding it desperately hard to continue working. Now the pain had spread up his arm and persuaded him to visit a doctor, who sent him to an x-ray clinic, where his lower arm and hand were x-rayed. After examining the x-rays the doctor told my mother that Dad had a bone-eating cancer called sarcoma, which meant that he would now die slowly and painfully. I think Mum may have told him that he had bad rheumatism and needed rest.

To try to cut down the noise which might upset my father, Mum used to send us younger boys up to our aunty and uncle and grandparents, who lived in Georges River Road – a bus and tram route passed their front fences, which was an added attraction. White buses used this route to travel to Sydney. The big attraction for me was my cousin Arthur Murch's art studio at the back of Uncle Jim's place. I used to stand and watch Arthur busy painting at his easel and I dreamed of one day having my own art studio to paint pictures in. It seems my uncle thought art was a waste of time and when Arthur wasn't around he would give me a lecture on how stupid artists were. He used to repeat over and over, 'Don't ever be an artist, boy.'[2]

My grandmother was a lovely silver-haired old lady and was, as my mother put it, 'A Christian lady who was loved by every living creature around her.' My grandfather had worked desperately hard all his life and was stoop-backed, wrinkled, and his fingers were twisted out of shape; he presented a fierce sight to a small, nervous boy who used to shelter behind his older brother for protection.[3]

The high point of interest in visiting my Nana and Nandad, as we used to call them, was at fowl-feeding time. We would watch Nandad enter the fowlyard carrying a bucket of mash, and he would tip some into a trough. As soon as this happened a large black Orpington hen would push forward and thrust herself in front of the other fowls to get at the food. Nandad would then give her a good boot in the tail. Now the huge black rooster would come for Nandad in a swift attack using spurs, claws and beak. There would come a haze of dust, curses and flying feathers, and Nandad would suddenly emerge through the gate, one hand dripping with blood. Nana would rush out of the house carrying an enamel dish of water, soap, towel and iodine. And while she bathed his hand in water and started dabbing iodine on the wound, Nandad would be shouting, 'I'll kill that old bastard! I'll cut his bloody head off!' Nana would say, 'Now, Dad, don't swear in front of the children,' and then she would lecture him, saying, 'You can't blame the rooster; you attacked his wife and he defended her.'

You could see a showdown coming between Nandad and the rooster, and Jim and I were there the day it happened, unfortunately for me. It began with old Nandad boldly entering the fowlyard with the bucket and a large stick, and looking to me like a Roman gladiator with sword and shield entering the arena. Peering through cracks in the paling fence, we tried hard to get a view of the fierce duel which ensued. Soon the sounds of battle stopped, and Nandad emerged through the gate triumphantly holding the rooster by the legs. Striding to the chopping block he seized the axe, chopped off its head and quickly set it down on its feet. What happened next was totally unexpected, by me anyway. The rooster without a head, blood spurting everywhere and neck bone popping up and down, charged straight towards where I stood. I turned and, running to a nearby peach tree, climbed up into the safety of its branches. Nandad and brother Jim were both doubled up with laughter at the spectacle. Remembering how nervous I was at that age, I feel I must have suffered some shock from the event.

Fortunately, my grandmother had a lively sense of humour and viewed my grandfather's bursts of sudden temper and somewhat eccentric behaviour with amusement, and she would often become helpless with laughter describing some event, such as his confrontation with Darky. Darky was one of the two big Clydesdale horses that used to pull my grandfather's flat-topped wagon and he could get very obstreperous at times and would try to catch Nandad off guard and nip him on the behind, or stand on his foot. These sly attacks didn't endear him to his master and there was continuous friction between them. He arrived home late one afternoon and was taking the bridle off

Darky when the big horse suddenly bent his head and nipped Nandad on the shoulder; he let out a scream of pain and then, leaping up off the ground he seized Darky's jowls with both hands and swinging in mid-air he sank his teeth into one of Darky's nostrils. Dropping to the ground he shook his fist under the big horse's nose and yelled out, 'How do you like it, you cranky big black bastard?' Nan was watching from the back verandah, and promptly collapsed again as she told the story to my mother.

Typical Australian houses of that period used to have a hallway or central passageway. Thus, when you opened the front door the wind would blow down your hallway and slam your back door shut. And of course, the reverse would happen when you opened the back door. They were draughty, but most houses were built this way. Most people laid down linoleum except when you could afford a long runner carpet. Nana and Nandad had just finished tea when she asked him could he tack down some lino which had come loose in the hallway. Armed with tacks and a tack hammer, and a lighted candle in a metal candle-holder, he set to work. He would stand the tack up between thumb and forefinger and raise the hammer to hit it, but then a draught would come, the candle flame would flicker and he would hit his thumb. After this had happened several times he finally lost his temper and, raising the hammer high, he brought it down hard, pulverising both candle and candle-holder, and yelled out, 'Now flicker, you bloody flickering bastard!'

There was a neighbour who was a retired Guardsman from England, named John Dark. He was a fine figure of a man and he would stride past, his back as straight as a ramrod, and raise his hat to my grandmother and bid her 'Good-day'. Nandad would scowl every time he witnessed this event, and after one such greeting he tried to force his twisted old work-worn body up into an erect position, and glaring at Nana he shouted, 'Why can't I walk like that upstart Pommy bastard?'

'Now Dad,' said Nana, soothing his injured pride, 'Mr Dark is a military man and has never ever had to work as hard as you have. The army trained him to walk like that.' After that Nandad confined himself to just glaring in contempt at the man as he passed by.[4]

My mother used to say that my brother Jack and myself were very like her father, and had more sensitive, introverted types of personality, and as Jack and I grew older we looked more and more like him, which means we threw more to the Welsh than the English side of our forebears. He was religious, a Sunday School teacher, played the violin, and was a carpenter by trade. Jack became a Sunday School teacher and, although a baker by training, he became a carpenter and became lead violinist in an orchestra. I used to study the Bible. I was interested in carpentering, made a rough violin at one period, and later built my own house. But I was never ever able to play a violin properly. I also made a lot of toys during my lifetime. Mum kept an old photo of her father and people often remarked how like Jack and me he looked. If we had been dressed in old-fashioned style, they said, we would have passed for three brothers.

Another hereditary trait I exhibited was worrying over tools lost or mislaid, and this worried my mother. 'Lost tools can be found in daylight,' she would say. 'Don't lose sleep over worrying what you did with your pliers, or whatever.' I learned later that her father had fallen down an excavation one night whilst searching for a hammer.[5]

Although he was somewhat eccentric in his behaviour, Nandad, my other grandfather, was also a decent man. I probably inherited some of his eccentric characteristics as well.

My mother had a hard life, full of worry and trouble and sickness, and this would follow right through her life, as though she were under some malignant curse, ending in a slow, horrible, agonising death, and yet she remained a Christian right to the end. I learned from my brother Jack that because my father had decided to stay home when World War I started so he could work and help to support a sick wife and children, some vicious woman sent my mother an addressed envelope containing a white feather. Although she recognised the handwriting on the envelope she never revealed the identity of the sender and she carried the secret with her to the grave.

My father's arm was now giving him lots of pain and I spent some time rubbing his arm with Sloane's liniment, which seemed to relieve him a little. I used to pick flowers from a kind neighbour's garden and take them up to some friends of ours who lived further up the street. There were three young women in this house who loved flowers and they used to give me money whenever I brought them some. I would then have money to spend at the Croydon Picture Theatre, which was a large corrugated-iron shed. When brother Jim had also raised enough money we would both be ready for entertainment, watching the silent pictures which were mostly cowboy films, Charles Chaplin comedies or the Keystone Cops.

Mum would send us off wearing clean clothes and she would pop a clean handkerchief in my pocket. First, Jim would find two vacant seats near an exit door just in case the picture theatre caught on fire. My father started giving us kids safety-first lectures from as soon as we were old enough to understand, and we never forgot those lectures, and one day they were passed on to our children.

There was a serial in those days featuring a beautiful blonde girl who used to get herself involved in all sorts of adventures. It was called 'The Perils of Pauline'. It usually featured Pauline as the helpless victim of a villain or villains, about to be murdered in some cruel, dastardly fashion. When the film reached the suspense stage, with Pauline tied down onto the railway track and the train approaching, I would unconsciously pull my handkerchief out of my pocket and start biting holes in it. By the time the hero galloped up on his horse, dismounted, slashed the ropes with his bowie knife and dragged Pauline clear of the line and the oncoming steam train – just in the nick of time – my poor handkerchief was full of holes. Mum always knew what sort of film we had been watching just by inspecting my handkerchief, which sometimes looked as though it had been put through a shredding machine.

As time went by, the dreaded cancer ate through all the bones in Dad's hand, then started on his arm, till eventually I could not massage it anymore for it just hung boneless and limp by his side. I was too young to know the misery and frustration of events surrounding my father's condition, and the terrible difficulties my mother faced during those days. My brothers and sisters were older and three of them would have been out at work all day, but I believe our neighbours may have been helpful. My mother explained that this cancer would go on eating out my father's bones like white ants eating out the whole framework of a house until the body covering has no support, and that all the doctor could do was inject morphine to dull the pain some of the time. She said doctors weren't allowed to put people out of their misery like a kind old vet could do to a suffering animal.

Sometimes Jim and I would wander up to Ashfield railway station; we would walk out on the overpass and when we were above the railway line we would sit down and dangle our legs through the iron fence rods so that we could look down onto the funnels of the railway engines going past underneath and feel the hot smoke on the soles of our feet. This, together with the smell of sulphur, was quite an intoxicating experience. As I remember, they were high funnel engines with a sort of emblem on the side with the words 'Beyer and Peacock'. But now and again we would see the new 36 class engine with their hump back and the thrill of seeing one of these huge monsters was enough to make a small boy tremble with excitement, and thus we passed the time and amused ourselves.

My mother's sister lived at Parramatta, and before my father became ill my mother would sometimes visit her and take me with her for the day. These trips were sheer joy, the absolute pinnacle of pleasure and excitement for me. We would first catch the tram to Ashfield station, where we would travel by steam train to Parramatta. There I would be allowed to watch the steam trams for a few minutes as they chugged down Phillip Street, puffing smoke and blowing their shrill whistles, and then we would travel by bus to North Parramatta where my Aunty Maude lived.

Aunty Maude's house was close to the old original reservoir which used to supply the population of Parramatta. This area was a real wonderland. The expanse of water surrounded by bushland with its beautiful trees, native shrubs and flowers was like something out of Paradise to me. We would walk down bush tracks to look at the dam and carry back sticks for aunty's fuel stove. There were many bush birds and small animals still in the area and a walk there during springtime, with the smell of bush flowers, was a rare and beautiful experience for me.

As time passed the cancer ate through my father's rib cage and even his cranial bones were being eaten away by this insidious creeping thing. He was finding it hard to speak and sometimes he didn't seem to know the people who were around his bed. We all knew he couldn't last much longer and my mother started to plan for us to move to Parramatta, not only to leave this place on account of the coming sorrow, but also because her sister was suffering ill health; unknown to us her sister had cancer slowly forming in her lower spine.

I awoke one morning and was told that my father had died during the night. I cried, mainly because of the memory of all those months of pain he had suffered. To me it didn't seem fair for a good, kind man to suffer like that. My mother lost one burden, but fate had another one ready for her to carry.

I was filled with joy later when Mum announced that we would move to Parramatta. Our eldest brother and sister were living away, so that meant Mum would take four of us to Parramatta. I was sad to see the last of the old house where I had spent a happy childhood, but as the furniture van left I knew we were heading for a beautiful place at Parramatta, although I wasn't looking forward to entering a new school and I wondered if I was going to be subject to more harassment from the boys at this next school.

I didn't know what the rest of the family thought, but I thought we were in a beautiful position, close to the old dam, or Lake Parramatta as it was now called. Looking back, I can see that this was an ideal place for a young boy to grow up in, for there was still lots of country to move around in. The lake was full of carp and large yabbies, as big as English lobsters. I soon built a fish pond and started roaming around the lake surrounds, checking out all the animals, reptiles and general wildlife.

I had to start school at North Parramatta and my old trouble started again as the bigger boys started antagonising me to see if I could fight. I put up with this for a while till one day a boy followed me around entertaining his mates by punching me with short jabs to the chest. Then suddenly something seemed to explode in me and I drew back my arm and gave him a terrific right uppercut to the jaw, knocking him flat on his back. He hit the ground with a heavy thump and after lying there for a few seconds he scrambled to his feet and held out his hand. We shook hands and I said, for the benefit of everyone, that I didn't go around picking fights. I heard one boy telling another that he should keep clear of this new kid. 'He packs a terrific right hook.' And from then on I was left alone.

A young ginger-coloured dog wandered into our backyard with an old piece of rag tied around his neck and he had big patches of raw skin showing. He had a skin infection and was showing signs of malnutrition. I asked Mum if I could keep him if I could make him into a healthy dog and she agreed on those terms. First, I cut off the filthy rag, then I bathed him in a tub of warm water with phenol in it and used a cake of strong soap. Then I dried him and rubbed the bare places with a mixture of olive oil and sulphur. My friend the vet across the street stocked worm tablets and condition powders. With good care and food the stray was soon a very healthy dog and I was then allowed to keep him. Now I had a mate to wander around with.

We were studying the early history of Australia at school and here I was right smack in the middle of hundreds of historical remains. We had the very beautiful church where the hypocritical, cruel and sadistic Reverend Samuel Marsden used to preach.[6] Then we had the magnificent stone arch bridge built by the Scottish stonemason, David Lennox, which carried road traffic from Church Street across the freshwater section of the Parramatta River.[7] I had been told that the interior of Lennox Bridge was hollow. Armed with a torch, I determined to see if this story was true. I searched around the southern end on the eastern side and found a square hole near the base which had to be the entrance. Crawling around inside, I shone my torch about and learned to my amazement that it was indeed hollow inside. I marvelled at this amazing young Scot who could build a bridge with a self-supporting arch over the river using only shaped stone and, further, build an interior locking arch of stone to support the weight of traffic passing overhead. Then I noticed large iron rings set in the wall. Shining my torch about, I could see convict prison numbers chiselled into the sandstone rock; that prodded my memory as I remembered seeing prisoners' numbers and rings set in the rock out at the old reservoir. After exploring the rest of the interior

I came back and sat down in complete darkness with only the sound of a horse and cart or noisy motor truck to break the silence. I tried to imagine those poor wretches chained up to the rings every night like dogs, whilst the Reverend Marsden knelt by his beautiful four-poster bed with its clean white sheets, praying, and no doubt thinking of all the floggings he had ordered and supervised and enjoyed on that day.

This was a happy period of my life, wandering through bushland with my little ginger dog, inspecting anything that interested me, and enjoying myself. After inspecting Lennox Bridge I journeyed right back up the creek till I reached the spot where a miniature dam was built. Here I found evidence of a camp site and here were the iron rings set in the rock and the prison numbers chiselled out of the rock. I sat down at the edge of the large pool of water backed up behind the small dam wall and I tried to dream my way back into what went on around this area, and it seemed as though I was surrounded once again with the ghosts of the convicts and they were describing it all to me: the floggings, humiliation and degradation forced on them by their haughty English masters. I spent a lot of time daydreaming and frequently received the cane at school for being inattentive.

It was the normal accepted thing in those days to learn about sex in a corner of the school playground and I proved no exception. Learning how babies were actually conceived shocked me with its animal crudeness, but what upset me most was what was said concerning abortion. One day I heard some boys discussing a young girl who was being taken to a doctor to get an abortion and the conversation went something like this: 'Today is the day Nelly gets her little bastard chopped up, isn't it?' asked one boy. The other boy answered the query with, 'Yeah, that's right,' and added, 'The doctor will probably flush it down the toilet,' and then they both roared laughing. I asked rather timidly if the girl's baby had died inside her and the doctor was going to do what the vets did with stillborn calves, cut it out with a wire instrument. They both looked at me with shocked unbelief, wondering how anyone could be so naive. They then took me aside and explained that a lot of people thought it was all right to get rid of babies if you didn't want the bother of rearing them, or if you thought a baby was going to interfere with your social life. To say I was shocked would be an understatement. This information devastated me and threw all my conception of human values into utter confusion. I was in trouble at school for inattention and brought out in front of an amused class and given the cane. But I never felt the two cuts of the cane on my hand or heard the loud ripple of laughter. My mind was on the parcel that had been dropped over the school fence at Croydon Park school and all I could see was a tiny, white baby's hand. From that time onwards I became more wary of my fellow man and became subtly more anti-social.

Mum, as usual, was looking ahead and now with the Depression on the way and things looking bad, she saw that we would all need to be occupied. Jim was only earning small amounts as a caddy at the local golf course, I would soon be leaving school, and brother Jack had served his time as baker and pastrycook. Sister Aileen was getting married and would have a husband providing for her. And thanks to Mum's plans, carpenters were soon adding a small shop to the front of our house, which was to turn out to be a very wise decision indeed.

One of my problems at school was sports day when we all went to Parramatta Park and were expected to organise teams and play some sort of game. As soon as the sports master took his eyes off me I would sneak away down to the banks of the beautiful freshwater section of Parramatta River. Here, under the lovely weeping willows with their branches drooping down and touching the water, I would do my nature study. I watched a cicada on one occasion crawl up out of a hole, shed its skin and then dry out its wings in the sunshine. Another day I was fortunate enough to witness the emergence of a beautiful butterfly out of its cocoon. I watched entranced as it spread out its wings in the sun and I could see the pattern of colours forming as they dried. This to me was more thrilling than football, even if boys called me a sissy.

I had become good at catching snakes, unbeknownst to my mother, and requested permission to build a snake and lizard house, but this was met with a firm 'No.' I smuggled a large frill-necked lizard under my bed, but was later caught whilst feeding it and, pointing towards the reservoir, Mum said, 'Take that creature back.' On one of my expeditions I stopped to rest and I heard a faint barking sound, such as you would expect to come from a very, very tiny dog, yet I knew there couldn't possibly be such a small dog anywhere near. I searched around some rocks and suddenly there he was, crawling right out on top of a rock in full view, and I realised I had set eyes on my first barking lizard. A tiny chap with big solemn eyes and a real bark, like a dog.

When I turned fourteen I left school. I failed to pass the Leaving Certificate, I was such a dunce, but having gone close to passing I was granted a special pass. The only subject I received big marks for was art, and it wasn't considered an important subject.

Mum was right in thinking things were going to get worse and her idea of the little shop and everyone pitching in to keep it going was a good one. Not that I played any great part in this success; it was largely due to the efforts of Mum and Jack that the shop survived. But it did keep going and we were able to weather out the first years of the Depression. I will never forget the long dole queues of gaunt-faced people and men wearing army clothing which had all been dyed black and which added the appropriate funereal atmosphere. I often wondered why the government dyed the uniforms black: at the risk of being declared paranoid I reckoned privately it was because of all the communist activity at the time. I thought some politician had read Henry Lawson's poem about the Revolution and reasoned that in the event of trouble the army would at least be able to shoot at the right targets, but fortunately it never came to that.

I would say that the communists were the greatest trouble-makers at the time. There was an organisation formed to counter the communist threat, calling themselves the New Guard. We were listening to the wireless when the New South Wales Premier, Jack Lang, was due to cut the ribbon which would signify the official opening of the Sydney Harbour Bridge. Suddenly the New Guardsman Francis de Groot made his sensational entrance mounted on a horse, and riding up, he slashed the ribbon with his sword. The ribbon was rejoined and the Premier cut it with his scissors as de Groot was hustled off by the police. I'll bet the Premier was very thankful that de Groot hacked at the ribbon and not his head! Anyway, old Jack Lang survived and brought in the Widow's Pension, which was a beautiful act and went down in history. De Groot has probably been forgotten together with the New Guard movement that he led.[8]

During the Depression, halls were thrown open to the public and community singing was organised and entertainers donated their services. It was somewhere for people to go, especially young people who were in great moral danger during those years. Many a romance or marriage broke down on account of a girl or a wife seeking those men who could afford to give them a good time. I was a loner, and being so helped me to avoid trouble, but eight of my acquaintances were charged with rape and another shot whilst attempting rape.

The aspect of the Depression that hurt me personally was that unemployed youths were desecrating the lake, burning the bush, killing the little bush creatures, and generally spoiling this magnificent place.

It didn't take much foresight to see that every beautiful thing would eventually be torn down and destroyed. I don't know what my convict ghost spirit friends thought of this terrible invasion into their very beautiful and peaceful domain.

There was one home-breaker who came to a sticky end during the Depression. He was a businessman's son, and one of the biggest playboys in Parramatta. I was walking home and approaching the intersection of two arterial roads where one driver was supposed to give way to a car driver approaching from the opposite direction. I could see the familiar Hudson Straight Eights, loaded up with women as usual, coming from the direction of Pennant Hills, and as I watched another car flashed past me heading for the point of intersection. The two cars met and the big Hudson just seemed to explode into a mass of flying glass and pieces of flying metal glinting in the sunlight. A girl came bursting out through the front windscreen and seemed to hang in the air surrounded by glittering glass before hitting the concrete road with a sickening thud and rolling into the gutter. Other bodies were flying out from the Hudson in all directions and landing on to the road.

I looked down at the girl lying in the gutter covered in blood and broken glass and seeing her pretty face, long blonde hair and torn dress she seemed like some poor discarded doll. Later it would remind me of a popular song that was being sung at the time, 'He left me like a broken doll.' I was brought out of my shocked state by a man yelling, 'Run for it, lad, or you will be called up as a witness.' Hearing the siren of a police car, I headed at a run for home. Someone told me later that the pretty blonde girl with the doll-like face had been one of the most popular girls in Parramatta before the accident and doted on by her proud, loving parents. She was returned from the hospital a living vegetable in a wheelchair.

Preoccupied with other things, I had neglected to check Ginger for ticks and by the time I learned that he had picked one up he was paralysed in the hind legs. I carried him over to old Jim the vet, but it was too late to save Ginger with the medicine available in those days and he died in my arms. I was grief-stricken and very depressed for several days and it didn't help matters to get a lecture from my mother on the way I put more value on my animal friends than any human friends. I pointed out that human friends may desert you as though you had the plague when you are in trouble, but animals are faithful and loving until they die.

Legend had it that Jim's wife had a vicious, lying tongue, and that one day there was a terrific thunderstorm over the district and the vet's wife was suddenly struck by lightning and felled to the ground. When she was taken to hospital it was learned that she had lost the power of speech.

Next door to the vet there lived a Mr S. who was a breeder of fox terrier dogs and who worked as a storeman at Parramatta Asylum. There was a story going the rounds that this man used to chop his dogs' heads off if any of them kept him awake at night with persistent barking. I found this very hard to believe. This man had a strong, well-built, blond-headed stepson named Derek who preferred his father's name. I asked Derek if the story was true, and he verified it, adding that, 'If the old mongrel ever catches me sneaking out in the old Chevvy he'll want to cut my head off too.' It seems that Derek would run the Chevvy downhill and clutch-start it, then go for his joyride, later coasting downhill from the top end of the same street and quietly pulling up again inside his stepfather's place. This Chevrolet had a distinctive whirring, whining noise, which I was told came from a hard-fibre cogwheel and could be plainly heard when the engine was started.

One night I heard one of a litter of young puppies yapping loudly and persistently, and then loud cursing from Mr S. 'I'll cut your head off, you mongrel, I'll stop you yapping.' There was a loud chopping sound and then silence. I realised then that the story was true after all.

Old Jim owned a lovely whistling canary and the big tomcat belonging to Mr S. was always trying to lift the latch on the door of the canary's cage. One day he succeeded and was gulping down the canary when Jim caught him. When the cat hopped back over the fence Jim called out to Mr S. who was in his yard, 'Your confounded cat just gobbled up my canary.' Mr S. called the cat over to him, then grasping it by the nape of the neck he swung it over the top of the fence and held it with its belly facing towards old Jim. Reaching in his pocket he pulled out a large penknife and, after pulling out the large blade with his teeth, he leaned over the fence and ripped the cat's belly right open. Then with a quick flip of the wrist he flung the cat's intestines at Jim's feet. 'Now you've got your bloody canary back,' he shouted. Jim promptly vomited up all his breakfast.

Mr S. was bitten by a rat whilst shifting a box in the storeroom where he worked; blood poisoning set in and he became very ill and nearly died. He came in the shop and was telling Jack in a loud voice, 'Me old ticker nearly stopped, Jack.' Being closer to Jack than he was, Jim and I clearly heard Jack mumble, 'Pity the blasted thing didn't stop, you cruel, sadistic old mongrel.'

As I have said, being a loner kept me out of a lot of trouble, but against my better instincts I entered into a friendship with a local lad named Arthur. When I gained a better knowledge of him, however, I realised my mistake. This Arthur was a vandal and a bit of a psycho type. One day I went for a walk with him and he took his .22-calibre rifle with him and was showing me from time to time what a good marksman he was. We pulled up opposite a private old men's home, which consisted of a group of galvanised-iron sheds. We could see through a window of one hut an old man just bringing a white crockery cup up to his mouth.

I vaguely heard Arthur say, 'Watch this for marksmanship.' Then a shot rang out, a hole appeared in the man's window, the cup disappeared and the shocked old man sat rigid in his chair with the white ring of the cup handle still around his index finger. As we ran off I mentally resolved that this friendship must end. I might have seemed a strange boy wandering around catching snakes in the bush, but at least I knew what the snakes would do. I could see that I could never judge what humans were likely to do. I don't know if the lady who ran the old men's home ever rang the police, or if perhaps the old man was too scared to report it, but I was very thankful that he was still alive.

My sister Aileen married a man whose recreation was speedway riding and motorbike club events such as hill climbs and speed trials, so I became interested in motorbikes early in life. Charles used to repair and sell motorbikes in our backyard in Parramatta. Sometimes I would go with him to club events. I was telling a Wollongong lad about the club picnics and how a whole line of motorbike riders and their wives would go on a picnic to the Royal National Park, boil the billy, have a picnic lunch, stage races and games, etc. He asked me did the clubs have wars and bash each other up with bike chains and when I explained that all clubs competed in a friendly rivalry and how several clubs may be at large, friendly gatherings, he appeared dumbfounded. 'What a corny, weak way to go on,' was his comment.

The old reservoir at Lake Parramatta had a sixty-foot drop at the back of the wall, onto jagged rocks. The wall had a smooth surface down to about seven feet, then a ledge jutted out running the full length of the wall. This ledge was about six inches wide, and in places was green with lichen moss. The daredevils or idiots (depending on your opinion) used to walk the wall or, to explain it in detail, used to shuffle across leaning back against the wall and carefully moving one foot after the other. It was more than I could bear to watch as a boy would scrape the lichen moss away with the heel of his shoe and test it slowly to see if his heel would grip the wet surface. To slip meant a frightful death. To deliberately risk life needlessly and for no logical reason was sheer idiocy as far as I was concerned. On today's values, these boys would be featured on TV and their actions would be considered very brave and very clever.

There was a man named Adolf Hitler being mentioned in the newspapers, who was blaming the Depression and all of Germany's problems over the years on the Jews and they were being persecuted all over Germany. The Jews were the scapegoats as usual and I couldn't help but feel sorry for them.

The old diggers who used to come into our shop said, 'This bloke will trigger off World War II.' The civilians argued that Germany was a Christian country and would not plunge the world into war. I learned that before World War I a young American inventor named Henry Maxim offered his machine gun patent to the American government. The generals knocked his offer back, claiming that no machine gun could surpass the good old Gatling gun. Maxim journeyed to England and offered the gun to the British army. The British generals said they would retain the good old Lee Enfield rifle, and knocked him back. He went to Germany and the German generals were so impressed with this gun and its high rate of fire, that it was bought immediately and German factories were given orders to go into mass production of what would prove the ultimate infantry weapon. When war with Germany broke out, the German army was slaughtering the English forces in thousands with their machine gun. Earl Haig, the commander-in-chief of the British forces in France, gave the order that any English troops refusing to face this new weapon would be shot for cowardice. Many did refuse and tried to desert and hundreds were lined up and shot. Finally, the Lewis and Vickers guns emerged on the battle scene, after many young men had been foolishly sacrificed.

So far our family's progress had been good and we were surviving the Depression nicely, but now we made a wrong move. It's no good apportioning blame to anyone, as it was just in essence a very unfortunate mistake. Mum and Jack decided to move to Batlow into a bakery. As this was a painful experience for everyone concerned I won't spend much time in describing it. Our first bitter lesson was learning that things were not as good in Batlow as we had been led to believe. There had been a bitter feud going on between one business section and the other and we blundered right into it.

The climate was about ten months winter and two months cold weather and the people matched the climate. Jack was baker, Jim was assistant baker and carter, and I was pastrycook. Mum did a bit of everything. I saw snow and quickly learned to hate it. Soon we received a black frost, followed by a hailstorm. What the first failed to destroy, the second did. People crowded onto Batlow railway station with bags, ready to move by train to friends and relatives in Sydney. We soon joined in the general exodus from Batlow.

After living in several locations in Sydney where Jack managed to get temporary work, we moved to Old Toongabbie. I took one look at this little old house and suddenly I felt as though I was being reassured; things would be all right. I can't explain this strange feeling, but it was very strong. Jack managed to get work on a farm and so did Jim, but all I managed to get was a heavy dose of influenza. It was a bad virus and even when I recovered I was so weak that there were no prospects of me getting strong enough to take on a job and I had to go on the dole.

The house was on a long block of land with water laid on and when I saw Mum carefully examining the rich soil I knew she just had to be planning a garden. A big strong man drove up with a cart and two magnificent Clydesdales. Mum went out and talked to him whilst my attention was focused on these beautiful horses. I heard Mum say, 'The yard is a big one, but can you manoeuvre those large horses in such a confined space?' I'll never forget the way this man looked indignantly at Mum and said haughtily, 'I will have you know I am the champion ploughman of the whole of Cumberland County, Missus. There isn't a ploughman who can beat me in the area. I have a mantelshelf crowded with trophy cups, and a hatrack covered with sashes.' I heard Mum say in a very timid voice, 'Thank you, Mr Powers, very much.'

So our wonderful garden was born as the first step was made. From now on it was a case of smashing up the clods with the only tool we possessed, a large three-pronged hoe. I would work a little and rest a little until we had our first bed ready for planting. Still weak, I tired very quickly, but I plugged along feeling very happy. Mum went out shopping and finding out about the district, and with what she and the rest of the family learned, I discovered we were on an early convict settlement. The dairy farm at the back of our place was where the guards' huts had been and where our garden was being formed had been the original cultivation area. We were actually on a very historic site and I was thrilled; it was all very interesting to me. When I made enquiries about the early convict history I was shown a nearby hill with an ancient eucalyptus tree, and my informant pointed out a branch from which the prisoners would be hanged, where they could be seen from the road. Later when I pointed it out to Mum, she shuddered and said, scathingly, 'Typical English history – man's inhumanity to man.'

As our garden flourished and we were soon eating huge platefuls of our own vegetables, I began thinking how uncanny it was that everything seemed to go right with this garden. Whatever Jim and I planted grew and produced bountifully and we were able to help feed our neighbours also. I often wondered if the spirits of those poor wretches who had once gardened on this spot were in some mysterious fashion assisting us. Many years later Jim would visit the place and find everything just the same. 'It was uncanny,' he said. 'Not a thing seemed changed in any way.' The red rambler rose still trailed over the front verandah entrance and the old place stood impervious to time and tempest, looking just as we knew it so long ago.

I managed to get a job on a poultry farm with a religious man known locally as 'Henry the Hen'. I received morning tea, dinner, and fifteen shillings a week and spent most of the day working very hard whilst Henry squatted on his haunches scratching about in his quest to grow a super breed of spinach.

He did eventually succeed in developing super spinach, but the workload was too heavy and I was forced to leave poor Henry.

Whilst I was away from the house, a man called asking Mum if one of her sons wanted a half-day job on his dairy, cleaning up, and so the following day found me cleaning bails only a short distance from home. Whilst sweeping with a yard broom I noticed a large, red, ugly, hammer-headed horse inspecting me over the fence. There was something unusual about this horse, and if he had been a man I would have said he was looking at me with a look of amused contempt on his face. Then the boss came along and, seeing this horse giving me a contemptuous look, he pointed to him, saying, 'Watch out when he is around. That's Toby and he will steal, bite, kick, buck or stand on your feet. He's nothing but a rogue, he is anti-social with other horses and doesn't like humans.'

When the boss walked away I very warily patted Toby on the nose and said, 'I don't like humans either; we should get along just fine.' Nearby was the hay shed and yard enclosed by a fence and a gate, and pausing in my labours to check on Toby, I was in time to see him pull back the gate latch bar, push open the gate and start nibbling hay. The boss had also spotted him and we both chased him out of the yard. He retreated back to a safe distance and stood watching us.

'I'll fix him,' said the boss, and with those words he began tying a piece of rope securely around the gate and post. A few minutes later I just happened to turn around in time to see Toby untying the last knot in the rope and as I watched in amazement he proceeded to pull back the latch bar with his teeth. I yelled out and forced him back and then grabbing some tie wire I bent over to tie it around the gate. Then suddenly it felt as though someone had seized hold of my shoulder with a pair of red-hot blacksmith's tongs and I let out a scream like a Sioux Indian. Toby had notched up another victim.

This boss was hard to get along with and in the eighteen months I worked with him, eighteen milk carters started work and left again and my red mate, Toby, bit every one of them. I would warn them and then watch them harnessing the horses through a peephole in the bails shed. I would see the new man being very wary at first, but as Toby just stood quiet with a placid look on his long horsey face, eventually the new man would relax. Then, as quick as a tiger snake, Toby would strike once again.

A new chap arrived one day and I waited until he had stored his dunnage in the milkmen's hut before introducing myself. He was short, thick-set and had red hair, and said his name was Matt. He looked at Toby standing in the yard, his legs all covered with dried mud and pretending that he hadn't even seen the new man and Matt said, 'I think I had better get the scraper and clean the legs on the big red horse.' I warned him that Toby would bite him and he turned and gave me a contemptuous look, saying 'Don't ever try to tell me anything about horses, mate. I've handled hundreds of horses during my lifetime.' I decided this was going to be worth watching and retired to the shed to watch through my peephole.

Matt warily led Toby to a stable and backed him into it with the horse facing the doorway. Matt was very alert as he scraped Toby's chest and Toby never moved. Then I noticed Toby had that innocent, placid look on his face. Matt continued working downwards, even scraping Toby's knees and Toby still looked placid and half asleep. I could see Matt beginning to relax. 'Any time now,' I said to myself. As Matt scraped his knees, one of Toby's eyes opened and I could see him looking down his nose at that great mop of red hair. Then Toby swooped on Matt's hair and, seizing a mouthful, he started lifting Matt slowly upright and then suddenly he let go and backed into his stable. I watched Matt seize his head and moaning loudly he retreated to the milkmen's hut. He left two days later and didn't even glance in my direction.

I knew that there just had to be some sort of early warning system to beat Toby, and the next day I found it. It was a beautiful day and I was in the paddock raking manure into heaps. I heard Toby edging up closer as he nibbled grass and I knew he would be waiting to see how close he could get to me without me noticing. What Toby didn't realise was that I was watching his shadow on the grass as he stalked his prey. I let him get close and then I saw that he had raised his head; bracing myself, I saw the movement of shadow and, dropping the rake, I brought up my fist with a beautiful right hook which landed square on his nose. Snorting, he retreated to the corner of the paddock to sulk and puzzle out how I had outwitted him. Next day he got his revenge, for I did a very silly thing as far as Toby was concerned. I was in the bottom paddock wearing gumboots and wanting to get back to the bails and I thought I would ride Toby barebacked. He let me lead him over to a stump and even let me climb on his back. Next thing I knew I was getting an upside down view of Toby's grinning face as I turned a complete somersault to land back on my feet, feeling very stupid.

When I got home there was a letter telling me to report to a place in Parramatta for a medical examination prior to being sent to a military camp where I would undergo a period of sixty days' compulsory military training. I had turned twenty-one and now I was going to have to mingle with a herd of human beings, which upset me just to contemplate, even if it was only to be for a period of sixty days. And so it was that shortly after that letter I was in amongst a group of strange young men sitting in a train bound for Liverpool. We were met at the station with several General Service wagons pulled by huge Clydesdales and English Shire horses and were then roughly transported to our destination, Holsworthy Remount Training Squadron. The camp was a cluster of tents and pre-fabricated huts. A lean, tough-looking colonel lined us up and told us we were now members of 2nd Remount Squadron and if we learned to take orders and behave ourselves we would have a real good time. These were the last days of the horse units, just before mechanisation came in, and I little knew then that I would see sights that would never be seen again.

Startling things were happening. Adolf Hitler was in total control of Germany and neighbouring countries were becoming very nervous. Japan had moved into China and stories of terrible atrocities being committed by Japanese troops were filling the newspapers. Joseph Stalin had developed severe paranoia and was conducting purges against people around him and ten million people were executed by communist death squads. Strange as it may seem, Australians were mainly apathetic. 'After all,' they would comment, 'it is only Orientals killing Orientals,' or, 'the Russians are only killing Jews.' These events were all taking place far away and it wasn't affecting Australians.

Closer to home, a large Catholic seminary was being built on what used to be a dairy farm on the old English penal settlement guard block section at the back of our place. The young builder, Ernest Foster, would become my next-door neighbour some thirty years later.

Meanwhile, in the Remount Camp a group of young recruits were being allotted horses by the old militia hands who were there to train us. I was on the end of the line and having seen many photos of jockeys with short stirrups I had shortened mine and I sat perched up on my horse like the jockeys in the photographs. I was suddenly startled to hear a crusty old militia sergeant scream out, 'Who the hell does that man think he is on the end there, Jimmy Pike?' Jim Pike was the jockey who usually rode Phar Lap, the famous Australian racehorse. I had made a stupid mistake first time up in the saddle and I was quick to let my stirrups right down again whilst a ripple of laughter went along the ranks.

Eventually, led by the colonel and a lieutenant, the squadron moved out onto the road. In amongst the new chums rode seasoned horsemen of the militia. Then the order came to trot and not being an experienced rider I bobbed up and down like a cork on the ocean. I got alarmed and yelled to the sergeant, 'I'm going to fall off!' to which he snarled, 'No you bloody well won't! Hang on.' Then a piece of paper blew across the front of my horse and he bolted right along past the whole squadron and next thing I found myself wedged between the colonel's horse and the lieutenant's. The sergeant arrived and the now red-faced colonel screamed out, 'Get him back!' The sergeant seized the bridle and led me back to the rear and as we passed the column there were plenty of comments from the rest of the men and more ripples of suppressed laughter.

I was given Rosie to learn on and it was a blessing for although she had a tendency to fall asleep and fall on her knees and I was always last in the column, she was ideal for beginners. I saddle-galled one horse, though, through not learning to tighten the girth before the horse blew out its stomach.

Later on I was given Brownie and I soon realised I now had a real good intelligent horse to ride. In fact, getting Brownie was just another of a long line of strokes of good fortune which befell me. Brownie knew all the commands, which was just as well because when the colonel screamed out an order I didn't have the faintest idea what he was saying but Brownie did and he would carry it out whilst I let the reins hang loose to let him know he was boss. I let the rest of the troop know that Brownie was my horse come hell or high water, and it was accepted that Brownie was Holman's mount.

I'm sure if that horse could have talked he would have said to me, 'How come of all these men in this camp I have to be landed with an idiot like you?' He would certainly have had just cause to complain about me. We went for rides and for me compulsory training was a life of lovely picnics in the bush. But I am afraid Brownie wouldn't have agreed, especially when on one occasion we lined up along a farmer's boundary fence to use it as a hitching rail and I tethered him right over a bull ants' nest; what with Brownie dancing and me trying to untether him, we provided the troop with great entertainment. The anger and contempt was plainly visible on poor Brownie's face.

One day we noticed that our militiamen instructors had wheeled out two box trailers with a long pole bar on the lead trailer. As we watched, they harnessed a huge Clydesdale each side of the pole bar and attached them to it, with the second trailer linked to the first. On the back of the nearside horse was a saddle. The sergeant explained that this was known as riding postillion, a man rode the nearside horse and directed both horses. The man would have a steel-plated legging on the right leg that would prevent his leg from being broken or smashed by the pole bar. A second man would stand in the front trailer holding the brake. These trailers were used for carrying ammunition.

As I stood watching, the sergeant suddenly turned to me and said, 'Right, on with the pad and up you go.' I managed to get the pad on and it was so heavy I could barely lift my leg. I looked up at these huge eighteen-hand Clydesdales and they looked as big as elephants. I had no hope of reaching the stirrups. This was soon solved by my mates as I was hoisted up to where I could reach them. I heard a man get in the limber and release the brake and I was thinking I was just like a flea on a Great Dane's back. 'Do one circuit of the training ground,' shouted the sergeant and he slapped one of the Clydesdales on the rump.

Away we went with the horses trotting along steadily. Then across the training area fluttered a piece of paper borne on the flurry of a sudden gust of wind. I saw the offside horse's ears go back and the next thing I knew they had bolted. The brakeman, seeing what had happened, panicked and leaped out of the limber, landing on his side and rolling over and over in the dust whilst my team thundered on, heading straight for a clump of turpentine trees. There was a narrow gap in the trees and I closed my eyes and hung on, frozen with fear, waiting for the end to come. There was a brushing noise as the hubs on the wheels tore bark off the two trees each side of the gap and then we were through and heading for a barbed-wire fence. Screaming, 'Whoah!' at the horses and pulling the reins as hard as I could, I tried to stop their mad rush. Gradually they responded until eventually they started sitting back against the thrust of the pole bar and drew to a halt with their noses inches away from the barbed-wire fence.

Surrounded by mates, I was helped down and militiamen took charge of the rig. After removing my steel pad I walked back to where I'd started with an admiring group escorting me. My mates reckoned it had looked like a spectacular sequence out of a Wild West film. I checked on my brakeman, but apart from gravel rash, bruises and torn clothing he was all right. I started thinking how hard it must have been in World War I with horse transport, having to control horses under stress and get vital food and ammunition to the front lines. And I remembered the famous American transport song: 'Over hill, over dale, till we hit the river trail, And our caissons [limbers] go rolling along.'

Arriving home on leave and walking in the front door, the first view I got was of brother Jim seated behind Mum's old Singer sewing machine. Spread out all over the floor were pieces of air force uniform. It was patently obvious that brother Jim had joined the RAAF and had been issued a uniform that didn't fit. I said, 'They'll shoot you if you don't get that all back together.'

Jim said, 'I'll not only get it all back together, but it will fit perfectly when I do.' He did make a good fit out of it, too.

While on leave, I spotted a little boy astride a pony and slowly wending his way down the road. Unbeknownst to me and the little boy, this pony had swelled his belly as the boy was tightening the girth strap. Unlike me, this little boy hadn't learned to trick the horse by pretending to be interested in the stirrups and then suddenly seizing the girth strap and pulling it tight.

I decided to impress this boy with my military presence and after getting permission to ride the pony I put one foot in the stirrup and the next thing I knew I was looking up at the pony's belly. Fortunately this little boy didn't roar laughing, or at least not in front of me, anyway. After this blow to my ego I went up to the dairy and asked permission to go for a ride on Toby. The red horse seemed glad to see me and never once tried to bite me and I had a nice short ride before bringing him back. I decided that in his old rogue heart he actually had a soft spot for his former workmate. I left the dairy hoping that no one would ever break his proud spirit of defiance towards the world.

When I returned to the camp we were taught to jump over brush hurdles and I loved every minute of it. One day we took a great string of horses out along the road for exercise. Fortunately I was holding two Clydesdales who were fairly stable and reliable, also I was up near the front. I heard a rumble behind me and someone shouted, 'Stampede!' Then one of the militiamen shouted, 'Run outwards!' Pulling the outer horse back hard with his rope I rushed past him across the road and dived into a deep drain as the mob of horses thundered past me heading down the road.

Later, when order was restored, and we had collected the horses, some of the old militiamen almost cried at the shocking injuries to some of the horses. Our old vet especially was terribly upset and complained, 'Why use chain leads when ropes would have been strong enough? Look at these poor chewed-up horses.' Brownie, intelligent horse that he was, had run to safety.

I had one more frightening experience a few days later as we were riding through bush when Brownie saw a snake and bolted. It was a wild, frightening ride over logs and dodging trees and ducking my head. When we broke through the bush I managed to calm him down and bring him to a standstill, but it was a ride no horseman could ever forget. It finally ended sixty lovely happy days of compulsory training.

When I returned home I learned that Jack had joined the AIF, which left me now on my own in the garden. I decided I would join the AIF too and rode on my pushbike to the recruiting centre at Parramatta where I was told they weren't taking any more at that time. Then I tried to join the RAAF, but I was told the same thing.[9]

Mum decided we would move to Northmead as Jack was getting only day training at Parramatta and Northmead was much closer to Parramatta. Then a letter arrived which said I should report to an Army Horse Transport Unit at Greta in the Hunter Valley, west of Newcastle. Here, as at Holsworthy, I spent several enjoyable weeks; I rode around in former bushranger country, and soon I was involved in a second horse stampede. We were taking two lines of horses towards the horse trough, leading with two massive English Shires in hand. Hearing the thunder of hooves behind me I leaped into the air, slapping the cheeks of both horses with the back of my hands, forcing them to turn outwards, and running forward to the end of the long horse trough I threw myself underneath. I had succeeded in splitting the horse herd into two lines that veered out away from the trough, and as they thundered past I knew no horses would get hurt.

These horses could be dangerous when they bolted as the sergeants in the Sergeants' Bar found out. One moment they were lined up at the tent opening, mugs of beer in their hands, then thundering straight at them were two massive Clydesdales, white-eyed and panic-stricken, pulling a GS wagon. I didn't see it, but the driver's account was enough. 'You shoulda seen the shocked look on them bloody sergeants as they scattered like fowls as bang right into the middle of the tent we went, scattering beer barrels everywhere and taking tent an' all with us,' he said, slapping his leg and shaking with hearty laughter.

I did a bit of unrehearsed entertaining one day. I was leading two huge English Shires towards the water trough in full view of the whole troop when suddenly they lifted me off the ground and holding on to their bridles I found myself floating along in mid air as they trotted towards the trough. On reaching the horse trough they just as suddenly dropped their heads and down I went, full-length face down in sloppy mud and horse dung. There were roars of laughter and much hand-clapping.

I should have said to myself, 'Serves you right', because I had had a hearty laugh at poor Eric when we were at Liverpool for the sixty-day camp. It was a Sunday and we were all clean and our uniforms brushed and leggings, bandolier, belt and boots all polished. It had been raining and there were pools of water on the parade ground. A pretty blonde girl appeared at the gates with a decrepit old horse and asked one of the older militia chaps very sweetly if she could water her horse at our trough. There was a commotion as a group of us nearly trampled each other to death to get to her horse. Eric, the good-looking dandy militiaman, seized the bridle of her nag and cutting a fine figure with all his polished leather, he led it to the trough. After watering the animal he led it back to the girl, his non army issue Mexican spurs glittering in the sunlight. He asked her could he ride her horse and she gave him permission.

I don't know if it was the six-pointed rowels on the spurs that caused it, but next second there was the girl's horse trotting through the largest muddy puddle dragging Eric along with his foot caught in the stirrup. Someone grabbed the horse's bridle whilst other troopers freed his boot from the stirrup and helped a very wet, muddy Eric onto his feet. It should have ended there but the girl apologised, saying, 'I'm terribly sorry, if I'd known you couldn't ride I wouldn't have let you get on my horse.' Eric made a choking sound and headed for his tent; being possibly the finest horseman in the squadron, for him the girl's comment was the very last straw. Poor Eric, for days after as he crossed the parade ground voices would call out, 'I wouldn't have let you get on my horse if I'd known you couldn't ride.' But it all seemed very humorous at the time.

The transport camp ended and back to Northmead I went, to learn that Jack was now in the 2/19th Battalion, commanded by Major Charles Cousins at Tamworth AIF Camp. Jim was stationed at Evans Head RAAF Coastal Surveillance base.[10]

I obtained a job nearby on a racehorse resting yards farm and this time I was amongst dangerous horses. Nervy, highly strung, highly bred racehorses who could play with you one minute and then try to kill you the next. The owner of the yard was a very religious man, which was another untrustworthy feature of the place as far as all my previous experience and judgment was concerned. It was only light work and I'll give Jackson his due – he didn't let me feed or care for any horse he knew to be dangerous. The mares were all right to handle and so were the geldings, but the stallions needed watching. The owners would give Jackson a list of expensive foods their horses were to get, but I had my doubts about whether they received it and I wondered if the horse owners still paid for it later on.

There were other animals to feed, including pigs, which were new to me. I used to watch the huge boar walking around and I wondered what would happen if I leapt on his back and tried to ride him. The thought was father to the deed and one day I did leap on his back. He lurched around the yard and off his back I tumbled. I had only just gained the outside of the fence when Jackson arrived on the scene. 'That's a bloke you want to keep clear of,' he said. 'It took five men with big sticks to force him into that pen; he's a vicious character.'

A big chestnut arrived one day and when placed in one of the yards he retired to one corner and just stood there. I took a tin of food into his stable and dumped the contents into his feed box but, unlike most horses, he never followed me inside the stable to eat it. I mentioned this to Jackson and he said, 'That's Thunderclap, and at the moment he has a scuffed ankle and he is sulking. When that foot heals he'll be cheeky enough.'

One morning when I heard 'clip clop' behind me I realised Thunderclap had decided to follow me into the stable. I raised the bucket and was just about to empty it into the very strongly built feed box in the stable corner when I happened to look back up at the stallion's head, near my elbow. One glance at those flattened ears and killer eyes and I dropped the bucket and ducked down under the feed box, not a split second too soon as he reared and struck at me with his forelegs trying to get at me.

As I listened to the drumming of hooves on that feed box I was very grateful for every nail and piece of wood that had gone into its very strong construction for otherwise my skull would have been crushed to pulp. And now I had to get out of that shed. Scooping up two handfuls of manure, I threw them up in his face, bringing my hands back to hit the corrugated iron with a loud bang and yelling at him with all my lung power. Startled with this commotion, he retreated and leaving the shed trotted a few steps out into the yard. Then I made a frantic dash through the doorway and across the yard towards the pole fence, with Thunderclap wheeling and coming after me. When I got near the fence I threw myself down and rolled under it, just clear of those striking hooves as chips of wood flew off the bottom rail. I got to my feet and was trembling and feeling thankful to be alive.

When Jackson arrived on the scene I told him what had just happened and he sneered and suggested I was exaggerating. Then when he heard I had dropped the feed tin he snatched up another and said, 'Now I'll have to give him his feed, I suppose.' I waited on some excuse to see what would happen. A few minutes later Jackson was visible running for the fence and rolling under the rails as I had recently done. His face was chalk-white. Seeing me, he said, 'Don't go near that horse again, he's a killer horse,' and with that he walked away.

I saw him again a few minutes later with another tin of feed and a whip. This time he forced Thunderclap to walk backwards all around his yard whilst he cracked the whip in his face then Jackson took his tin of feed into the shed and a sulking Thunderclap didn't dare try to follow him inside.

A week later Jackson accused me of not filling the water bucket of one of the two-year-olds. I repeated that I had filled the bucket and that the young horse must have drunk it dry and that I wouldn't accept being called a liar, so I gave him a week's notice. Whilst I was away from home one day weeks later, Jackson called in and told my mother that he wished to apologise. My mother told him, 'You called him a liar. He'll never work for you again.'

When I was about fourteen I had gone down camping to a place called Werri Beach, and I had later talked of thousands of rabbits running around, abalone, fish and lagoon mullet to be obtained for food and stressed what a beautiful place it would be to live in. Mum now decided we'd move down there to a little house. I enquired about work and was told that any work would only be farm work, which would be very hard and for little money.

I set about trapping a lot of rabbits and then drying and selling the skins. I was trying to support myself as best I knew how, but the more I saw of the local people the less I liked them and I knew that unconsciously I was trying to avoid setting down my roots here.

I became friendly with a local old soldier and one day his two young daughters invited me to go swimming with them; I accepted and we spent hours swimming in the local pool. While we were harmlessly enjoying ourselves a very religious man living nearby came and reported to Mum that I had gone swimming with young girls under the age of consent. Mum assured him that the girls were in no moral danger. When I learned about this I wanted to go over the road and punch him on the nose. I informed my old digger friend that perhaps the girls should have a chaperone to protect their moral reputation and then he also wanted to go and punch this man on the nose.

I was getting very frustrated and despondent and I often indulged in my Robinson Crusoe fantasy, which I had been doing from the first time I had read the book as a child. An island away from all civilisation with a few goats and a garden. I must have read and re-read that book a hundred times. Finally one day I told Mum I would have another go at getting into the services. I travelled to Sydney by train and then caught another to Parramatta and eventually arrived at my Aunty Maude's. She seemed a bit worried about my decision but never queried it. However, as I lay in bed sleepless with anxiety I heard my uncle say, 'They may as well shoot that boy here. He's an artist, not a soldier, and you can't make soldiers out of artists, musicians or poets, and all those sensitive types.' I was to learn the hard way, like all my lessons in life.

Sitting in the train I pondered over all of this and upon reaching Sydney I had decided that perhaps I had better try to enlist in one of the other services. I went into the navy recruiting centre where I was handed a details form to fill in. Having completed this, I was told to sit down and wait to be called into a surgery where I would be medically examined. Just as I sat down, a large, well-built young man came bursting out of the doctor's surgery and was still engaged in dressing himself as he approached me, looking absolutely furious.

'What's the doctor like, mate?' I enquired.

'What's the doctor like?' he echoed. 'He just seized hold of my testicles and giving them a downward tug he said, "Geeze, there's a pair of beauts!"'

'What did you do?' I asked.

'I grabbed him by his white coat and socked him on the jaw. Over he went on his back, slid across the polished floor and hit his head on the skirting board,' he said angrily. As he walked away, he said as a parting remark, 'I'm going to join the AIF.'

'Wait a second,' I yelled out. 'I'm coming with you.'

Shortly after that I was signing a document and listening to a jocular army clerk saying, 'Now you've done it, mate. Signed yer life away.' And as we were being transported to the big mob camp at the showground I wondered if that was what I had done. When we arrived we were issued with a bag filled with straw, known as a palliasse (or in civilian terms, a mattress) and given an allotted area to bed down in the Dog Pavilion. This fact wasn't lost on the recruits and soon the pavilion echoed to the sounds of male voices imitating every type of dog from a Pomeranian to a Great Dane as our humorists expressed themselves.

I bunked down next to a chap who at first glance looked like a big, shy country boy. I learned later that big and tough as he was, and he did come from the country, he wasn't shy by any means and we became very good mates. Roy wanted to roam around Sydney at night and our leave passes were only issued on alternate nights; we soon found a way around that by collecting a lot of old leave passes from other chaps, then with a bit of delicate forgery we turned them into new ones and so we were able to get plenty of leave. Of course, there were MPs all over the place, but our system stood us in good stead except for one time. The plan was that if you saw an MP you didn't avoid him but instead you walked straight boldly up to him with an unlighted cigarette in your mouth and asked him in a real friendly, casual manner for a light. By the time he had produced a lighter and the cigarettes had been lit and we had thanked him very politely and walked away, he had become convinced that all was well and in order.

One night on Central Station we suddenly found ourselves confronted by two MPs right near the phone booths. They examined our passes and wouldn't let us go. 'Who's this Captain Harden?' they asked suspiciously, and I cursed inwardly at Roy's impudence in using his own name of Harden to sign our passes. Knowing only bluff would get us out of it, I said blandly, staring the man straight in the eyes, 'He's our Duty Officer, and if you want to check that out there's the phone just over there.' Still obviously only half convinced, they let us go.

As we walked away I whispered, 'Walk real slow, they're probably watching us.' We decided to get back to camp while our luck was in. After we had had a good laugh about it, Roy asked me, 'What would have happened if they had rung up?' I told him we would have been cracking rocks at Holsworthy Detention Camp a few days later.

One aspect of army life we both detested was PT or physical training. One morning Roy suggested we go on strike and refuse to attend the parade. I doubted the wisdom of this, but he was my mate so I, too, went on strike. Soon afterwards we were both taken to the Commanding Officer who gave us seven days confined to barracks and we had to clean out every toilet in Sydney Showground. But as they say, all good things come to an end, and a few days later we were transported to Dubbo Military AIF camp.

We were in 2/33rd Infantry Battalion at first, where we met a good mate named Kelly. When they called for volunteers for machine-gunners later, the three of us stepped forward one pace. We became like the Three Musketeers and we went everywhere together. We competed against each other on the rifle range and firing the machine guns. Also seeing who could assemble or dismantle the Vickers in the shortest time; everything was one big competition.

Then on 7 December 1941 the Japanese struck Pearl Harbor and there was a call for reinforcements for the 8th Division which had two brigades stationed in Malaya. Roy and Kelly went to 2/29th Battalion whilst I was placed in the 2/19th.[11] Final leave had become a bit of a joke in those days and you would hear the comment, 'I'm on my semi-final leave' or else, 'I'm on my grand final leave.' Errant wives suffered extreme embarrassment when their husband, who had recently gone back to camp after spending his final leave, suddenly walked in the door catching them in bed with one of the neighbours. It was very unsettling and a big emotional strain with these sad farewells.

I spent leave at Werri Beach and told Mum that it was probably only a semi-final leave. I visited my eldest brother, Bert, in a room of the Sir John Young Hotel and as we chatted and looked down at a newsagent's opposite, the owner walked out and placed a placard out in front of his shop. On it, printed in big black capitals were the words 'Australia Declares War on Japan.'

Later, my sister Aileen and I were travelling by ferry for a trip to the zoo and we could see a huge ocean liner with four funnels berthed at a wharf and we both took note of the fact that this was probably a large waiting troopship.

Back in camp at Dubbo it was a hive of activity as we were all issued battle dress and tin helmets. One look at Roy and Kelly and I realised that these two men were real soldiers. Roy suggested I try to sneak out to see my girlfriend, but it had been declared a closed camp and I didn't want to get into trouble at this stage. My girlfriend was an atheist; unlike her family and myself who believed in a spiritual force which surrounded us, she didn't believe. Actually, her family had accepted me with great affection as a son and I became very good friends with her sister. I thought it over and decided to stay in camp.

At about this time, an American woman pilot had become lost and when those searching for her checked her flight path, they noted that it passed close to several islands. Someone came up with the theory that she had unwittingly landed on a secret landing strip being used by the Japanese for transporting Jap troops and that this island was a secret training ground for the Japanese. Although the theory was ridiculed at the time, we of the 8th Division wondered later, where did the Japanese get their jungle training in crowded Japan with its lack of any type of dense forest areas? Why were they all so adept at climbing trees? Why were they all issued with special shoes with a cleft between the big toes and the rest of the foot, so ideal for gripping liana vines for climbing? We had never read of rainforest in Japan with trailing liana vines hanging from the trees; nor the deadly little machine gun with the sharp steel spike on one side which could be banged into the soft bark of a rubber tree and held very firmly for a quick, accurate burst of gunfire; nor the special little mountain cannon which was built for quick dismantling and carrying through jungle. They must have trained in some jungle area.

My family, although steadfast in adversity and with close allegiance, were not given to emotional leavetaking and when we were on board the troop train at Dubbo station I was embarrassed by all the handshaking, hugging and kissing. I remembered in the shop at Parramatta when Mum had heard her sister had been taken to hospital, she turned to me, a boy of fourteen, and said, 'Right, you're the only one expendable. You go and take charge of your aunty's household till she returns. You will cook meals, make beds, cut lunches, get the children to school and do everything to help.' And as I stood gaping in sheer amazement she said, 'Go on, off you go. You can do it.' I remembered with amusement that I did do it, and very capably too. Now the band was playing and the huge green 38 class loco was whistling loudly and we were off on our journey to adventure.

The departure of troop trains was supposed to be a closely guarded secret, but all along the route platforms were covered with cheering people and the driver of our loco blasted the air with a loud 'cock a doodle doo' practically every chance he got. After reaching Sydney we were taken in trucks to a wharf where we looked up the side of a large ocean liner. I asked one of the wharfies near at hand, 'What ship is this?' And he answered '*Aquitania*, mate.' Once aboard and with our gear stowed in our allotted bunk space we adjourned to the top deck to catch streamers thrown by people among the crowd that thronged the wharf. Soon ropes were unwound from bollards and with a loud blast from the ship's siren we moved out from the wharf. I watched as the streamers parted and contact was broken with Australia as the last ribbon snapped. We proceeded down the harbour escorted by a multitude of small craft and with just about every ship, ferry and large launch blowing their siren full blast as we passed them.

Later as I stood watching Sydney Heads fading into the distance, I noticed the colour of the water getting perceptibly bluer and bluer until I was reminded of my mother swishing a Reckitts Blue bag in the concrete tubs full of water to make blue rinse water on washing days. I now realised why men who travelled in ships that sailed out of harbours and bays were known as 'blue water sailors'.[12]

Singapore

I thought this would be a fun cruise, but officers soon had us attending lectures and detestable PT. One day I discovered a rope locker where we exercised and quickly slipping into it I hid and missed out on all the PT. I repeated this trick on several successive days before I was eventually caught in the locker. From then on the officers checked to make sure that this Holman character was actually there.

Going down the coast on the *Aquitania* was all right, but when we started crossing the Bight she rolled like a porpoise and most of us were seasick. After bringing up breakfast I stepped back from the ship's rail and accosted a passing sailor.

'Why does this old tub roll so much?' I enquired peevishly.

His reply was terse. 'This old tub, as you call her, was built for speed and is streamlined to cut through the water and although she rolls a bit she'll outrun any enemy submarine afloat.'

I now viewed this old ship with new respect as I looked out over the forbidding expanse of cold blue sea.

It is said that on every ship there is a clown, but in this case he could have been called a fop or an idiot. He was one of our officers and could have been described as tall, fair-haired, slim build and wearing a toothbrush moustache. He obviously came from a wealthy upper-class family and was fresh from a military academy. He swaggered up and down the decks with a cane tucked under his left arm. With his superior, arrogant posture he seemed to me to be trying to imitate some English film actor. I think he probably watched every Pinewood Studio film ever made about World War I. I was instantly reminded of David Niven in an English film, endeavouring to play the part of an English officer. There had been an old, threadbare joke going the rounds for about twenty years about the passenger who reports the loss of his life preserver to the captain, who asks him, 'Do you know any good prayers?' When I found mine was missing I realised what might be the idiot's answer when I reported it. Sure enough, he gave me the same answer and rushed off to retell it all to his long-suffering fellow officers.

Finally we crossed the Bight and proceeded up the west coast to Fremantle harbour where our ship anchored. I soon noticed barges coming alongside and then all along the ship, as each barge was ready to leave, soldiers could be seen throwing ropes over the ship's side and clambering down for some unexpected shore leave. I wondered if they were actually deserting and I thought of poor old Mum and the white feather and how she had told me never to do anything dishonourable such as running away in the face of the enemy or being caught trying to desert. Breaking in on my thoughts, I saw men throwing ropes over the side right in front of me. After several hundred men had gone over the ship's side I was talking to a nearby sergeant when out of a doorway burst the idiot, brandishing an army service revolver. Seeing the ropes over the rail of the ship he turned, and striking a dramatic pose, he pointed the gun at me and shouted, 'I'll shoot the first man who tries to go overboard!'

The sergeant said, 'Half the ship has already gone over the side. Now give me that gun you stupid bastard,' and he snatched the gun off the clown.

He seemed to drop out of sight after that and I don't know for sure, but I heard of an officer who tried to get his men to rush across open ground to attack a bunch of Japs in the cover of underbrush at Singapore. This officer is reputed to have rushed forward in a very dramatic fashion brandishing a .45-calibre revolver and shouting 'Charge' at the top of his voice. He ran a few steps before being chopped to pieces by machine gun bullets. Fortunately his sergeant held the men back or they too would have been cut to pieces. It sounded like the idiot in action.

Eventually those who had gone AWL were rounded up ashore and brought back to the ship [13] and shortly after the *Aquitania* was heading north along the coast of Western Australia with escort warships guarding us. They were a grand sight and for hours I watched them bursting through large waves and signalling with Aldis lamps to each other.

We had been receiving wireless messages for days. The Japanese were taking island after island in their great drive southward and a large convoy of troop transports was supposed to be headed for Singapore. Later reports came of more troopships sailing up into the Gulf of Siam. Next came reports that Japanese troops that had landed in Siam[14] were crossing towards Malaya. From what I learned after, there was an aerodrome on what is now named Thailand near the Malay border and lined up on the tarmac was a long line of sleek, fast Hurricane fighter planes which had recently been brought from England. Just across the border in Malaya was another aerodrome equipped with only a few serviceable obsolete Brewster Buffalo fighter planes bought from America. The Japanese knew this defence weakness and all the other weaknesses in the British defence plans for the area. There had been a network of Japanese spies all over Asia. In fact, they knew when, where and how to strike at all the British forces.

My brother Jack had been in Malaya for twelve months and was still in the 2/19th Battalion under Major Anderson. In the base camp at Johore Bahru they had been hearing of the exploits of the other divisions overseas and they were all itching to play some part in the defence of their country in the great world conflict. Meanwhile, between their times of pleasure they were training very hard indeed. To relieve boredom they paid the small Malay paper boy who sold his papers at the base, and who couldn't speak English, to shout out what they said was good news. This was usually some insult to someone in the camp. However, once they went too far and Major Anderson was startled to hear the little lad shouting out loudly, 'Major Anderson is a bastard.' Giving the boy money to point out the nice men teaching him English, Anderson soon located the culprits.

Whilst Australians trained hard in jungle and malaria-infested swamps or paddy fields and were hard, wiry and well trained, ready for action, the English did parade-ground drill. General Arthur Percival,[15] leader of the Allied forces in the Malaya campaign, observed this Australian display of jungle training with ill-disguised contempt and appeared to favour the old English Redcoat mentality of troops advancing towards each other across open ground with kettledrums beating and standards flying. From information I received, it seemed he had learned nothing from the newspaper reports I had read about savage troops ravaging Chinese cities, including the Rape of Nanking with all its atrocities. Singapore was like an impoverished English aristocratic family trying to survive merely on their former reputation. It was no longer the so-called bastion of the Pacific with a huge garrison of well-trained troops and warships. The spectacular parade-ground drills and immaculate uniforms at the huge Changi Barracks were all part of a false front like the false fronts on the buildings in the early movies of the American

West. The people too were imbued with this false feeling of absolute security. The native population were absolutely subservient and, as servants, did just as they were told. Even the British army had native servants right down to the ordinary private soldiers with mess servants. And Japanese eyes were observing everything about them.

We were now in the Sunda Strait and in touch with Malaya and Australian Command. The Japanese had attacked and the British army was retreating in disorder down the Malayan Peninsula. I think this would have been the Australian version, while the English version would have been 'conducting a strategic withdrawal'.

What actually happened was that the Japanese attacked with great force. With captured Hurricane fighters, and Zeros, they were strafing retreating British soldiers and advancing on them not by sticking to the main highways or any arterial roads, but by crossing all terrain in front of them. Not being jungle-trained, the British troops were bewildered as Japs chased them on pushbikes, dropped down on them from tree branches and came wading across paddy fields after them.[16]

Lieutenant General Gordon Bennett[17] advised the officers on the ship to turn about and head for Australia. Thus we waited at anchor in the Sunda Strait while our Prime Minister was contacted by wireless.[18] Meanwhile, the Japs were using abandoned pleasure launches to land their forces behind the retreating troops near the coast. Australian troops moved up the peninsula to form a defensive line, using their three brigades spread across the peninsula to hold back the foe.

Word came from our Prime Minister that we were to proceed to Singapore. Now three Dutch ships had arrived and we were told we would be transferring on to them. We boarded these vessels and were soon headed for Singapore. Once aboard, we discovered that the toilets consisted of a steel trough with seats over it. Sea water was pumped along the trough and instead of using toilet paper you used your hand dipped in sea water. The Australians now had a name for the Dutchmen; they became known as the 'blot washers' and that name would stick.

We found a dark chap named Ali sharpening his new bayonet on the ship's grindstone and boasting how he was going to rip the Japs to pieces. I was to see Ali later as a pathetic shell-shock case and he never ever did get to ripping any Japs to pieces.

I never found out whether you see Singapore first or smell it first. As we sailed closer I saw men looking nervously upward and as I looked up at a few dark clouds in the sky I heard a chap say, 'If they come now, we are sitting ducks.' We had no navy escorts now and there was no visible sign of any English escort planes to shepherd us safely into Singapore harbour.

Then we saw them: twenty-five Mitsubishi bombers getting ready for their bomb run. We groaned with frustration – and then, as if from a clear sky, came the rain. It covered the three ships like a blanket, hitting our hats and cascading off our shoulders. One chap shouted, 'Send her down, Hughey!' and down it came as a screen, whilst frustrated Japanese pilots eyed their fuel gauges and turning slowly above us headed back for Thailand. And then, as though a tap was being turned off, as soon as the Jap bombers receded into the distance, the rain stopped, the sun came out and we sailed under a canopy of blue sky. I couldn't reason why, but I had the feeling I had just become involved in a miracle and feeling very grateful I mumbled a prayer of thanks to God. With the ship's engines throbbing steadily we entered Singapore harbour and I remember how quickly and efficiently we disembarked off these ships. Even foreign land felt good underfoot.

Whilst our reinforcements had been approaching Singapore, the 8th Division was forming a rough battle line across the peninsula. At Gemas on the south-west side of the peninsula a trap was being set for approaching Japanese bicycle troops by the leader of Australia's

2/30th Battalion, Lieutenant Colonel Frederick 'Black Jack' Galleghan. AIF sappers mined the bridge over the Gemencheh River and hiding in amongst the ferns they waited with plunger ready to detonate the charges. They had been instructed to first allow two hundred Japanese to come off the bridge where they would be ambushed by the 2/30th Infantry Battalion hidden in brush each side of the road. But the trap was yet to be sprung. As they watched, Japanese troops appeared on bicycles riding five abreast. The leader held up his hand to halt his troops, and laying his cycle down he walked warily over to the bridge and carefully inspected it. Satisfied that nothing was amiss, he remounted and rode forward. The sappers silently counted two hundred in fives and then down went the plunger. The bridge exploded with a roar, showering pieces of pushbikes, timber and Japs everywhere. Those off the bridge lay down their cycles and frantically tried to unstrap their rifles but they were bowled over like ninepins by Thompson sub-machine gunfire. Five hundred Japanese had died in about five minutes. Now troops fired at each other across the river. Later, under fire, Japanese engineers formed a tank support pontoon bridge. The first five tanks across were blown up by men of the 30th and then the battalion slowly withdrew.

Meanwhile, the 2/29th Battalion was dug in at Parit Sulong near Muar on the south-west coast of the peninsula, and advancing towards them was the cream of the Japanese army. One division consisted of men measuring six feet in height, the Imperial Guards, whilst the other was the terrible Chrysanthemum Division which had been blooded in China with a reputation of sadistic, senseless atrocities credited to them by observers from all over the world.

The Japanese speak of the cult of *bushido*, the code by which Japan's samurai warrior class lived, as though it pertains to something noble and Christ-like when it really means that you have no regard for anything or anybody smaller or weaker than yourself. Japanese children were taught to trap rats alive and torture them slowly to death to nurture manliness in them. If a Jap soldier is humiliated in battle he loses face and so he quite literally vents his spleen on the nearest living thing, especially if that animal or human is too small or weak to retaliate. This to us in the West is cowardice but to the Japanese it was the noble *bushido* spirit.

The 2/29th Battalion held a Japanese division at bay and even inflicted severe losses on the enemy. But with half their number dead or severely wounded they were forced to call for help from Base Camp and soon the 2/19th Battalion were on the way. Clambering out of trucks the men charged forward singing 'Waltzing Matilda' and soon the fierce pressure was eased and the wounded men were brought out from the battle area in ambulances. Indeed, the men of the 2/19th had poured so much firepower on the enemy that the Jap divisional commanders thought they were facing a force of at least one division of Australians, at the time. On the right flank were untrained young troops of the 45th Indian Brigade and these were the weak link in the chain of the defence line.

The Japanese generals must have been puzzled by all this resistance because up till now they had swept down the peninsula, replenishing food and fuel with what a generous enemy had left for them, together with luxury motor launches, cruisers and yachts filled with all sorts of goodies as well as stocks of petrol. These vessels proved handy for ferrying loads of well-trained Japanese troops down the coastline where they could move in behind hard-pressed retreating British troops and ambush them. Firing loud noisy grenades from little mortar tubes in amongst the young untrained Indian boys, the Japanese caused confusion and panic and soon the 45th Indian Brigade was retreating in disorder, allowing the Japanese forces to surround the 2/19th and cutting off any retreat towards the Muar Bridge.

Now the Japanese attacked fiercely in 'banzai' suicide charges to try to break through the 2/19th Battalion perimeter. Charge after charge ended in heavy losses. For several days and nights without food, water or medical supplies the 2/19th held back the crack Guards Division and then the tanks arrived. When they heard the clanking noise coming from the bridge the infantry groaned, 'Now they are going to attack us with bloody tanks,' and it seemed as though nothing was going to save them now.

Soon they were treated to an amazing sight as a young Australian gunner ran to a truck, seized a shell and slammed it into the breech of a nearby 25-pounder. Then he climbed over the gunshield and sitting astride the barrel bumped his behind up and down, forcing the barrel down, then he hopped back down again and pulled the lanyard. The turret of the first tank was blown off and it tilted over. Rushing back to the truck he seized another shell and as the second tank came along the gun again spat flame and the tank was put out of action. His artillery mates ran to help him but by then the third tank was retreating.

On 22 January, as night came once again, 2/19th commander Anderson ordered all men to try to break through the encircling foe in small groups. Carrying compasses, each group quietly silenced any Jap that blocked their retreat to the Muar River.

My brother Jack was one of the men who made it through, swimming across the river and collapsing near a Chinese house. These brave Chinese farmers carried Jack for miles on a pushbike and then by boat until they reached the 5th Norfolk Regiment of the British army, who were just about to blow up a bridge behind them. Grabbing Jack, they hoisted him on to a truck and tore off south towards Johore Bahru and the Australian base.

One of the last men to escape across the river was able to hear the screams of the wounded Australians who had to be left behind. The noble *bushido* spirit was evident again as these 'knights' subjected their gallant enemy to degrading, humiliating torture and abuse before dousing them with petrol and setting them on fire. This man survived to report this terrible atrocity. The true facts of the Muar battle would eventually become snowed under by English historians giving an entirely different and misleading account of what happened but those who know what really happened in Malaya are proud of these brave men at Gemas and Muar and the other areas of battle. The Japanese owned up that they lost two thousand at Muar, which was probably only a very weak conservative guess. The poor civilians at Muar would pay dearly because the Japs had lost face against the Australians in battle but – no problems – civilians couldn't defend themselves.[19]

After we reinforcements had landed on Singapore on 24 January, we were taken by train up to a point not far from the base camp at Johore Bahru in Malaya. I listened to some old hands who were escorting us on the train and observing the shocked looks on my mates' faces I realised they were just as terrified as I was by the descriptions of the Japanese and the terrible atrocities they were committing against old people, women and children and even small animals. To suggest the young reinforcements were totally demoralised would be correct, for even the dullest recruits had gathered by now that, should you become hit with shrapnel or be wounded in any way and be picked up by the Japs, you would die by torture.

When we left the train we made our way through rubber trees to the base camp. I had hardly entered the camp when I became aware of someone shouting, 'Bob Holman, where is he?' I shouted, 'Here I am,' and was immediately seized by the arm by one of the original 2/19th Battalion men and taken to where Jack was being supported by two of his mates. I walked up to Jack and shook hands. Swaying on his feet, he said, 'They got poor old Len. The rotten cruel swine murdered him.' Jack's best friend had been amongst the helpless, unarmed wounded who had been humiliated, tortured and then burned alive after the battle of Muar. Jack's mates said he was suffering from battle fatigue and badly needed some sleep so I had to leave him in their charge.

Orders were issued for troops to cross the causeway to Singapore.[20] The reinforcements were all assembled later on the golf course. Whilst we were milling around I was told I wasn't wanted in the 2/19th Battalion as the now Colonel Anderson, VC, wouldn't have brothers in his unit. This was his official reason but had he seen my arrival with buttons all undone and one puttee dragging, any self-respecting officer wouldn't have wanted me in his unit.

I was reminded of an incident at Dubbo camp when in typical style I was last out of the hut after assembly had been blown on the bugle. With my rifle tucked under my left arm and frantically trying to do up my coat buttons, I was on my way to join my unit who were already lined up. Then I became aware of an officer's voice saying with heavy sarcasm, 'You have no doubt observed, men, how Farmer Holman carries his gun in the accepted duck hunter's style, loosely held under one arm.' And I remembered when our machine gun crew was under instruction at Dubbo (I was in number four position at the time) as we paused to listen to some instructions I fell asleep with my head on a box of ammunition. I was shaken back to consciousness with the heavy sarcastic tone of the sergeant's voice in my ears, 'We don't want to put you to any inconvenience, Holman, but we could use some ammunition.' In both these instances I caused quite a ripple of laughter. Perhaps as a soldier I was quite a success as an army entertainer.

Roy and Kelly came to see me to find out if we could get together again, but since we had been separated I had fallen back into my old inclination to avoid friendship ties and go it alone. I said I would wait to see what turned up and that I wasn't going to volunteer to go anywhere.

What turned up were the barrels of the Japanese artillery guns as they blocked up wheel to wheel on the opposite side of Johore Strait. If I remember correctly the artillery barrage started early on 8 February. I know that when it first started I took a flying leap into a slit trench and I remember getting a fleeting glimpse of a snake lying at the bottom of the trench as I descended. Fortunately, it was dead and in between shells I was able to throw it out.

It was a concentrated barrage lasting from about 8 am to 8 pm as far as I can remember and old-timers from the First World War said it was equal to any barrage they had ever experienced; they estimated sixty shells were airborne during every minute. The shells were mostly directed at the two Australian troop areas.[21] Of course there were many questions being asked as to why the English troops weren't delivering some sort of counter barrage with their huge supply of field guns. Somebody said, 'Percival has ordered 60,000 English troops to guard the swamps and that's a good place for 'em.'

Next day a truck pulled up and a no-nonsense sergeant ejected from the cabin. Pointing first at me, he yelled out, 'Right, you, you and you,' as he counted six men, 'grab your gear and hop in the back of that truck.' I felt a sickening tug at the pit of my stomach, thinking, this is it, up to the front line we go, and I climbed up into the truck. I didn't know it then, but if I had been sent to the Australian troops area I would have been right where the Japanese intended to make a landing. Instead we stopped near a deserted English mansion which had been appropriated as Australian Headquarters. As we de-bussed I noticed a chap spraying camouflage paint onto a tent and I asked, 'Where are we?'

'You are at 8th Division Headquarters, Bukit Timah,' he answered. We were escorted into an area encampment and told we would serve as guards to protect all the Australian officers and staff.

A chap told us we might get a last letter home if we wrote straight away and soon after I sat at a little table trying to compose a letter which would let Mum know I was in a safe place now; she would guess I was actually in HQ, which, as everyone who has read or heard of the events of World War I knows, was the safest place on the whole battle front. I wrote, 'I cannot mention names of places or military units, but I am now in a very safe – ' and then the first shell landed smack in the centre of the camp area. After the explosion I ran for the nearest slit trench, where I foolishly lay face down, and next second there were about six pairs of army boots bearing down on different parts of my anatomy. The chap who caused me the most discomfort was the one who placed one boot on the back of my neck and the other on my shoulder. Then I could hear the whine of shells as they straddled the whole area and shock waves shook my body.

Looking up through the tall trees which were growing around us, one chap spotted a group of planes. I heard him yell out, 'Oh Gor blimey, here comes twenty-five Mitsubishis now to bomb us. We are going to be bombed and shelled at the same time.' In amongst the noise of shells whining overhead I heard the roar of bombers coming in on a bomb run, then the whistling of the tailfins of the bombs, followed by the cracking of branches as they pierced the foliage above.

The noise was terrific, and my body was jolted by a series of explosions as aerial bombs rained down on our camp area. Now the bombers were leaving and the Jap gunners were dropping a creeping barrage, gradually elevating their gun barrels, and now we could hear shells exploding further down the road, possibly towards the crossroads as they sought out passing troop trucks. In amongst the whine of shells passing overhead I heard a voice screaming, 'Don't let them hit me, don't let them hit me,' over and over, then a voice above me yelled out, 'It's Ali and he's shell-shocked. Look at him running round and round.'

Next a voice of authority ordered, 'Grab that man, you chaps, and hang on to him.'

As men clambered out from on top of me I gradually managed to rise painfully onto my feet. I saw Ali sitting on the ground with bowed head and he was trembling all over and couldn't answer me when I spoke to him. The ground all around was pockmarked with shell and bomb craters but surprisingly there were only about six soldiers killed and I think they died because they had obviously failed to take adequate cover.

Now the shelling ceased and I ventured back to my tent, which was still intact. Snatching up the letter I screwed it up and threw it away. So much, I thought, for old diggers' tales about how safe you were at Headquarters, and how you never ever hear the shell that is close. I was in Headquarters and had just been bombed and shelled simultaneously and I had heard the shells that were close because they made a definite buzzing noise. Then I heard it again, a buzzing noise, and I went through the tent opening in a leap and was nearly swept off my feet as a shell landed behind me. Still running, I heard someone running behind me and the buzzing noise came again. Glancing behind me I was able to get a fleeting glimpse of a shell bursting behind a running soldier, and to my horror shrapnel tore his right arm off at the shoulder and blood was spurting out as he ran. I reached the edge of a gully, the sides of which were covered with ferns and scrub. I went rolling down, taking broken branches and pieces of fern with me as I went, finally ending up in a dense bush at the bottom of the gully.

Gasping for breath, I listened as the shells were now landing further away, and I realised it was another creeping barrage. Then I heard voices; one man said, 'I just saw one of those new reinforcement blokes running in this direction. He was doing about fifty miles an hour when he passed me – poor little bugger was completely demoralised.'

I decided to sneak out of the area. The ground flattened out at the end of the gully and as I proceeded I saw a young English soldier gazing at a deep bomb crater. 'Me myte was standing right 'ere when ah last seen 'im,' he kept muttering.

'Well, if he was here when the bomb dropped it's not much use looking for him now,' I said, and suddenly realising I was in an English perimeter, I headed back before some stupid Pommy officer wanted to declare me a deserter and have me shot.

The shelling had stopped and I reached the cook-house, and there I met a dispatch rider who had an interesting story to tell me. It seems that Malayan Command and Australian Command had been worried over the murder of dispatch riders, and it seemed as though some person or persons had declared open season on all dispatch riders as one by one their bullet-ridden bodies were being found by the roadside.

One day an Australian rider pulled off the road and sheltered under some shady trees to make some minor adjustment to his machine. After this had been effected he restarted his machine and was adjusting the broad belt carrying his Thompson sub-machine gun when he looked back up the road. Coming down the road was another dispatch rider. Following the rider was a black Ford V8 saloon car, and as he watched, a side window came down and the muzzle of a machine gun was thrust out through the opening. Then as he watched on in horrified fascination the car drew alongside the hapless dispatch rider and flame spat from the gun muzzle. The dispatch rider crumpled, the bike wobbled and bike and rider slewed off the road.

In cover of the dark shade the Australian waited, revving his engine, then as the saloon car passed he took off in hot pursuit. Drawing close to the rear of the vehicle he flipped the lever on his gun to full burst, and slowly lowering the muzzle down onto his steering damper he moved it to and fro as he pulled the trigger, aiming at the rear tyres of the car. Slowing to a standstill he put a fresh clip of ammunition onto his gun and proceeded after the vehicle which had wobbled and gone off the road. Drawing within range he stopped again, and hosed the saloon car from one end to the other till it looked like a colander and blood poured out from under the car doors. The dispatch riders' killer had been executed.

I learned that Australians have a strong feeling for real justice, and real justice was often a kangaroo court and very swift. I heard of one English officer who didn't get the chance to use his connections to defeat justice.[22] Of course, should one be questioned one would plead complete ignorance. A supposedly loyal Indian was caught arranging his white washing in the shape of an arrow pointing towards an Australian battalion perimeter so that enemy planes knew where to bomb. He didn't return to India.[23] Jap infiltrators were everywhere and there were Malayans caught in treachery who were shot just where they stood. Even Australians weren't immune from execution.

In Headquarters I could hear the exchanges of fire and the thunder of guns but I had to rely on grapevine news to obtain some idea of what was going on, or eavesdrop on what was supposed to be private officers' conversation. It was apparent that the Japs were going to attempt a landing soon.

Even when the Japs did cross, the news sounded unbelievable. I met angry men drifting in wanting to know, 'Why were the artillery not allowed to lob shells on the crowded Jap troop train at Johore railway yards? Why were the 2/4th machine-gunners, with their guns trained on barges full of Jap troops, ordered not to fire on the Japs but to allow them to land – and then retreat? Why did Percival order sixty thousand English troops up one end of the island to guard the swamps where the Japs would have sunk up to their armpits in mud anyway, and leave two Australian battalions to face the entire Jap landing force?' There were bitter words being exchanged but it wasn't the English private's fault how things were going.

Anyway, when the Japs did cross, the two Australian battalions bore the full shock of the attack and lost heavily in troop numbers. This was the confusion that reigned supreme. Since the shelling had started I had been sleeping sitting up in a slit trench or lying on the edge of one. One morning, however, whilst I slumbered a Bofors anti-aircraft crew moved in right behind me in some shrubbery. Dawn broke, and suddenly a Zero appeared searching for unsuspecting dispatch riders or patrols moving in the area. Then suddenly the Bofors gun started firing and, although I had just woken up, the noise gave me a terrific fright.

There was a chance that Jap tanks might break through and someone had produced a Boyes anti-tank gun; another chap had put a Bren gun together and was looking for a number two. Having heard how firing a Boyes gun could leave you with a broken collarbone from the breastplate recoil, I promptly yelled out to the Bren gunner, 'I'll be your number two, mate.'

The sergeant detailed us to scout the area for possible infiltrators, and off we went with me lugging ammunition boxes and trailing behind. Moving from cover to cover we had viewed the area thoroughly and were returning to camp. As we passed a native kampong we paused to look at a pond nearby. It was obvious that this pond was the dumping ground for all of the residents' garbage – it smelled vile and duck or chicken's entrails were floating on the surface of the water. It had a high bank on one side of the pond, and whilst observing this I heard the now-familiar buzzing noise. My mate threw himself down flat, and I dropped my ammo and leapt forward to land on the side of the bank.

As the shell exploded nearby and shrapnel whistled overhead, my feet were slipping, and down into all the filth and slime of the pond I went, right up to my waist. I climbed back out onto the bank, and immediately my mate seized his nose between thumb and forefinger and in a nasal twang said, 'Don't come near me, Holman, you stink like a polecat.' We made our way back, skirting a dirt road. My mate had abandoned all concealment now, and just seemed to be trying to put as much distance as he could between me and himself.

Then I saw the ambulance, just standing there as though abandoned. Sneaking up and peering over the tailgate I saw to my delight a clean pair of trousers and a shirt lying on the floor, and further down the grassy slope was the blue of water reflecting the blue sky. After climbing into the ambulance and grabbing the clean clothes, I headed for the patch of blue. Down in a hollow trickled a small stream passing through several small ponds. Stripping off my smelly clothes I lay down and luxuriated in a lovely cool refreshing bath. Later, wearing fresh clean clothes, I headed back to camp.

At the camp there was a group of Gurkhas who had become separated from their unit. They seemed very friendly towards the Australians and were smiling and shaking hands with everyone. Not realising that they spoke English, I asked one of my mates, 'Why do they wear loops of string threaded through pink seashells around their belts?' Glaring at me he said, 'Wake up, Holman, they're Japanese ears hanging from loops of cord.' I must have turned a shade pale and the Gurkhas burst out laughing, then one of them walked forward and after slapping me on the shoulder he pumped my hand in a vigorous, friendly manner to indicate he liked me. I was very glad they were on our side. Then I noticed a group of Englishmen who were as lost as the Gurkhas. Like the Gurkhas, they had been enjoying the hospitality of tea and biscuits and as they rested I thought they may have a story to tell.

These men looked terrible, with clothes in tatters, long straggly beards and hair hanging down behind collars. They had gaunt, haggard faces and hollow cheeks. But what shocked me was the way they kept glancing around them with fear-filled eyes. They could have been described as young men suddenly grown old. I was a young untried, untested soldier and I felt very sorry in my heart for these pathetic young men. They said that they had been up at Kota Bahru on the north-east coast of the peninsula when the Japanese landing force attacked and after throwing away anything that might impede their progress, they had quite literally run most of the way down the peninsula. After managing to sneak across the strait in boats at night they had moved around Japanese positions and blundered into Australian Headquarters.

On asking them how the Japanese had attacked them, I was told that the Japs had behaved like a large tribe of monkeys swarming all over the British forces from every conceivable position by sea, air, road, jungle and rubber plantation. I gained the distinct impression that these men had expected the Japanese to sound the 'charge' on a bugle and to advance down roads, sports fields and airstrips with standards flying and kettledrums beating, like the War of Independence in America. Wherever these poor chaps went the Japs hounded them with Hurricane fighters, English-built launches, pushbikes with bars made of Australian hardwood. They shelled them with Australian scrap iron and jumped down on them from the branches of trees.

During their wild, fearful flight down the peninsula they approached a causeway road separating two large paddy fields. After looking fearfully behind them for a sign of the Japs who must now be very close, they started to run across the causeway. Then out of some scrub appeared an English officer. 'Hello, chaps,' he said, 'don't worry about the Japanese, my men will take care of them.' Looking wildly around, they were just beginning to think he'd gone mad when, pointing to some neat piles of clothing, he said, 'My men are concealed in the paddy fields.' Looking closely they saw that the Gurkhas had lain down in amongst the rows of young rice, smearing mud over themselves and picking up rice shoots to place them on each other's backs. They held their long, curved-blade *kukri* knives in their hands.

Getting themselves under cover, the Englishmen watched the road for the approaching Japanese. Soon the Japs hove into sight jogging down the road. Seeing the brush at the end of the causeway they joked amongst themselves and pointed towards it, no doubt savouring what fun they would have torturing these helpless unarmed Englishmen. The Gurkhas allowed them to fill the full length of the causeway before they arose, screaming out loud and surging towards them swinging their *kukris*.

The young Englishmen shuddered as they recalled the horror of this scene. The grins had left the faces of the Japanese and instead of laughing they screamed with fear and ran for their lives. They were tripping over severed Japanese heads as they twisted and dodged to avoid the slashing knives but there was no escape for them and the Gurkhas chased them until the whole of the causeway was littered with bloody heads and bodies. The English officer turned to the group of shocked young men and with an air of intense pride he remarked, 'Jolly efficient little bastards, aren't they?'

I was wondering next morning about how some men seem to be born soldiers with courage and fighting ability whilst others, without any conscious wish to fight or kill any living thing, suddenly find themselves involved in a war. Had my parents been wealthy, I would now have probably been in an art class enjoying myself. Instead, I was here, and listening to the sounds of a fierce battle going on.

My thoughts were interrupted by our no-nonsense sergeant after volunteers. 'Righto, Holman,' he said.

'What's the job?' I asked.

'We are going to try to find out where the Japs are,' he answered. Now, I had realised that at some time the Japs would come to me and

I would have to kill as many as I could, but going out into unknown territory looking for them wasn't in my scheme of things. 'Can't you get someone else?' I asked in a shaky, tremulous voice.

'No, I can't!' he snapped. Later, as the boys started moving out I tried to hang back but the eagle eye of the sergeant was watching. 'Come on, keep up, Holman,' he said. I began to think of how I felt about the Poms when I first heard of them retreating in disorder. I wasn't feeling very brave at all now.

I had seen on films how soldiers enter a village on patrol, kicking doors in and then charging in and searching for the enemy in the house. Thus when we quietly sneaked into a village I knew all the things a soldier was expected to do. Fortunately I never found any young Japs hiding in any of the houses I searched after kicking the doors open, and I was very thankful for that. If I had met a Jap I would have had to bayonet him; that is, unless he got me first.

I had always avoided aggressive body contact sports whether serious or in fun, and in sports like rugby league when chaps hugged one another after one had scored a try, I viewed this comradely demonstrative act with an acute feeling of nausea. Yet, despite this former revulsion, when a tough-looking 2/19th Battalion soldier suddenly appeared asking, 'You looking for Japs?' I was so relieved I could have kissed him. He gave our sergeant the present Jap position.

You always wonder about meeting the enemy face to face. It is one thing to fire at a concealed foe, who can kill you by firing back at you, but actual physical animal contact, that is another. There was a strange case when, during a bayonet charge by the 30th, one big tough Australian had his rifle taken off him and he was thrown on his back. He was so startled he got to his feet and ran back through his advancing comrades. He had to toe the carpet later and explain, and he was exonerated from any charge of cowardice. But why did the Jap drop his own weapon and disarm the Australian? Did he respond to judo training, not army training? I heard stories of men facing each other and both signalling they wanted to retreat, refusing to use the bayonet.

Next day several men were nearly shot by Jap sniper fire. The snipers wore camouflage net and split-toed sandshoes, and carried beautiful precision-made carbines, weapons greatly admired and feared by Allied troops, unlike the crudely made ordinary Japanese service rifle, which made our troops wonder how Japs ever managed to shoot any of us at all. With his camouflage net strung with leaves, if a sniper sat quite still in the fork of a tree branch he became invisible. The special cleft in his shoes enabled him to grip vines and so climb trees easily.

Feeling guilty over my previous day's reluctance to become introduced to the Japanese, I decided to repair my image and foolishly set up a plan to flush out the sniper by setting myself up as bait whilst my mates hid and watched all the surrounding trees and palm tops for the slightest movement. Either our sniper had sneaked away during darkness or he realised he was being set up, or perhaps he was only after high-ranking officers. I will never know, but I stayed uninjured and there was no more sniping.

Further over, another sniper wasn't so lucky for as my friend Roy walked across an open space he fired at him, missing Roy but hitting the large tin of biscuits Roy was carrying. Once under cover Roy carefully examined the acute angle made by the bullet and where he had been at the point of impact, and he decided that this bullet could only have been fired from someone in a very tall coconut palm growing in the area. With some help from his mates he set up a Vickers gun and, aiming at the base of the palm, he started firing. Chips of fibre were torn off as the bullets chewed a deep gash at the base of the palm. With a soft breeze riffling through the tree tops Roy stopped firing, there came a soft scuffling sound, and the palm started to fall. About a quarter of the way down, out flew a figure screaming loudly, plummeting downwards to eventually hit the ground with a sickening thud. Roy knew how to deal with snipers in palms.

During the campaign there had been little or no air cover and the British forces had taken a battering from Japanese Zeros and Mitsubishis. I don't know if it was true but we were told that the pilots who had fought so bravely and well during the famous Battle of Britain had been sent here to Singapore to rest and repair their shattered nerves. If this was true, a terrible blunder had been made.

It was horrifying to watch about three old worn-out Brewster Buffaloes flown by crack British pilots facing about twelve Zeros. The Japanese would fly circles around them, shooting bits off their wings, until finally the pilots would bail out. The Japanese would follow their progress downward in the parachute and just as the pilot thought he was safe, they would fly towards him and chop him to pieces with their machine guns. Here was this noble *bushido* spirit again, when faced with someone who was helpless and unable to fight back. They hadn't shown much bravery when the Gurkhas chased them on the peninsula. During one of these acts of bravery by the British pilots I saw a great big tough Aussie with tears of frustration streaming down his face. He was shouting, 'You magnificent, stupid Pommy bastard!'

Lieutenant General Gordon Bennett, or 'Old Cocky' as he was affectionately known by lesser ranks because of his parrot-shaped nose, was very busy in conference with English generals. He was usually angry when I did get near him and would be mumbling to his driver, 'Retreat, retreat – that's all the Pommy bastards can say – retreat.' One day he refused to eat with the English officers and shared a thermos of hot tea and some bully beef sandwiches with his driver. This was the typical Gordon Bennett we all knew and admired.[24]

One day we received the order to retreat and after piling onto trucks we headed towards the coast. We moved back to an abandoned British mansion in Holland Road. Getting out of the truck with my mate, we debated whether this place had a garden with edible fruit or vegetables in it. Instead of doing what guards are supposed to do, stand on guard at the entrance door, we found pineapples growing at the back of the house. After sampling them we began pointing at each other's mouth and were soon dabbing at our lips and looking at the bloodstains on our handkerchiefs. Unripe pineapple, we later learned, contains an acid that takes the skin off your lips. After also inspecting a weird-looking fruit known as Chinese five fingers, which also seemed unripe and which hung down from its tree like a green plumber's glove, we left the garden and returned to the house.

Unbeknownst to us, Japs were watching us and had reported our position. After inspecting Bluey and myself through binoculars they must have thought Australia was scraping the bottom of the barrel to come up with recruits such as us. Then to add further to their amusement, while Bluey and I dabbed at our skinned lips, a large staff car carrying generals advanced with a very large Union Jack, lashed to a long pole wired onto the radiator, flying proudly in the breeze. Japanese Headquarters were receiving vital intelligence, but Bluey and I were still poking about looking for food, unaware of all the generals left unguarded on the top floor of the mansion. Perhaps it was just as well the 'big brass' didn't see us guarding the entrance because I don't think my mate even knew how to do a full 'present arms', which was the required salute for high-ranking officers.

Not that I was ever very good at these rifle salutes. Several times I had fumbled them at Dubbo AIF camp and once I had given a carload of drunken sergeants a full 'present arms', which was reserved for high-ranking officers. This effort brought forth loud cheers and handclaps and gales of drunken laughter. My star performance, however, was when caught unawares by a carload of officers entering the camp; I failed to give any salute at all. A red-faced lieutenant was sent back after the car stopped to enquire how long I had been in the army. I said, 'A couple of weeks, sir,' and so I was excused. I had learned to tell lies like an old veteran.

Bluey and I eventually found the fridge and with our pockets stuffed with bananas and bottles of lemonade in our hands we proceeded to search the house, eating mouthfuls of banana and taking periodic swigs from the bottles. I walked up a carpeted stairway and seeing a heavy, ornate door instantly had a vision of a large banquet room containing a massive long dining table piled high with mountains of glorious food.

Turning the doorknob, I stepped into the room and became frozen with shocked surprise. There stood the large long banquet table covered with maps, not food, and all around it were officers with canes pointing at various features on the maps. I recognised the foppish, effeminate-looking man with immaculate uniform and white topee as General Percival. Then there was a large, broad-shouldered, grey-haired general wearing an officer's cap, with a distinguished appearance and air of authority as he drew attention to some position on the map. I recognised this man from photographs I had seen in newspapers as General Wavell. Opposite these two stood Lieutenant General Gordon Bennett and other officers. I slipped out before they noticed me and went back along the hallway and down the stairs looking for Bluey to suggest we start trying to look like soldier guards or sentries near the entrance.

The Japs' reaction to the blatant showing of the flag was to arrange for three fast fighter bombers to fly very low on a bomb run designed to land direct hits on this Headquarters and these generals. Actually, if they had known who was on guard they could have sent a Jap over whilst my mate and I were checking out the garden and he could have walked up the stairs, entered the room and with his machine gun mown down all the generals.

Stepping out onto the verandah, I heard the roar of aircraft engines. I ran across a lawn and leapt into the middle of a bed of flowers. The planes roared overhead and bombs exploded all around, one of them in the centre of the front lawn just as I landed face down in sweet-smelling flowers. I heard one of the bombs burst right next to the house.[25]

I heard later that all the officers with the exception of Gordon Bennett dived underneath the large table. When they emerged, there stood Bennett, cap and shoulders covered with white plaster off the ceiling; he grinned and said, 'Cheeky little bastards!' His driver told me how on one occasion they had run smack into a Jap patrol. 'I nearly turned the car over wheeling around and roaring down the road as the Japs shot all of the glass out of the windows. When I glanced back to see if our General was still alive, there sat Bennett with a grin on his face. Chuckling softly he said, "Cranky lot of little bastards, no sense of humour."'

Bennett's bedroom was the front lower room with large French windows. That night, shadowy figures fired a burst of machine gun bullets, missing Bennett and the night guard. The following night I was on guard and our sergeant handed me a Thompson gun and, pointing to all the bullet holes, said, 'They're not playing games, Holman. You see someone, you shoot. If you hesitate even for a second, you're dead.' He showed me where he would approach when bringing up my relief guard so that there would be no mistake. Then I settled down, watchful and alert. I remembered how as a child I had noticed that crickets stopped chirping when footsteps vibrated the ground and that frogs were susceptible to the same vibrations. Here now I could hear crickets and frogs out in front of me.

I was startled later when a pyjama-clad figure appeared through the French windows and Bennett stood chatting alongside me for a few minutes, puffing on a cigarette. The glow of the lit cigarette didn't bother me as fireflies flittered all around us, but white pyjamas could get us both killed. I was trying to listen politely to what he was saying so I could give him the right answers and yet keep an ear out for the frogs and crickets. With a final 'Goodnight, soldier,' he retired inside, leaving me to concentrate on frogs and crickets.

Just as I reckoned my relief was due there came the tiny snap of a breaking twig and the insects stopped their noise. Slipping the catch on full burst, I pointed the gun at the direction of the sound, and I could just make out two shadowy figures. I started to squeeze the trigger, but just at that instant a tiny shaft of light outlined an Australian helmet, and I stopped and eased my finger off the trigger. 'Blimey,' the sergeant gasped, 'that was close. Sorry, Holman, I came from the wrong direction. But you hesitated,' he added. 'I told you, you shoot fast, never hesitate.'

All day I had listened to the thunder of the guns and it seemed to sound louder and closer.[26] As I looked down the long gravel driveway towards the main road and the sound of trucks that came from that direction, I tried to identify the different types of guns firing. In my mind I was saying, now that's a Vickers, that's a Bren, or that's a Thompson, and they sounded very close indeed. Then up the gravel driveway ran my mate, shouting, 'The nineteenth have retreated down the front road and the thirtieth down the back road!' I'd worked it out that we were now in the front line when our sergeant screamed out, 'Dig in, men! We have to defend this area till the officers get clear!'

The officers were leisurely strolling out with bags, slowly getting into cars and slowly driving away. It seemed as though they didn't realise we were in the front line and as the suspense built up, I remembered the films I'd gone to see as a little boy, and how I'd bitten holes in my handkerchief. One officer strolled out, paused and said petulantly, 'Oh bother, I've left my jolly toothbrush back in the house.' I felt like screaming, 'Bugger your toothbrush!' and trembling, I thought, here's where we all get massacred, knowing that about twenty-five men couldn't beat the whole Chrysanthemum Division of the Imperial Japanese Army.

The last officer left and it was too late for us now, unless some miracle occurred. Our brave dispatch rider set out to try to find a way through. Then I decided that the best idea would be to arm myself with hand grenades and get next to the man with the Bren gun. It grew dark as night came on and I turned to the sergeant and asked, 'What was all that rumbling noise?'

'Tanks,' he snapped, adding, 'For your information, Holman, we are now three miles behind the Japanese front line.'

I wanted to say, 'You've got to be joking,' but seeing the look on his face I kept quiet. Then up raced the dispatch rider, yelling out to follow him as he knew a way out. We ran for the trucks and as the first truck started off we came under very heavy fire. Our driver tried to start the engine but it only spluttered and died. Again he tried, with the same terrifying result, and then as I was just about ready to jump out and run, the engine started and we were off. It sounded like the whole Japanese army was shooting at us; how they missed us was a real miracle. For sure we owed our lives to that brave dispatch rider.

We pulled up at Tanglin Hill just around a bend. Each truck was held while the men were told to dig in, and then the trucks moved off as soon as we had unloaded. We thought we had been followed, and so a large anti-tank cannon was set up facing the bend in the road, with gun crew tense and expectant.

A Bren gun crew crouched alongside with their gun ready. I moved up the hill overlooking the Bren gun crew and started digging. Then the shelling started and it was a case of dig, flatten out and dig again and all up the side of the hill men were digging in to get away from the shrapnel that was flying around us. Eventually we did and then the shelling eased off.

I was thinking of Vickers guns and on impulse I ran up the hill to where a whole lot of gear had been unloaded. Rummaging around I found a Vickers, in pieces but it was all there. Then I began making trips up and down the hill carrying pieces of Vickers machine gun whilst under a barrage of shells. The Japs still had not made any charge forward and were apparently content to stay and shell our position. Eventually I had bits of Vickers machine gun all around my slit trench plus a large pile of hand grenades. In between ducking up and down I eventually got the gun set up and loaded ready to fire. I could now finish up in accordance with how I had been trained: before they blew me up, I would take as many of the enemy with me as I could. I felt very calm and I wasn't afraid anymore. If they were going to charge, I was prepared.

Things had been happening all around us. The Australian cruiser, *Perth* and American cruiser, *Houston*, were sunk by the Japanese light fleet in the Sunda Strait. Ships had left Singapore with nurses and women and children aboard and had been chased by the Japanese light fleet. The Australian naval sloop, *Yarra*, tried to hold off the Jap fleet and was blown to pieces, leaving nurses and women and children undefended. The *SS Vyner Brooke* was sunk and the nurses made it ashore on Banka Island where they surrendered to Japanese infantry. The Japanese forced them back out into the water and machine-gunned them. Sister Vivian Bullwinkel survived by pretending to be dead. And after three and a half years in captivity, she was able to testify at the Tokyo war crime trials.

My brother Jack, after a strenuous period as infantryman and stretcher-bearer, had collapsed from battle fatigue and been taken to the Cathay Theatre, which was being used as a hospital and had a large red cross painted on the roof. A Jap bomber flew over and dropped a bomb on the centre of the building, which already held many shell-shocked victims.

Now as we prepared to fight to a finish, mixed nationalities led by an Australian officer had ordered women and children off a ship at bayonet point and were preparing to desert by this ship to Sumatra. They would be arrested at Sumatra by Australian medical officers.[27]

On Tanglin Hill we were copping an intense artillery barrage and, rising up after one shell burst, I was in time to see the effect of what old diggers referred to as a 'daisycutter'. There stood a straight-up palm gently rocking to and fro before finally crashing down showing a trunk cleanly sliced through as though with a giant razor. Next, I was amazed to see a man running in mid air as a shell drove in on an angle underneath his trench and quite literally blew him up. When his feet reached ground he took off like the proverbial Bondi tram and he was brought down with a beautiful rugby tackle executed by one of the 8th Division signallers. Somewhere close behind me, a man was groaning and calling out for help. I saw his mate wriggle along and look down into the trench as an anguished cry came up, 'It's me leg, it's cut orf at the knee!' His would-be rescuer was chuckling and answered, 'Get up, you dopey idiot, it's only a clod of dirt resting on the back of your kneecap where it fell on you.'

I saw one of my mates carrying a dispatch bag and I was curious. 'Let me see the dispatch orders,' I said.

'Now you know I can't do that,' he protested and then after a quick look around he flipped open the top and quickly lifted a paper up in full view. It read, 'All Australian troops will fight to the last man.' A deadly calm came over me and I thought of my mother and how she and the people of Australia would learn that the Australians fought it out right to the last. I wondered how the English troops would explain why the Australians were left to fight on alone and not surrender, which seemed a possibility the way things were.

At the bottom of the hill the ground flattened out and on the opposite side of the road was a large hospital of *attap*-roofed huts made of bamboo. Red crosses were painted on every hut roof and a large red cross signboard at the gate read '45th Indian Brigade'. I had noticed looking down on these huts that the Japs hadn't bombed them and I wondered if some of the stories of Japanese ruthlessness were being exaggerated. About this time, Japanese soldiers were striding into a large English hospital. Behind one of the front doors hid a terrified orderly who would later testify to this brutal massacre in a war crimes trial. They slaughtered nurses, doctors, orderlies, patients – even stabbing one man on the operating table. Their general would later give the feeble excuse that his troops were rough, incorrigible men who were hard to keep under control or discipline, and said he was very sorry this massacre had occurred.

Back at Tanglin the shelling eased and now I heard a Jap bomber. It swept into view flying low over the hospital, dropping dozens of incendiaries onto the tinder-dry *attap* roofs of the huts below. I looked in horror as flames swept through the huts until the whole hospital was a roaring inferno and I could hear men screaming as they burned to death. Orderlies tried in vain to get helpless victims out of the huts.[28] The pilot circled around the area as though he was gloating over his handiwork. I shook my fist and screamed, 'You rotten filthy bastard!'

and collapsed in a sobbing, trembling heap at the bottom of my trench. I was no hard, tough soldier. And all the shelling, bombing and general tension was starting to catch up with me.[29]

Although the hillside was pockmarked with shell holes, I wondered why we hadn't received more intensive fire. It never occurred to me that Yamashita[30] might be short of ammunition and was dreading a desperate Australian counter-attack any moment. It was getting very depressing with the smell of burnt flesh and everyone waiting to be attacked – and then there was a loud 'bang' and I sat in the bottom of the trench stunned and shocked, not realising what had happened. I must be dead, I thought, perhaps in some in-between state where I am floating in a semi-conscious void.

Then I heard little particles of dirt falling onto my steel helmet and, looking down, I could see that they were black and I could smell cordite. With the gradual realisation that I was still alive, I managed to scramble to my feet and look around me. The top of my trench had fallen in on me and was blackened all around the edge. The Vickers gun lay in a torn, twisted heap, having taken the full impact of the shell. Then a chorus of happy voices yelled out, 'He's all right!' and I looked around me at a bunch of 8th Division signallers who had been concerned about this strange young bloke who wouldn't join in with any of the other groups in trenches but insisted on being alone in his own trench.

I learned later that after a particularly heavy barrage, a signaller had crawled down to my trench to check on my state of being, that is to say, being still alive or being dead. He returned with his report. 'Gor blimey, it's like a bloody arsenal down there. There's Mills bombs everywhere in shelves cut into the sides of his trench. He's scrounged a case of Nestle's cream and eaten it all and he's lying on his back fast asleep and snoring!' I remembered the bit about the empty tins later. One thing a good soldier would never do would be to leave tins around his trench with the shiny metal lids reflecting sunlight and flashing like a mirror to be seen by observers miles away. It had become very obvious to me that I would never be a real soldier.

I was wondering how long it would be before we would be attacked when I heard a voice shouting, 'Lay down arms! All men lay down arms!' A warrant officer was running forward telling everyone that a surrender had taken place. Apparently General Percival had countermanded the Australian order, him being the Supreme Commander, and now we were helpless prisoners of the Imperial Japanese Army, who showed no mercy to anyone.[31]

There was bitter comment as men piled their guns and the queries were, 'Why were we sent here when all was lost, anyway? Why weren't we disembarked at New Guinea or Darwin to protect Australia?' Five thousand men and millions of pounds' worth of equipment all handed to the Japanese. Why didn't Percival train his men in jungle warfare instead of barrack square parades? Then when the Japanese were obviously going to seize all those Hurricanes, why didn't the English move into Thailand (or Siam as we knew it then) and fly them over into Malaya? The West Australians in the 2/4th machine-gunners would gripe about not being allowed to massacre the Japanese whilst they crossed the Johore Strait. I'm glad for his sake that Percival didn't appear grinning and shouting, 'Hello, chaps!' at this point in time.[32]

We were organised into a column of march and set off for Changi barracks. The route to Changi was littered with the wrecks of tanks, trucks and cars. Dead Japs were everywhere, bloated and giving off a very offensive smell. It wasn't pleasant and I remarked on it to my travelling companion. He looked over the scattered Japanese bodies and made a very prophetic statement, 'You will never ever see better Japanese than these.'

Changi barracks consisted of a large square of two-storey brick buildings surrounding a large barrack square. From stories told by the old veterans one could imagine hundreds of immaculate soldiers on parade with polished buttons and boots and officers strutting about with swagger canes giving orders, whilst Australians hacked paths through steaming jungle and waded across muddy paddy fields. And for years as these glamour parades went on, the Japanese had obviously been training hard on some island developing skills in jungle warfare. Changi barracks was a classic version of a fool's paradise.[33]

We, late of Headquarters staff, were billeted in what used to be the married quarters. Being a loner I decided a large broom closet would do me fine because there was barely room for one small man. Having scrounged a new English ground sheet, I indulged in my favourite pastime, drawing on the fine canvas. Roy Whitecross, who was a typist in administration, paused in passing to comment, 'Very mediocre.' Roy and I had already crossed swords previously when as he boasted how many words he could type per minute I had adjusted my Tommy gun on its broad shoulder strap and said, 'Not as fast as I can hose bullets out of the Thompson.' Highly intelligent, Roy later wrote of his wartime experiences in his book, *Slaves of the Son of Heaven.*

Next day I found Jack and we discussed our present circumstances and debated what might happen in the future, and then I went to check up on old friends. I learned that most of my friends had died in brave but very foolish and ineffectual circumstances, not advancing the progress of battle or in the act of rescuing someone, and this fact angered me. Rudyard Kipling must have experienced similar emotions when asked to write an epitaph for his son, who had been killed during the Great War. He submitted this: 'If our fathers hadn't lied to us, there wouldn't be so many of us here.' His proposed epitaph was not accepted, for it would have added to the bitterness of thousands of English parents whose sons had been sacrificed needlessly.

I walked past a mild scholarly-looking officer wearing steel-rimmed glasses and mentally dismissed him as one of the office types from administration. I was abruptly pulled up by an original 2/19th Battalion man who confronted me, snarling, 'You don't bother to salute our VC winner?' I was dumbfounded and looked once again at this mild-looking gentleman gazing into the distance. Then a large Japanese staff car with a general's pennant flying from a rod fixed to the radiator pulled up close by and a stocky Japanese general armed with an ornate samurai sword and scabbard attached to his belt descended from the vehicle. He asked the 2/19th Battalion man, 'Could you direct me to Colonel Anderson?' and the man pointed to Anderson. He walked towards Anderson and stopping in front of him, saluted smartly. Anderson returned the salute. The Jap officer said in perfect English, 'I just had to see this man who held up two divisions with just one battalion.' After saluting again, he returned to his car and was driven away.

As I remember now he had finished his little speech with, 'You proved a worthy foe.' Not that any of this hypocrisy impressed Anderson, who would have been concealing his anger and contempt knowing credit went to his men, not him. It may have impressed some of the English officers and yet the Japanese didn't seem to be commending any of them. Although Anderson was an able leader, he always gave credit to his men, not himself.

In Changi we were allowed to be supervised by our officers and the Australians, being realists, relaxed discipline. The English appeared to be living in some fantasy state whereby everything would carry on as before, with spotless uniforms and all the pomp and ceremony of English barracks discipline. We goggled in amazement at the spectacle of Japanese slaves drilling on the square and marching to the skirl of the bagpipes. One mate commented, 'Gor blimey, these poor silly Poms don't seem to realise we lost the campaign and we are only slaves of the Japanese now.'

Jack filled me in on how after he collapsed with battle fatigue and was taken to the converted Cathay Theatre hospital, upon recovery he joined orderlies in trying to coax shell-shocked patients to relax so that they could urinate and others to relax and use their bowels again. They had just managed to coax some men's bodily functions to work again when a bomb landed, killing some and injuring others whilst putting many back into shock. Jack also gave me his account of the Muar battle, and he related an incident when as a dispatch rider he was attacked by a Zero pilot. Jack did a broadside, and leaving his motorbike he rolled towards a ditch as machine gun bullets raked a line of dirt along the side of the road only about six inches from the side of his head.

Jack was full of praise for the Chinese farmers, many of whom lost their lives helping Australians to get back to their units. Treacherous Malays and Chinese handed to the Japs lists of names of those who had helped the Allies and the penalty was usually having their heads cut off. But the traitors' names were also going on secret lists ready for when the Japs would be driven out. These traitors would suffer shocking deaths as retribution came later on.

Crossing the Muar River had been a problem for the retreating 2/19th Battalion and 45th Indian Brigade; the Indian troops solved the problem for those unable to swim by tying turban cloths together to make a long lifeline stretching across the river and so men were coaxed across holding one hand onto the turban and the other on their mate's shoulder.

For a while we were on our own rations at Changi but we had been warned we would eventually be on a rice diet. However, when the rice did become our only ration, one Englishman refused to eat, saying that he couldn't eat rice. It seemed like the action of a sulky spoiled child, but he went through with it, not eating any rice, and he weakened and died. Thus we had our first victim of the rice diet. The Japs also refused to give us any salt in our rations. Instead of sitting down and whingeing about it, the Aussies showed their adaptability by organising water parties to go down to the sea and cart back sea water to use with the rice. This became a very unpleasant task because of bodies washing up on our beach. Traitors were now supplying the names of Singaporeans who had assisted the Allies, and the Japanese were carting these people out to sea in barges. They would tie two people's hands together with wire, shoot one of them, then push them off the barge.[34]

Returning from one of the salt-water parties, we came upon an amazing sight. There stood three ranks of English soldiers lined up, standing stiffly to attention, and at one end of the rear rank an English officer lay down on his stomach and was sighting along his swagger cane at the backs of all the men's boots to check that they were exactly in line. We first gave three rousing cheers and then began a slow handclap. I don't think it was just the exertion of getting to his feet that made the officer's face turn red. The next day our water party was reprimanded because of our lack of respect.

I called on my friend Roy who was billeted further down the square and found him in miserable dejection with scratches all over his chest. It seems he had climbed a palm in search of coconuts but on reaching the top his strength had given out and he had come sliding down again, hugging the palm. I told him that you are supposed to use a rope looped around the palm and also around your feet or make a logger's loop around your waist. It sounded all right to me but Roy snorted and said, 'That's you all over, Holman. Still the same old bloody know-it-all professor.'

In the barracks was a man with neck and shoulders encased in plaster. During the campaign he had been captured, tied to a tree and a Jap sergeant tried to cut his head off without striking the tree with his sword. He cut through the muscles and sinews of the neck but failed to cut the man's jugular vein. As the man's head lolled over sideways the Jap assumed that he had killed him and departed. When an Australian patrol discovered him they were amazed to find him still alive. It seems his wound had become fly-blown and the maggots had eaten away the dead tissue surrounding the wound, preventing it from going gangrenous. Now he was safe and getting well again.

Another chap recuperating had been captured by the Japs together with several of his friends. The officer in charge of the Japanese force was apparently anxious to brutalise and blood some of the younger men. Stakes of saplings had been planted all along the bank of a nearby creek and the Australians were tied to these and then they were used for bayonet practice. During this practice session some of the stakes collapsed and the bodies rolled down into the creek. This man's body had been pierced right through in three separate places without the bayonet touching a vital area. When he rolled into the creek his head lay supported above water by a small log whilst the rest of his body was submerged below the cool flowing stream.

The patrol that discovered this man was full of amazement to find that he was still breathing. It seems that although he was in a very bad way, the cool waters had congealed his blood and then prevented more blood oozing from his wounds. He was a survivor and it was survivors who would later testify in a war crimes court and their testimony would bring grim retribution.

If the English thought this honeymoon existence was to continue they were in for a rude shock. Officers were badgered into signing a document saying we were not to escape and some British men were actually shot after being found outside the wire. There had been work parties leaving the area so that when we learned of a work party being organised we didn't take much notice at the time. I suppose it is a typical human reaction to not be much concerned about things that do not immediately involve one personally. This work party, however, would go to Borneo and would be subjected to numerous horrific experiences, ending in the infamous Sandakan death marches from which there were only six survivors. I have learned since of terrible atrocities committed against civilians in the Borneo area by the Japanese but in the interests of world trade these have no doubt been hushed up.

After this party left, rumours were spreading about another large work party being organised and rumour had it that these work parties were actually prisoner-of-war exchange parties to be conducted somewhere in the Pacific. It all sounded like wishful thinking to me and in consultation with my brother Jack we decided an exchange was fantasy but that a work party for some Jap project was possible. Jack suggested that if the Japanese were going to put us to work they would have to feed us, and while we were being fed we would remain alive and of course, while there's life there's hope. Of course Jack didn't know then what was happening to the Borneo party or the six million Jews in Germany, or he wouldn't have been so confident with his advice.

When the time came we both joined work parties. Jack joined Colonel Ramsay's force, whilst I joined A Force, Colonel Anderson's, which meant that this Holman wasn't going to be any asset to Anderson as the other Holman had proved to be. We were warned to be ready to leave any day.[35]

Burma

The day finally arrived when we were to leave the camp on a work party, and we boarded a fleet of trucks which took us down to the wharves. We clambered out and massed along the wharf, hardly giving more than a glance at two rusting Clyde-built hulks with their tall funnels and square-shaped superstructure, renamed *Toyohashi Maru* and *Celebes Maru*.[36]

I was looking at other ships when a disturbance broke out nearby. It seems several of the guards had an Aussie pinned down on the wharf and were about to administer the water treatment. This torture was effected by forcing a hose nozzle into a man's mouth and turning on the water, to inflate his stomach. Then a ring of barbed wire would be placed on his stomach and someone would jump up and down on it. This usually resulted in the man's death, but this man proved an exception as, marshalling his strength he suddenly erupted, throwing Japs about like rag dolls. Getting to his feet he ran along the wharf and soon blended into a large group of fellow Australians, managing to evade recapture. The guards rushed around looking at these white men who all looked alike, just as they all looked alike to us at this point in time.

Soon afterwards, much to our shock and consternation we were ordered to go aboard the rusting hulks. My mob boarded the *Toyohashi Maru* whilst Jack's mob went aboard the *Celebes Maru*.

I heard a story that the *Celebes Maru* was later used as an ammunition carrier to ferry munitions to the islands and was painted white with large red crosses prominently displayed all over it. This proved futile as agents of British intelligence managed to contact the Americans and a bomber dropped a bomb on it. The resultant explosion could have been seen forty miles away, proving she was no hospital ship. But for now she was to prove a real hellship. Down in the hold we were herded and on the bottom of the hold were grass mats, each man being allotted just enough room to sit down. Then the engines started and we headed out past the harbour buoys and into the Strait of Malacca. It became very hot in the hold and the Japs rigged up a long canvas ventilator wind sock which brought just enough air to prevent us from suffocating. We were allowed brief periods to come up on deck. I learned later that on the *Celebes Maru* the men were kept below deck most of the time. The toilets were a rough wooden structure suspended over the side of the ship; noting the skillion roof, I realised that if I could sneak up onto that roof at dusk I could at least breathe the cool night air without anyone being able to see me lying down.

We called into Medan in northern Sumatra, where three Dutch POW ships joined us plus some sort of little escort ship. That night found us hugging the coast and heading towards Victoria Point in southern Burma. I had sneaked up onto the toilet roof and lay breathing in the cool night air. The old ship creaked and groaned. I found the sounds very soothing and I felt like dropping off to sleep but first I thought I would tie my wrist to something secure to avoid sliding off the skillion roof. It had grown completely dark now and reaching around I felt a piece of steel cable nearby so I decided to tie my wrist to this with a handkerchief. Before dropping off to sleep, I felt thankful to be alone and cool and I felt very sorry for the poor wretches who were now sweltering in the intense heat of the hold.[37]

Dawn came, casting a faint light over the sea, and I woke up to the now-familiar creaking and groaning of the old ship. The light was soon touching objects around me and looking around I was shocked wide awake with the realisation that I had anchored myself to a large coil of wire rope lying loose and untethered on the slanting iron roof. I shuddered to think what might have happened during the night if the ship had rolled heavily and I had a brief mental picture of myself plunging down through the murky depths of the sea with my wrist firmly tied to a coil of wire rope. Before it became light enough for anyone to discover my hiding place I descended and made my way down to the hold.[38]

That day was pure hell, for several chaps had now developed dysentery. In their efforts to get across their mates squatting on the floor, they had defecated on them and tears of frustration coursed down their cheeks as they eventually gained the ladder which led up out of the hold, apologising to men who cursed them every foot of the way. Soon the whole floor became fly-blown and maggots crawled over the mats and the stench of human perspiration was really nauseating. I learned later that conditions on the *Celebes* were even worse. Looking back I think that our freedom to be able to move more freely on our ship and the ventilator canvas shute that was secured to the mast and brought some air down into the hold could have been attributed to the efforts of our three wonderful officers, Colonel Anderson,[39] our interpreter Captain Drower,[40] and Doctor Rowley Richards.[41] We of A Force had been blessed with some very wonderful men. We stopped at Victoria Point, where some of our men went ashore.[42]

Our battered hulks steamed on and later we pulled into a little cove and anchored whilst brother Jack's mob went ashore. I could see the sun shining on gilded pagodas in amongst the green shrubbery on the hillside. Someone said this was a place called Mergui, a coastal town in lower Burma, and I remember spending a pleasant night breathing cool, fresh air whilst men below sat in misery. Next morning our ship moved off and then later that night we anchored again. Sometime next day we went ashore in a barge and walked to a rice mill where we spent the night sleeping on a mound of unhusked rice grain.[43]

The following day we marched through a little Burmese town which would have fitted well into one of Rudyard Kipling's stories. I was informed that it was Tavoy in lower Burma. As we marched along there were sights and sounds which boggled the imagination and it served to take my mind off the fact that Jack and I were separated; I wondered for just how long. A Burmese appeared, ringing a hand-bell and shouting, 'Unclean! Unclean!' and someone said he was a leper. Everybody appeared to be smoking cigars of some description and even pot-bellied little boys puffed away at cigars with the aplomb of a New York businessman. I caught one Australian gazing at a young Burmese baby suckling on his mother's breast. He had a long cigar in his baby fingers and in between sucking on his mother's teat he would take a puff at his cigar. The Australian was dumbfounded. 'Gor blimey,' he ejaculated, 'now I've seen everything!' I too was amazed and I realised I was to learn a lot over a short period.

Rowley Richards, the young doctor who would be our guardian angel over the next few years, forced his weary body up and down beside the slowly moving column of men from front to rear and back again, warning us not to accept gifts of water from these warm-hearted friendly people. There could be large stomach-worm eggs in the water or any of a multitude of tropical germs in it, he advised us. One little boy pressed an English penny into the hand of a big rough-looking Australian who had tears in his eyes as he accepted what must have represented a fortune to this little Burmese boy. I also saw children playing war games with wooden swords and garbage can lids as shields and it was brought home to me how children the world over treat war as a game, just as I had done as a child.

We spent the night on the rough blue metal floor of an airplane hangar and there was no way you could dig a hole for your hip.[44] A Burmese had tethered a goat near a barred window and soon hands reached out, seizing its chain, and the animal was pulled up through the bars. It was promptly killed, skinned, cooked over a makeshift fire and eaten. I could see that this would be the pattern for the future.

We were moved from the aerodrome to a camp nearby. We called this Tavoy Camp and here we would see and experience a glimpse of the horrors to come. We seemed to be left to our own resources for the first few days and then one day we were all called out on parade by our Brigadier Varley. A Jap placed a soapbox on the ground and a Japanese officer stood up on the box and, thumping his chest like a filmstar version of Tarzan, he said loudly, 'I am Chiina. You will now work for Japanese Imperial Army,' and he went on to say that if we did just as we were told everything would be all right. One look at this cruel, arrogant man was a warning of what would happen should anyone upset him. In his neat uniform with polished leather belt, samurai sword and high leather polished boots, he was a typical Japanese officer.

It was here that we heard of the execution of an Australian at Victoria Point for being caught outside the wire.[45] After hearing this, I went off into my favourite fantasy, trying hard to imagine being on a remote island right away from human beings, living a Robinson Crusoe life with a few goats and unable to even hear another human voice. But there was no escape from reality. Captain Chiina gave orders for sentry boxes to be placed around the camp. Prisoners were ordered to take turns in these boxes as guards and the idea was that should any prisoners try to sneak out of the camp at night the guard would talk him out of it. What was to happen to the guard if the other prisoner ignored him and still went out, wasn't declared, but we knew what punishments the Japanese gave to law-breakers, even to their own fellow soldiers who broke the law.

One of my mates was on duty one night and next day he came and told me he thought he heard a low growling noise during his watch period. We went down to where the Jap guard was on duty at this box and with a lot of gesticulating and using the words '*Mira, mira,* tiger' (Look, look, tiger) I managed to convey the message that we wished to look for tiger pads in the soft ground, and he grunted an okay. We soon found them forming a circle around the sentry box and they were as round as dinner plates. At this point in time Burma was largely covered with dense tropical rainforest and full of wild animals. Today it may be rapidly becoming like the Gobi Desert which, if you can believe science, was once a dense tropical rainforest teeming with birds and animals.

That night I trod a well-worn path towards where our toilets were situated on a slight rise, when a voice came from the direction of the toilet, 'Stop, mate! There's a great big python crossing the path in front of you.' I stopped and listened to the sound of a large undulating reptile sinking down into the groove of the path and up out again as it moved and tiny dry sticks cracked as they broke beneath the weight of its body.

Unlike the small deadly yellow South American scorpion which has a bite as lethal as a funnelweb spider, the Burmese scorpion is six inches long, brown in colour, and although very painful its sting is not fatal. Walking across the floor of our hut with bare feet one night, I touched one with my big toe. It immediately seized my toe in its big nippers and drove its sting right into the end of the toe; it felt like a red-hot darning needle. I screamed and up came my foot, tossing the scorpion in amongst a group of sleeping companions, which caused quite a lot of mad noisy confusion until it was finally located and crushed.

I began suffering from diarrhoea and Dr Richards sent me with some other chaps to our only hospital of sorts, which was situated a mile or more from the camp. Recovering after a few days, I was told by an orderly that I could walk back to camp. Alarmed, I asked for some sort of explanatory note to be able to show any Jap why I was alone outside the camp. He assured me I only had to walk straight down the road towards the camp. Nervously I set off, towards a scene that would haunt me for the rest of my life.

I came upon a paddock in the middle of which knelt eight Australians before eight freshly dug graves. In front of them stood a line of Japs with rifles held at the ready. Behind them stood a group of Australian and Japanese officers and our Australian padre. The Japanese were behaving as though they were having a picnic, laughing and joking, and Chiina swaggered to and fro laughing and smacking his polished boots with an officer's cane. Then he wheeled about and, drawing his sword, screamed out in Japanese: 'Ready, Aim,' then holding his samurai sword aloft in a grand gesture, he screamed, 'Fire!'

There came a volley of rifle fire and eight young Australian soldiers toppled forward into the open graves dug ready for them. I walked on towards the camp, shocked and terrified, and with tears of anger and frustration coursing down my cheeks. To the gate guards I mumbled, 'Bioki' and pointed back towards the hospital, indicating that I had come back from there after recovering from sickness. They both grunted okay and I rushed blindly forward until I reached my hut, which was fortunately empty, and sitting down, I burst into tears.[46]

Later when I ventured out, the camp was buzzing like a hornet's nest with angry men. I learned that the eight men were 2/4th Anti-Tank personnel who had been caught outside the wire. We were paraded for a lecture by Brigadier Varley about what to expect from the Japanese in the future. He described the execution to everybody so that any survivors from this camp would be able to name names and to testify to everything later when and if called upon to do so. I was glad the men remained disciplined although trembling with fury, for I had noticed the muzzle of a machine gun poking out the side of a hessian screen in front of the guard-house. We were also told work would begin on the aerodrome.

We went to work on the 'drome using a large deep-bladed hoe known as a *chunkal*, and picks and shovels. We didn't have wheelbarrows but used bag and pole. A bamboo pole was carried on the shoulders of two men, one walking behind the other. The bag was a rice bag with rope tied to each corner, one rope to the two front corners of the bag and another rope tied to the two rear corners and these were suspended from the pole. When the prescribed number of shovels of dirt had been put in this hammock type of conveyance, the men would walk to where the dirt was to be tipped and the man at the rear would seize one corner and tip the contents over, shaking it and replacing it again.

In areas where we worked near trucks, prisoners would pretend to be involved in a big brawl with a lot of abuse being shouted and wild punches being thrown. This noisy diversion would bring Japs running to break up the fight by shouting at us and slapping faces. All of this would give one man time to lift out one of a truck's spark plugs, pour sand through the hole and replace the plug. Soon we began to notice trucks being dumped because they had broken down. But one would not have been wise to be caught with a plug spanner.

As I never kept a diary, I am a bit hazy on many things that happened around this period. I think we were receiving about one pint mug full of rice three times a day and a watery stew and I think any man working received about ten cents per day. There was a man who came into the camp with some kind of cart. I'm not sure if he was Turk or Indian but I remember the Aussies christened him Ali Baba and he laughed and seemed to understand. He carried fruit and slabs of beetroot sugar. We were starting to trade objects among ourselves and I traded a slab of brown sugar for a small carved elephant which stands on my kitchen mantelshelf to this day. [47]

In spite of all our sabotage, the runway on the aerodrome was eventually ready for a trial landing by one of the Japanese bombers available for the test. As I waited on the edge of the aerodrome for this momentous event to occur, a nearby guard kept extolling the virtues of Japanese pilots and making gestures to indicate how every Jap pilot always made perfect three-point landings. One of my mates said, 'This stupid four-eyed bastard thinks we've never seen a plane land before,' and then we heard the bomber approaching. The pilot circled and came in for a landing. Someone said, 'His bloody nearside wheel isn't down,' and he was right, but we wondered if the pilot knew and how on earth he would be able to land on one wheel.

The plane came in low and the wheel touched and the next thing we saw was a Jap bomber sliding along the runway on its belly and making a noise like a thousand sheets of roofing iron being dragged along. The Australians, realising how the Japanese hated to lose face, roared laughing and cheered loudly. I felt sorry for the hapless pilot; Chiina would make someone pay dearly for this humiliation.

We were told that the Japs had other plans for us and a few days later we were marching out again and cigar-smokers increased their supplies as Burmese rushed forward presenting cigars to their friends whilst

Japanese rushed up and down threatening them. We were marched to a river where we were picked up by barges and taken up river to where an old steamer lay waiting for us. Someone said this was the Salween River. The ancient steamer was most likely an old Clyde-built vessel, now renamed the *Unkai Maru*. She was a pitiful neglected rusting hulk.

We pulled into Moulmein Bay next morning and an argument started amongst our intellectuals on the words of the song, 'An' the dawn comes up like thunder outer China, 'crost the Bay!' Some argued that it wasn't possible and some said it depended on just where you stood and at what angle you looked across the bay. Being a loner and not being an ex Boy Scout, I hadn't learned much about Rudyard Kipling and as far as the song 'On the Road to Mandalay' was concerned, to me it was only a stupid song Pommies sang whilst they enjoyed the warm water and suds of a bath.

If memory serves me right, we continued further across the bay or somewhere nearby.[48] I remember how we straggled through a Burmese town. I saw a leper with a hand-bell and this chap had nearly all the toes on one foot rotted off. Then I saw a chap with one thick leg and one thin one and someone said he was suffering from elephantiasis. The next object of curiosity was a normal brown Burmese man with one leg completely white from right hipbone to the tips of his toes. I had heard of this skin complaint which affected the pigment and I wondered what it would be like to go through life with one brown leg and one white one.

I could see the Burmese gazing with awe at our interpreter Captain Drower as he strode along, shoulders back, head held erect with very proud bearing and with a large white pith helmet completing the picture. I thought it was no wonder they stared at him, for this man represented all that the earlier generation feared and admired. I was glad that Malayan Command had placed him on loan to us, for this man would be an inspiration, not only to us but for every Burmese who saw him, that the British would come back again to free them from the cruel yoke of the invader. Our Captain Drower was a magnificent-looking man and the very epitome of the British Colonial Officer. He was going to prove a great asset to us during the next few years.

On our way we passed a Burmese timber mill where huge Burmese elephants were being used to handle the logs. These were large magnificent animals and unlike anything I had seen in a circus or zoo.

We finally reached a railway yard where we were told we would be taken to a place with a long name, Thanbyuzayat, which was pronounced Tam Bu Zi. At Tambuzi camp, which consisted of bamboo *attap*-roofed huts, were Dutch and American prisoners of war. 'The Yanks', as we dubbed them, were a Texas artillery unit. We were given a welcome by the Camp Commander, Colonel Nagatomo, who gave the usual flowery speech telling us that we were working for the Japanese Army and that now we would build a railway line across Burma.[49] I was to learn that the route we were to follow passed through some of the densest jungle on earth, for a great part along a valley that was known to the Burmese as 'death valley' on account of the terrible annual loss of life there through disease. The British had considered bridging the gap between Moulmein and Bangkok with a railway so that goods could be transported across and so cut out the long route around the peninsula by ship, but had been put off after considering the possible terrible loss of life which might be incurred. But the Japanese wouldn't worry about human life in their calculations.[50]

I had been thrilled at the sights and sounds of the jungle even when on its outskirts; now we were in it and I was excited to think of all the wild creatures living in those dark depths. I'm sure some of my companions thought I was already going insane because for them it was an Australian tradition to chop down anything that grew and shoot anything that walked on four legs or climbed up a tree. In contrast, I would be in a sort of seventh heaven just lying down in a hut at night listening to the howling rhesus monkeys and gibbons and then noting periods of silence followed by the sounds of a tiger or leopard growling as they came to the river to drink. Our camps along the route of the railway would be next to rivers so this would be a sound pattern that I would grow used to over the course of time. Unfortunately, my companions didn't share my great excitement and the sounds of animal noises in the night were accompanied by growls of, 'If I had my Tommy gun now I'd silence those noisy bastards.' When at Tavoy, in the hut I could hear slithering noises all night long as harmless pythons or frog-eating snakes went their way. I didn't like the sounds of the poor frogs screaming as they were seized though, but this was the jungle, where jungle law prevailed. When I first mentioned that I used to catch snakes and lizards back in Australia I received some strange looks from my companions and I'm sure they thought I was showing early signs of cracking under the strain.

We were first engaged in building up an embankment by digging wide, shallow excavations each side of where the railway would be. A lot of men had travelled over miles of railway in Australia and had wondered as they looked out of carriage windows why there were shallow, wide holes filled with water or weeds; now they knew. One chap said, 'I always wondered why that water was there each side of the line and I never realised soil had to come from somewhere to build the embankment.' Only over here, we would use pick and shovel, bag and pole.

The wily Japanese split us up into three groups and gave each group a quota of soil to be dug out with the promise of returning to camp as soon as the quota was removed. The Australians were stupid enough to be trapped by this simple ruse. Returning to camp seemed a smart thing till they realised the Dutch returned much later and abused them for giving the Japanese a work benchmark which all groups would be expected to carry out in the future, or be beaten with a bamboo stick for failing to work harder and faster. This was a bad start and one of many stupid things done by the Australians, but they would learn and adapt very fast. They had come from an outdoor, healthy environment and were used to working out in the hot sun. Nearest to them were, of course, the rugged tough Texans from hot, dusty cattle country. The Dutch were accustomed to soft living and wouldn't bear up so well in spite of their superior knowledge of the tropics and tropical diseases and treatment. The English troops were the most disadvantaged, coming from unhealthy factory areas and in poor physical condition. They had a barrack square mentality and had done no hard jungle training. We would learn from each other, but much would be learned from the resourceful, ingenious Australians.

We organised concerts and learned that we had a lot of very talented people in our midst. One performer was known as 'Ol' JB' or 'Hank the Yank'. He was a trumpet player and a real hot Dixieland jazzman from a jazz band in one of the small Texas towns. When Ol' JB mounted the concert platform, everyone stood well back to avoid shattered eardrums as he rendered a popular number.

I awoke one morning to see the monkeys gathering as usual in the trees all around the camp to hear the bugler play 'Reveille'. This singular event was a great attraction to them. A man walked out into the middle of the parade ground and there was complete silence as the monkeys stopped chattering. A voice queried, 'That's not our bugler.' And a voice answered 'No. Our bugler is sick and Hank is going to play "Reveille" for us this morning.' I had heard 'Reveille' played many times before but never like this. After the first few familiar notes there was a shocked silence followed by gasps of amazement and a man yelled out,

'He's bloody well swinging it. Old Varley will kill JB when he gets hold of him.'

With the last notes hanging on the still morning air, a sergeant was seen striding towards the bugler and then Hank and the sergeant walked towards Brigadier Varley's hut. We learned later how Varley, trying to look stern, asked Hank for an explanation. Hank responded by saying he was thinking of his little ol' jazz band back in Texas and he sort of got carried away. The sergeant said Varley seemed to be having a job to keep a straight face and after warning Hank not to do it again he was dismissed. They had only taken a few steps when they heard the sound of muffled laughter behind them. I shudder to think what would have happened to an English bugler if he had swung 'Reveille' in the centre of the barrack square at Changi barracks.

The Japs now decided to move us up to the next camp at Hlepauk, pronounced Lee Po. The camp we had been in was to be turned into a hospital and Brigadier Varley was to stay behind and Colonel Anderson would be our new leader from now on, from camp to camp.[51]

We had reached a river and now a bridge had to be built over the river. Axes were produced and a party including myself cut logs and slid them down a slope where they could be trimmed and made into bridge piles. Then I watched with excitement as the work elephants arrived on the scene. The logs were trimmed to a point on one end and a metal strap nailed on, then the elephants would be used to snig the logs forward to the river's edge, where a tall wooden pole gantry was being built.

A bout of dengue fever flattened me out for a few days, and when I arrived back on the job piles were being hammered into the mud at the river's edge. There was a large iron pulley wheel at the top of the wooden gantry and over this a rope was looped and tied to a large cylinder of iron which was the monkey, or pile driver. A long line of men with tropical ulcers on their legs would pull the rope which would raise the monkey up high and then the men would release the rope and the monkey would drop with a thump on top of the pile. The chant that was used sounded to me like, 'Itchy nee nar si o, nar si oh!' and on the loud OH men would let go of the rope.[52] The last man on the rope sat down, as he would be the one with the worst ulcers on his leg or legs.

A Burmese elephant driver asked me to tie a trailing rope around a log, and I became an instant elephant boy, or something like a dogman on a small mobile crane. I was thrilled just to be near these wonderful creatures. This was just like a boyhood dream fulfilled and I felt very privileged indeed.

When the guards called for a cool-off period, men, guards and elephants all walked into the river and playful young female elephants often squirted water over us.

Whilst I worked with the elephants a drama had been taking place with my work group up on the embankment. It seems anger had built up over the way the Japs had tricked them into a work quota and one man had elected himself as shop steward. It was this leader who was haranguing the men to go on strike for shorter working hours. The fact that we were helpless slaves and that men had been executed at Victoria Point and another eight recently shot at Tavoy seemed to have been forgotten. To make things worse, they threw all their work tools into a fire and burned the handles out of them.

My first intimation of trouble was when a mate appeared above me on the edge of the embankment shouting, 'Come here, Holly, you're wanted.' On enquiring why I was wanted, I was informed, 'We are all going to get our heads chopped off.' I could see my mates all lined up and an angry guard and Japanese officer stood in front of them. I measured the distance from where I stood to the edge of the jungle and to where the armed guard was standing and then seeing an Australian officer and our interpreter Captain Drower approaching, I decided to walk up and stand in line. I noticed some handy rocks nearby and was quickly planning how to clobber the guard and then shoot the officer because no way was I going to kneel meekly and be executed if I had a chance to escape.

Captain Drower did a magnificent job as Defending Counsel convincing the Jap officer that this sort of thing was going on all over Australia every day and wasn't looked on as being unusual by any Australian employers. The officer said he'd read all about Australia and the way Australians were always on strike, and stamping his foot, he shouted, 'That is why you are losing the war!'

By now the gravity of the situation had at last penetrated the consciousness of the Australians and it wasn't hard to look dejected and stand with bowed heads, which seemed to impress the Jap officer. Somewhat mollified, he removed his hand from his sword hilt. The Australian officer was apologising and assuring him it wouldn't occur again and the interpreter begged for leniency and no carrying-out of the death penalty. The officer ordered we be taken back to camp and go without food for forty-eight hours as punishment for our crime against the Japanese Imperial Army. Our officer and the interpreter had saved our lives and we didn't need anyone telling us how lucky we were.

The threat of execution hung over us like the sword of Damocles and yet men risked their lives to go over the wire to get medical supplies and special food for sick mates. Whilst I lacked the raw courage of these men, I was nearly executed, or under threat, three times. In the early camps the Japs insisted that we go on guard with a broomstick, with the admonition that we were to persuade any visible escapees not to go missing.

One night on guard I was taken short, and thinking I had plenty of time I defecated behind a nearby bush. The Jap guard caught me and I was taken to the guard-house before the corporal of the guard. The Dutch interpreter was brought to the guard-house and almost immediately I was told the Japs wanted to shoot me on the spot. My defence was that I had left my post to sing out to some men who were awake, to get them to send me relief. It was better than no defence at all, but it didn't satisfy the corporal.

The suspense was terrible, as the Dutch interpreter explained that it wasn't as serious as it would be to a Japanese soldier who was found to have left his post. After all, he explained, I wasn't a real guard, just a man who was ready to advise his mates not to try to leave camp. He finished his defence by suggesting that to give this man a hiding would be sufficient punishment.

And so the corporal laid it on to me with both hands as I rocked about like a ship in a gale, until finally I was dismissed. My head ached for hours. I was bruised but still alive, and once again some force had deemed that I should survive.

Our medical orderly told us that there are three strains of malaria. A1 was a one-attack strain; B2 was a permanent one or two attacks per month strain; and B3 attacks the spinal nerve. B3 or cerebral malaria was known to the Burmese as 'The Singing Death' because the victims suffered hallucinations and would sometimes start singing loudly or even reciting poetry before they died. Malaria is spread by the Anopheles mosquito and treatment was three five-grain tablets of quinine per day to be taken over a period of nine days.

Back in camp, I did my 48-hour starvation period and after a while my stomach probably thought that my head had been cut off, because our one pint of rice and watery, salty jam melon stew which we received three times a day wasn't coming down the red lane anymore. I started shivering, then I became feverish, and several times during the night

I became delirious. The doctor tested my blood and said I had B2 recurring malaria, which, as I would later learn, I would keep getting for about four years.

We Australians had come from a lucky country with a relaxed mode of life with few restrictions on liberty and because of this we had made silly mistakes on becoming prisoners, already losing men through executions because we had failed to grasp the gravity of our position. But now the Australians were settling down and our pattern of existence would be copied by others. The Australians showed great ingenuity and would prove to the Japs that even they could be outfoxed. The battle for survival had begun.

These were early days and I was allowed to stay in camp to recuperate for a period of ten days, during which I took my quinine three times a day. By the eighth day I was hearing ringing noises in my ears, but I was recovering and seeing others around me in worse condition. We were learning to avoid getting a scratch or cut on our legs because in the tropics any break in the skin could result in an ulcer. These were treated by placing hot wet rag foments over the ulcer to soften the dead tissue around it and remove it. If this treatment failed, a powder called iodoform would be sprinkled onto the yellowish core of the ulcer and it was very effective. I remember as a boy seeing missionaries going around visiting people, including my mother, and showing photos of black and Oriental people with horrible ulcers on their legs. The missionaries had mentioned how these ulcers had a very offensive smell, and now I could look around me and see and smell these same horrible flesh-destroying ulcers.

Another thing we were becoming aware of was that we were all carrying around with us a lot of very unwelcome guests in the form of body lice. These were not the lice found in the hair of some poor underprivileged children in Australia, not minute nits, but a real body louse looking similar in size and colour to a white ant or termite. We called them chats and the term 'sitting down to have a chat' literally meant just that, as men of different nationalities sat down together, peering at the seams of their clothing in the hunt for lice to squash.

I lay recovering from malaria watching men dropping their garments into tins of boiling water, and feeling too weak to get up and do likewise, I began plucking the lice off my clothes and squashing them. Then I accidentally dropped a live one on the ground. Raising my foot to stamp on it, I was prevented by the speedy action of two ants, who were now busy tugging their resisting prey towards their nest. Suddenly it occurred to me that here was the answer to my problem. I placed my shirt and shorts on the ants' nest and placed twigs inside my clothes to make it easier for the ants to get in and out. They cleaned out all the lice and even the tiny eggs in the seams. I tried to share my ingenious idea with others but they seemed to think I was joking.

We had a sort of canteen going and anyone with money could get slabs of beetroot sugar, known as *chindegar*, or bananas, and those without money traded shirts or shorts over the fence to the Burmese. To use our jungle slang, I whizzed off my clothes for bananas and soon my sole item of clothing was a khaki loincloth. Unlike the English troops, I faced up to reality, realising that survival was more important than showing the flag. I was a coolie and I might as well look like one.

Christmas arrived and our cooks showed their ingenuity by producing a more appetising dinner than our normal fare. We had visitors from the next camp and what was left of the 2/19th Battalion Band, with band instruments. I saw Jack with one of the instruments and I was able to talk with him for a little while before they played some music for us. Jack insisted that I accept a pair of shorts, not liking my loincloth at all. The improvised band played for us on Christmas afternoon and I had another talk with Jack before the guards from the next camp hustled them away. Jack and I promised to try to get news of each other's welfare to one another.[53]

As the men's ulcers grew worse, their legs were put in slings and suspended on ropes to ease the pain. Although we had become aware of the presence of bugs, they must have been a torment to these men as they crawled out of the cracks in the bamboo poles onto the men's bodies at night when they lay defenceless.[54]

Back working with the elephants, I was growing very fond of these beasts but I was learning that they could get very obstreperous at times. I saw one young female get in a tantrum, stamp her feet and scream, and then start pulling up saplings and hurling them around. When this sort of boisterous behaviour occurred I usually took off for the jungle like the proverbial Bondi tram until things settled down again. One day I stood beside an elephant I had been working with during the morning, a huge bull with long outspread tusks. The driver signalled for me to tie a rope to one of his tusks so that one end of a pile could be pulled into position. I went forward and was next to the tusk when I happened to look up, straight into a pair of killer eyes, and my memory instantly reverted back to the same look in the eyes of a killer racehorse named Thunderclap. Then he suddenly lowered his head and catching me under the rib cage he catapulted me backwards down a twenty-foot embankment, where I landed in a pool of sloppy mud. Getting up, I heard a mate say, 'He just tried to kill you, Holly.'

'No,' I said, 'this time he was just warning me. If I go near him again he will kill me.' So I resigned and after sneaking into the jungle for a few minutes I made my way back to my mob on the embankment, realising I was indeed lucky to be alive.

There had been talk around camp that we would be getting Koreans to replace Japanese as guards and we wondered what Koreans looked like and whether they would be like the Japs. Then one day a lorry arrived full of new Korean guards. The obvious leader was a brutal, cruel-faced man over six foot in height wearing the now-familiar polished leather Nazi-type knee boots. He strutted about like a storm trooper and we now christened him 'The Storm Trooper' or 'Stormy' for short. These brutal, cruel and arrogant men would become hated by Australians and Japanese, and especially 'Stormy'.[55]

Our guards had a little Jap cook who was the only likeable Jap I ever met. He seemed to like the Australians and imitated our slang. Occasionally he would slip a man a tin of milk, saying, 'You give to sick man in hospital.' One day one of the new Koreans was behaving in an offensive manner and after the cook had ordered him to leave the cook-house he refused. We never actually saw what the Jap did, only a large Korean flying in the air to land with a sickening thud on his back. Getting to his feet, he shook his fist and abused the cook before limping off to the guard-house. After he had left, the cook began putting his boots on. We asked him what the Korean had said and he replied, 'He say he come back and kill me. But I am ready for him. He come back, I fight him bootsenall (boots and all).'

We were working on the line one day when I heard a shot ring out. Looking about me I saw a Korean, minus his rifle, being escorted back to camp by several guards. We went back to camp and saw Anderson leading a stretcher party out. Anderson led them back later and a man's body lay on the stretcher. Anderson, who was a big-game hunter, said that according to the signs the Korean had made improper advances towards the Australian and when rejected had shot the Australian dead.[56]

Parades, or *tenkos*, were usually quiet but on one tenko as we finished counting there was a danger period. Down the bottom of the parade ground two guards were arguing with Captain Drower. Then suddenly he was down on his back yelling 'Help!' There was a rumble of angry voices as Colonel Anderson, with flashing angry eyes ran and faced the guards, calling out 'Stop!' Surprisingly as he confronted the guards they cowered back, even though they held rifles with fixed bayonets. Then our sergeant ran down the parade ground shouting, 'Don't break ranks! The bastards have a machine gun trained on you!' Looking towards the guard-house our quick-eyed sergeant had spotted the legs of the tripod underneath the hessian screen. The guards had been about to kill Drower but now he was safe, thanks to Anderson.[57]

Some English troops joined us and I wondered how long our meagre, almost non-existent stew meat supply would last. The next day we were treated to a rare sight as the Texans brought in some woebegone thin gaunt-looking yaks into camp. There were loud cries of 'Yahoo' and waving of Stetsons and one Texan mounted a thin-looking creature and waved his hat in a wide circle and then the poor weak, exhausted thing just dropped dead underneath him, amusing the Australians who cheered and clapped loudly. Then screaming guards broke up the Texans' rodeo.

Our toilet trenches were usually built the other side of the river if it was shallow enough to walk across. One evening a chap was perched over the trench when he heard a tiger growl. Shinning up a thin sapling, he hung on tight as a huge tiger with its belly nearly touching the ground hove into view, stopped, and after cleaning itself with its tongue like a giant tabby cat, padded off back into the jungle. The man said he made spray and foam like a speedboat getting back across the river.

We had two wonderful medical orderlies and as I remember, one chap, a gentle, kind, well built-man, was named Jim Armstrong while the other was a slim, fair-headed, freckle-faced chap named Rhodes, known as 'Pinkey'. [58] As the years passed, I noted this fair-haired young medical orderly and admired his bravery and his great service to his fellow man. I was thrilled and happy to see him after the war, seated in a railway carriage looking fit and well. I looked at those other passengers sitting around him unaware of all this man had done. He wore no decorations and would no doubt have refused them had the offer been made to him.

These two men did a marvellous job, worthy of medals and decorations for dedicated service. I came down with a malaria attack out on the line and, staggering up to Pinkey, I explained why I was there. He had just emerged from the jungle and was holding a flower and admiring it. As he gave me quinine, he asked my opinion of this dark flower.

'It looks all right,' I mumbled.

'All right,' he echoed. 'This, Holman, is a black jungle orchid; a rare orchid indeed. A black jungle orchid would be worth a fortune back in Australia.' He sent me back to camp and I proceeded down the road.

I hadn't got far when I saw approaching a column of sixteen elephants. To me it was an unforgettable sight as they moved, each elephant holding on with its trunk to the tail of the one in front. The man on the lead elephant recognised me and holding up eight fingers he pointed back and then towards the jungle. I had no trouble understanding him as I saw a massive bull elephant, head and shoulders higher than all the rest. It was my old antagonist, and should he see me he would kill me. Peering out from the fringe of the jungle with terrified fascination, I watched this gigantic beast pass by.

My mob moved on to a camp at Tanyin and here I would meet another remarkable Australian. Colonel Williams had been in Java with an Australian force. When I began talking to his men I realised they actually worshipped the ground he stood on and as days went by I could see why. This man would stand by his men till the last shot was fired. It was strange to find two brave men, both colonels in the same camp, both excellent soldiers, both very courageous men. Anderson, liked and respected, was like a surgeon – cool, calm and diplomatic and was more likely to gain any concessions for the men in the camp as a whole. Williams, although loved by his own men, was no diplomat and openly showed his contempt for the Japanese in every way.[59]

Captain Drower and Colonel Anderson both spoke Oxford English and seemed to get on very well with each other. The fact that both these men were well educated and that Drower could speak high-class Japanese as well as low-class coolie Japanese didn't go down too well with Japanese officers. The Japanese officers probably realised that our two not only walked about with an air of superiority but they actually were superior and this gave the Japs an opposite feeling of inferiority. To offset this they would frequently try to assert their superiority by calling either officer to stand still in full view of the guard-house whilst on some pretext they would be abused and have their faces slapped. On the loud summons '*Kara*' (Hey, you) everybody in earshot would stand still; thus I would find myself sometimes witnessing either Drower or Anderson being compelled to stand to attention, threatened, cursed and slapped. Williams was openly insolent and showed no fear at all. He didn't flaunt any superior education or any knowledge of Japan. He was no phoney samurai like some of them, but a real warrior and this knowledge really infuriated them and seemed to confuse them.[60]

A story I heard from one of Williams's men was that watching the Jap warships standing off Java, the Australian and the Texan artillery commander got together and worked out a simple hoax to fool the Japanese. Knowing a Jap army commander just had to be watching the shore area through binoculars, they moved truckloads of troops and guns around in a circle. Thus a startled Jap commander, seeing a seemingly endless line of troops, committed a second division to land on Java, convinced he faced an enemy in large numbers. After Java was taken, the Jap commander accused them of hiding troops, asking, 'Where is your other division?' They were beaten, tortured and had thin slivers of bamboo forced up under their fingernails in an attempt to force them to reveal the whereabouts of this hidden Allied division. Finally, forced to accept the truth that they'd been made to look foolish by a simple hoax, they took out their spite on helpless civilians and nurses.

After the war I lay in a bed in Concord Military Hospital. I saw Colonel Anderson visiting men who, after shaking hands with him would boast, 'I've just shaken hands with Colonel Anderson, VC winner.' Then I saw men who had served under Williams and when he and his lovely wife passed through the ward their faces lit up and with tears in their eyes they were mumbling, 'Thank God he lived to get back home.'

In this camp I met Shorty Bullivant off the cruiser *Perth*. He described the Sunda Strait battle and how the *Perth* and USN *Houston* entered the Strait in heavy fog. 'It was as thick as pea soup,' he said. 'Then our lookouts and the Japanese lookouts discovered that we were passing through the centre of the Japanese Light Fleet. Guns thundered, there were blinding flashes of light, explosions and fire, then suddenly there were men everywhere in the sea grabbing anything afloat and screaming as oil got into their eyes.' The *Perth* and the *Houston* were sunk and three Jap destroyers. Credit went to the *Perth* for the sinking of the destroyers as the Japanese Imperial Navy never officially panic and sink their own ships. When I talked to men off the *Perth* they didn't appear to be clear on who was being shot at or by whom. One thing was certain, however, and that was that no American ship was going to get the credit. [61]

These men were berthed in different huts and their naval slang and naval names for everything amused us landlubbers. There was good comradeship between these two groups. After the sinkings there had been bloody battles fought in the sea between Japanese and Allied groups with Aussies coming to the aid of the Yanks and vice versa and then as the battle drifted to the beaches Australians and Americans fought side by side, clubbing the Japs with bits of driftwood. There would be humorous banter passing from one hut to the other during the night when the Aussies would accuse the Yanks of sinking the *Perth* and the Yanks would retaliate by saying the Aussies pulled the plug out. Jap guards would usually break up these nightly verbal exchanges.

One morning I found I had a very sore mouth; seeing a mate walking about I told him and he said just about everyone in camp had it. Then we saw a Burmese man walking down the road and my companion said, 'We'll ask this bloke what you do for it. You never know, he just might have a cure.' We rushed over and opened our mouths, showing him they were sore. He gave a delighted grin and rushed across to a bush growing at the side of the road. Plucking off a handful of berries, he handed them to us, making signs that we were to chew them. He put one in his mouth, chewed on it, let the juice roll around in his mouth and then spat it out on to the ground. We did likewise and obtained almost instant partial relief. Realising we had a cure, we made signs indicating that others were affected and that our doctor would want to see the berries and the identifying leaves. He was an intelligent man and went back across the road to gather more berries and leaves and he showed us points of identification so that we could recognise them. We then shook his hand and assured him all sick men in the camp would be grateful for his kindness.

Rushing off to the doctor we showed our bush herb to him and told our story. He lost no time in consulting Drower and Anderson and soon a berry-picking party was being organised whilst Drower sought permission from the Jap commander to leave camp. I learned later that we all had pellagra caused by vitamin deficiency, a condition that could prove fatal if not checked.

We enjoyed this berry-picking party and it gave us a chance to see some scenery outside the fence without the fear of being shot. It also gave me an idea for an excuse to get out again. I had become friends with the Dutch herpetologist from the Amsterdam Zoo and I approached him to see if the Dutch interpreter could wangle permission for us to spend a few hours outside. The interpreter possibly cooked up a story about two professional snake-catchers who wished to keep their practice up. To our great surprise, the camp commandant gave us permission and I can only surmise that he was hoping that these stupid prisoners would meet a cobra and soon be dead.

We spent the next few happy hours catching and examining harmless pythons and frog-eaters, leaving the venomous ones strictly alone. The Dutchman demonstrated how clever he was but warned me never to show off, explaining that it was usually the show-off who eventually gets bitten. I learned a lot from this man about respect for nature and the environment and above all how one must learn to be vigilant if one wanted to survive.

All this time through the dry season the line forged ahead through the jungle. I helped lay out sleepers, build the embankment, carry rails, bore holes with a boring machine and drive in dog spikes. We marched from one camp to another and then came one march and one camp I would never forget, for it was the worst march and to the worst camp we had so far experienced.

I had carefully wrapped rags around my feet and tied my worn-out boots together with wire. I walked up to the head of the column, realising I would be steadily dropping back, and soon we were marching. We plodded on mile after mile, and I started dropping back until someone shouted, 'One mile to go', and right at the end of the column I slowly dragged one leg after the other. Then I heard a Jap guard screaming in anger and turning around I saw a burly Jap guard clubbing an Australian with his rifle butt. I recognised him as one of our very sick and weak dysentery cases who was struggling to keep up. With little red flecks dancing before my eyes I rushed back and confronting the guard, I screamed, 'Hit him again you bastard and I'll tear you limb from limb!' Surprisingly, he backed off, whereupon I got one of the man's arms over my shoulder and half carrying, half dragging him I moved onward.

Somehow we tagged along behind as the column halted at the camp gates. Anderson walked through six inches of a mixture of human and cattle excreta to reach the bottom hut where a group of men lay in their own filth, too sick to move and with legs half rotted off with ulcers. He was very angry when he returned to report to our doctors on what he had seen.

As if arranged to stimulate Colonel Anderson's anger to a point beyond control, a Japanese officer strode out through the camp gates immaculately dressed with polished belt, sword and highly polished knee boots and leading a pitiful, filthy mob of Indian coolies.[62] Anderson walked over to face the officer, his face grey with suppressed anger. 'Are you leaving those sick men behind?' he asked. The young officer answered, 'Yes.' Anderson burst out angrily, 'You can't just walk out and leave sick men to die!'

The officer gave him a contemptuous look and in Oxford English said, 'I am a Japanese officer. I should worry if these wretched men die – let them die.' And as Anderson stood trembling with anger the immaculate officer turned and walked away.

I managed to get myself and my companion through the gates, where we collapsed on one of the only areas of ground not covered with mixed excreta and stale urine. Recovering a little, I staggered after the other men, trying not to vomit at the foul stench of the camp. A group stood looking at the rows of skeleton-like figures in the bottom hut. Rowley Richards called out, 'Don't gape at them, boys, get those filthy bandages off and clean them up.' Our orderlies, Pinkey and Jim, hurried towards the nearby river carrying buckets whilst other men started building a fire to heat up the water. Some men rushed to remove filthy bandages; I went forward to within fifty feet of them and started retching at the nauseating smell coming from the tropical ulcers. Tears of frustration came as I saw these rough, rugged men turned into gentle angels of mercy and all I could do was stand and watch their good work.

Stumbling inside a hut through excreta I looked for a clean area on the bamboo slat sleeping platform to put down my kitbag. I stood in shocked amazement as I saw that the whole area was covered with human excrement. Even the sleeping platforms each side of the hut were covered with excreta and blood as the former occupants were obviously dysentery sufferers.

Finding the cleanest spot of the filthy area I put down my pack and stood with my spirits down at their lowest level since becoming a prisoner. This, I thought, was the lowest a human being could descend to. This was the bottom of the pit. Completely devastated, I looked about me and a bit further along the hut I noticed a dead Indian. He lay on his back, mouth open as blowflies buzzed in and out of it. Someone had left a bucket standing nearby with a piece of rag near it, so selfishly seizing the opportunity I was soon engaged in dipping the rag (tied on to a stick) into the bucket of water and trying to rub off the blood and excreta from the bamboo slats so that I could have a clean spot to lie down on. With tears of misery and frustration blinding my vision I brushed flies away from my mouth and eventually cleaned my sleeping area. I had heard someone say, 'Ashes are clean and pure', so I soon found a shovel that someone had carelessly left lying down and I proceeded to steal ashes from the edge of what was now a large fire, dropping them below where I would sleep. When this area was covered I made a thin path of ashes from the fire area to my bunk area.

Whilst I had been gratifying my own selfish needs, men had removed the corpse and buried it, cleaned up the ulcer patients and only now were proceeding with the cleaning of their personal sleeping areas. The clean-up extended well into the night until finally men just lay down and slept the sleep of utter physical exhaustion.[63]

Next morning I examined my feet and saw five little tropical ulcers forming on my left ankle, caused by the chafing of my boot. Fires were going, bandages being boiled, dried and re-applied to ulcers, everywhere men were cleaning up the camp area. Seeking attention for my ulcers I noticed hot wet rag foments being put onto other men's ulcers in front of our hospital hut. With my ulcers burning like five little fires I looked towards the cool water of the river and my eyes caught on to a tributary of the river leading away and forming several small ponds. Sitting on the edge of one of these ponds I dunked my feet into the cool, soothing depths. Almost straight away I felt a sharp pricking sensation and looking down I saw tiny piranha-like fish nibbling at the dead tissue forming around my five little ulcers. My first impulse was to quickly remove my foot and then it suddenly occurred to me that these little fish were like tiny surgeons snipping away the dead tissue. Perhaps they would do better than our doctor would with forceps – after all, these little chaps could even eat out the yellow pus at the centre. Realising my good luck, I dried my ankle and pinned a clean bandage around it and this would be the procedure day after day. First a visit to my 'surgeons' then later I would attend sick parade and the good Dr Richards would say, 'Much improvement, Holman, keep up with the hot foments.' Of course they improved so much I soon found myself back at work.

I heard scuttlebutt that some Englishmen had escaped and assisted by Buddhist monks one of them survived and reached the English troops in upper Burma. They said that as a result of his descriptions a British Government protest was sent to Japan via the Swiss Consulate regarding ill treatment of prisoners of war. The Japanese denied the charge and sent a Jap propaganda film unit to Burma to film how well we were being treated by the Japanese Army. I had been wearing wooden clogs that I had made when suddenly we were issued with new boots and some men were issued all new clothes, which they were instructed to wear when called upon in camera close-ups. It was a while before we realised the Japs were up to their foxy tricks again but there was nothing we could do about it except laugh.

Carpenters built a temporary mock-up of a hospital ward on the end of our primitive bamboo *attap*-roofed hospital, and clean beds with white sheets were set up and a couple of prisoners were photographed lying in bed attended by white-uniformed doctors and nurses. We witnessed this with anger mixed with amused contempt. Trucks loaded with fresh vegetables and meat were paraded in front of the cameras, inferring we were fed very good food. We lined up to receive fresh bread off a truck only to have to hand the bread back to the Japs out of view of the cameras. Meanwhile, our cooks cooked rice and jam melon for our vegetable stew whilst on private fires buckets were boiling up python snake and other types of 'meat'.

Men with new shirts, shorts and boots were ordered to file past the cameras and sound recorder singing happy songs. They all sang the rude army version of 'Bless 'em All'. The Japs wanted to stage an elaborate funeral, military style with flag-draped coffin, guns fired over the grave, etc. but their only delayed corpse was our much-loved Stevo, and Stevo, with our orderlies' encouragement, refused to die. After a frustrating wait they decided to enact the scene using an empty coffin. After the film unit moved out of the camp poor old Stevo sighed and gave up the ghost.[64]

In our camp we had a stupid guard with prominent front teeth and he wore glasses. We christened him George after the topical English comedian George Formby. He regarded this as a great honour without realising that English George was a professional, whereas our Jap George was a perpetual unconscious acting comedian. The Australians were always putting George up to some silly caper, such as the time they persuaded him to shoot at one of our local Burmese citizen's cows which happened to stray past the camp one day. The Japs had captured our heavy Lee Enfield rifles off the Allied army when Singapore fell and these were now carried by our guards. George was obviously not familiar with their heavy recoil as he raised his rifle and aimed at the cow. There was a loud 'Bang!' and one of the cow's horns flew off and the startled animal took off for the nearby scrub whilst George fell on his back in the dust.

It seems George had read books on big-game hunters as a boy in Japan and all about native bearers obediently following the great white hunter with the dead game suspended from a bamboo pole. Thus one Sunday some men suggested to George that he get permission to become the great white hunter. Much to our amazement, he did, and we suspected that the colonel was hoping a tiger would eat George and they'd get rid of him.

Not missing a chance to get back into that jungle I became an instant native bearer. Typical of George, he led us down the road where a track appeared on one side and soon we found ourselves in a bamboo jungle. These have to be seen to be believed, with stalks of bamboo six or eight inches thick rising to a height of forty feet with leaves blotting out the sun. We walked on a carpet of dead leaves. Looking up, I could only see tiny patches of blue sky. Then everyone began smacking at large leeches crawling up our legs. Here was the home of the bamboo snake which when exposed to sunlight showed a skin of brilliant flashing colours. To move about, this snake would hang down from a curved-over stalk of bamboo and start a pendulum motion swinging back and forth until, suddenly releasing its tail's grip on the bamboo, it would fly through the air until it contacted another stalk. The Burmese were terrified of this reptile and were very careful when obtaining house-building materials because if bitten, death would come in seconds. Bamboo was the main building material used by the Burmese for house piles, walls and slats for covering sleeping platforms. The split fronds of the *attap* palm provided leak-proof thatching for hut roofs.

We backed out of the bamboo and re-entered the jungle from another direction where it was beautiful rainforest. Moving forward, we eventually entered a large clearing with a lot of *attap*-roofed houses built high above the ground on tall piles away from tigers or leopards. We stood looking for any sign of movement but there were no visible signs that this village was occupied and we wondered if the people were shy and had retreated into the jungle or were hiding quietly inside their native houses.

Becoming more brazen we moved forward towards a row of cooking pots. Looking into the pots we saw a mixture of cold but fresh stew, and the ashes of the fire felt as though they had recently cooled off. Climbing up ladders still propped against the house platforms, we peered in through doorways to see plates laid out on grass plaited mats as though the families had been interrupted by someone or something and had run off into the jungle to escape from it, leaving everything behind. I heard someone say, 'Geeze, gives you the bloody creeps, don't it.' Another chap said, 'Just like that *Marie Celeste* ship mystery – where everyone cleared off the ship and the ship was found with cook pots full of stew and empty plates on the table.'

We discussed what may have happened, with several impatient verbal interruptions from George, who was promptly told to shut up. Finally, an intelligent member of our group said he'd read somewhere that the Burmese thought that cholera came floating along in a vapour or mist about four feet off the ground and anyone in the area would die. Thus when someone came into a village and collapsed with cholera people would evacuate the village area. This sounded feasible so we moved back towards camp.

We hadn't gone very far before we saw a wonderful sight. There in a small clearing stood a cow cropping some short grass. We licked our lips in anticipation of fresh meat as George, seeing it, slowly raised his rifle. Just then we became aware of a rustling sound in the kunai grass and looking around we saw the heads and shoulders of a circle of typical Burmese warrior types clutching large spears. George gave them a silly idiotic grin and lowered the rifle barrel and with everyone grinning the warriors stood aside, leaving an opening for us to retreat through, which we did. I felt cold shivers running up and down my spine.

We arrived back in front of the camp and there in some scrub stood a huge wild sow. We pointed it out to George and once again he raised his rifle. As he took aim there was an anguished cry of, 'The bloody barrel is going round in circles,' then there was a loud bang and a dull thump as George landed on his back, followed by a scream from the sow as she rushed into the jungle with a long bloody crease across the cheeks of her behind. 'Gor blimey,' said a voice. 'How did these four-eyed coots ever manage to shoot our blokes?'

A couple of days later I felt the familiar chills and shivering, and wrapping a blanket around me I went over to a hut where our medical orderly Pinkey Rhodes was standing.

Outside the hut stood Pinkey looking down on a man lying on an army stretcher. As I approached he called out, 'What do you want?'

I answered, 'Some quinine tablets,' and kept on walking.

'Stop!' he shouted, adding, 'this man has cholera.' Seizing a bottle of quinine tablets, he unscrewed the lid and threw some on the ground. I stood looking at this poor man on the stretcher and I mechanically kept all flies away from my mouth as I pocketed the quinine and turned to leave. It was probably just my imagination but he seemed to be collapsing bodily from inside even as I stood there looking at him.

The introduction of the cholera germ to the body is usually by drinking unboiled or unchlorinated water and once the germ is installed into the cavities of the stomach wall it divides itself with cells splitting and reproducing at a terrific rate and the germs literally eat the body away. Unlike amoebic dysentery, where the excreta show streaks of blood, the issue from cholera appears black and watery in content and the patient dehydrates quickly. It pays to drink only boiled water in the tropics, and mixing chilli with food keeps food from settling into these tiny cavities in the stomach wall.

Whilst I tossed about in high fever with the subsequent delirium common to malaria where one second you can be flying along on a motorbike and the next second jumping over hurdles on a horse, our doctors were in conference with our camp commandant. Through interpreters they asked for cholera serum to be brought up by rail very quickly because cholera had struck. The Japanese officer's attitude was,

'I should worry if your wretched Australians die.' The doctors pointed out that the theory of sprinkling lime around a tent, as the Jap and Korean guards were doing, wouldn't save the guards or their officers. When it was understood that Japanese officers would get cholera as well, they suddenly did an about-face and ordered cholera serum to be brought up by rail from Moulmein. The brave samurai spirit was dominant when it was thought that only Australians would die, but for a Japanese to suffer this horrible death was unthinkable.

Thus it was that we stood thankfully in line next day to receive our shots from needles so blunt it was like someone poking a two-inch nail under your skin. Our wonderful interpreter officer and the doctors had saved our lives. But in the camp further up our less resourceful English allies were in tragic pathetic confusion. With no apparent prior warning of entering the cholera belt and with poor leadership and poor hygiene, men marched into the camp, drank unboiled water from the river, filled their water bottles and retired to their huts in mobs, or *kumis*, to sleep. By morning's light they emerged in groups of only twenty-five men out of each hut. Out of each *kumi* of fifty men per hut, half of their number had perished during the night.

Now they appealed to the Australians for help and it was the Australians who set the survival pattern. They were generally very versatile and resourceful and had a strong will to survive. They rigged rollers for grinding the rice to make porridge for the sick whilst a former instrument-maker made instruments for the doctors and pieces of metal from the crashed plane at Tavoy appeared in all sorts of devices.

We were so weak now that we were seldom escorted back to camp but left to find our own way back. The embankment was wet and slippery due to the wet season, dusk had fallen and I was plodding along on my own one day when I heard a cry of distress. A man in front of me cried out, 'Don't leave me, the tigers will get me,' and after slipping over several times and getting back up again I heard him not far ahead. I yelled out, 'Hang on, mate, I'm coming', and after I reached him I assured this poor fear-stricken man that if we talked loudly and helped each other to keep upright we would both reach camp safely. When we did so, he was very grateful for my assistance.

Malaria hit me again next day and around me men were dying and the bugler and burial parties were busy. Every time I became conscious I heard a bugle.

Later in the evening I woke up and mumbled, 'I can still hear the bugle.'

A voice answered, 'No, mate, they've stopped. It's ten o'clock.' They went from eight in the morning until eight at night with those bugle calls.

The wet season put all the workers under stress as bridges washed away and embankments became eroded. We returned from work in groups, slipping and sliding on a surface like wet glass, and making noisy conversation to avoid a tiger or leopard attack. We ceased all pretence of organised military funerals and, enticed by extra rice for burial squads, I joined in the pathetic ritual of carrying the corpse out to the jungle, digging a shallow hole and after the Dutch padre had read the service I pelted the perching vultures and cringing wild dogs with stones.[65]

News came down from Thailand, or Siam as we knew it, of the terrible plight of F Force being forced to make rock cuttings and build suicidal high bridges and we realised we weren't so badly off.[66]

My first glimpse of vultures had been quite an experience. I blundered into a battle for the remains of some dead animal between the Burmese wild dog, which is a smaller version of the Australian dingo, and several vultures. With vultures in possession the dogs tried harassment by diving forward in short attacks, just keeping out of range of those long scrawny necks and vicious hooked beaks. Then as I watched, one dog was caught unawares. A vulture seized him on top of the shoulder and with a twisting, ripping action tore the skin right from over his rib cage, exposing his insides. I could see the dog's lungs and internal organs in movement. Feeling sick and nauseated, I turned away and continued my walk to work along the embankment.

Recovering from this shocking sight I saw approaching a Burmese man who clasped his stomach and gave vent to loud screaming sounds. My first thought was that this must be a man who had contracted cholera and compassion welled up inside me, but as he came closer it slowly dawned on me that this man was happy and he was singing in Burmese!

One day I was amongst a group of men sent back by train to repair the line in front of the gates of one of our early camps. After working for a while, someone said, 'I hear aircraft engines.' This man was a former RAAF mechanic so we stopped work to listen. Our guard rushed back and forth, shouting, 'No English plane. Only Japanese bombers. Japan is master over all of Burma sky.' But the mechanic grinned and yelled out, 'He's wrong, men. They're British engines!' Then, leaping up and down excitedly, he pointed towards a patch of blue sky and screamed, 'Lancasters!' and following his directions we saw five huge bombers bursting into view.

Our guard had vanished and down in the camp men were rushing about, including on-duty Jap guards who were blowing whistles and shouting at the prisoners, whilst Jap guards not on duty appeared wearing the usual white loincloths. The bombers circled and the air force man assured us, 'They've already dropped their bombs somewhere else. They are now just looking us over.' Then we saw a Jap guard preparing an improvised anti-aircraft gun out of a machine gun in the centre of the parade ground. 'Gor blimey!' yelled the ex-mechanic, 'they'll come in and blast him if he fires that thing.' Meanwhile, having circled the camp the bombers were leaving when the intrepid 'Knight of Bushido' opened fire. One bomber pilot banked his plane until his 'tail end Charlie' could aim his forty-millimetre cannon at the Jap guard and then came some loud bang, bang, bang noises and when the dust cleared there was only a big hole where the hero had stood. Looking down into the camp, we could see that the barbed-wire fence was decked out with strips of white cloth hanging on the top wire where some of our off-duty camp guards hadn't quite cleared the wire hurdle. As we watched the bombers leaving, our guard appeared from nowhere and we prepared to return to our camp.[67]

We crossed the Siam border and I remember looking up at three golden pagodas high up on the side of Three Pagodas Pass so the camp we were in must have been 105 Kilo camp. I remember entering the hospital hut one day and hearing men laughing, which was unusual even in the camp, let alone a hospital, so I made an investigation. An Australian sat up in his bed area and glassy-eyed and with fixed gaze he was giving a perfect imitation of a BBC news announcer giving a war news commentary. I was astounded, for he gave precise names and details of a tank battle going on in Europe, mentioning names of generals and army units involved. Finally he stopped his commentary and announced the next news time. I joined in the laughter and asked someone what was going on. 'Cerebral malaria,' said one chap, adding, 'we've got a whole hospital full of them.'

I went through the hut and saw some men sitting bolt upright with glassy eyes, reciting poetry whilst some lay mumbling and giving vent to occasional bursts of laughter. Slowly realisation came to me and I felt a deep sense of shame for laughing at one of them. I asked the orderly what chance they had and he said, 'There's eighty chances out of a hundred they will die. With cholera you have about ninety-five out of a hundred you will die.'

I left as another 'news broadcast' began and returned to my hut bed. Lying there, I began shivering and I went off to get some quinine. What happened after that became very muddled but days later I would gather information and piece the story together. I remember later that at one stage I heard voices which were deep and angry. One gruff voice demanded, 'How long has he been here?' and a voice answered, 'Three days.' I heard two angry gruff voices query, 'And who's been looking after him?'

There was a pause and then a weak voice answered, 'Nobody.'

Then a voice filled with angry contempt said, 'You lot are a pack of rotten selfish bastards,' followed by, 'Come on, Alf, we'll bloody well look after the poor sod from now on.' And look after me they did, like two rough nurses. It seems I had contracted cerebral malaria. The men who bunked around me and whose company I had sought in preference to the rougher types were men who were supposedly very religious and they studiously attended all church parades, regarding themselves as Christians. Now two men I had once looked down on were cushioning my head and pouring cool water into my mouth. Later when I told them I couldn't drink soup, a voice said, 'You'll bloody well drink it, Holman, or we'll pour it down you.' Too weak to resist, I started to surrender to force-feeding. Soup went down, rice went down and quinine tablets went down. As soon as it became obvious I would live, they directed my bunk mates to carry on, saying, 'You see that this poor bugger lives or we'll both be back to know the reason why.' Then they unobtrusively left me to men who started behaving like Christians. I had learned a lesson that I would never forget.

Malaria is a depressing illness and even though I had recovered I could have easily slipped back. The fact that the man who made the wooden crosses set up his workshop at the end of my bed did nothing to help my recovery. I would see him carve NX and I would start seeing

NX44861 and I had to force it out of my mind and try to concentrate on other things.

As I recovered, men started telling me what I had been doing whilst I had been out of my head for three days. Strangely enough, I was now remembering things and the general picture emerged like little pieces of a jigsaw puzzle coming together. At one stage I was found swaying about and glassy-eyed in front of the guards at the gate yelling out, 'The war is over, you bastards, and I am travelling home on Colonel Thyer's yacht.' My rescuer mumbled '*Takusan bioki*' (very sick) to the Japs and escorted me back to bed. Later, with glassy eyes and rapt expression I was remarking to a chap on how well the band was playing and was again escorted back. Another man found me peering around a corner of the hut at our orderly sergeant and when he asked me what I was doing I said I was a deserter and the sergeant was hunting me down.

We survived by caring for one another and my mate Don was an example. Don was very deaf and of course he often didn't hear when the Jap summons '*Kara!*' was shouted, whereupon one of his mates would rush to explain to the infuriated guard that Don was deaf.

Medical supplies were hard to get and various means were used to get them. For example, Jap guards were only allowed to contract VD twice and if they became infected a third time they would be shot. Here was one way to get iodoform for ulcers smuggled into the camp. Our doctors offered to treat the Japs secretly in exchange for medical supplies and this blackmail was very effective. Of course, there were also men who showed raw courage by sneaking over the fence to get food or some medicine for a sick mate in hospital to save their mate's life.

One camp I will never forget was the one governed by Lieutenant Naito. He was a real dapper figure, dressed in a spotless uniform, polished leather belt and high boots and armed with a samurai sword and a holster containing a .38-calibre revolver. We learned through our interpreter that Naito was a wealthy businessman's son, well educated and apparently a slave to alcohol. It is possible his family was happy to have him travel far away to a distant land. Not long after we had arrived in camp and set up our lines of latrines, our hospital and our cooking area, we saw Jap guards setting up sandbag gun-emplacements. Our interpreter, Captain Drower, learned from the guards that Naito was in a paranoid state through imbibing too much wine and imagined British soldiers were all about and preparing to attack the camp.

One morning the guards were lined up in camouflage dress clutching rifles with fixed bayonets and listening to a lecture by Naito. As curious prisoners gathered to watch, my gaze strayed down towards the line of thin scrubby bushes which only partly concealed a line of men sitting on the latrine – thunder boxes as they were called. Even as I looked at this line of battered slouch hats and brown shoulders showing above a rough matting fence, Naito raised his sword and screamed, 'Charge!' The Jap guards gave out demoralising screams and ran towards the men seated on the latrines. As they passed me, some of the guards were laughing and some were stumbling as they ran, seeing a line of Australians frantically rising up off their seats and trying to pull up their trousers. It was obvious the Japanese used the same expression as we did about not getting caught with your trousers down. With faces kept averted from Naito's watching eyes, the guards pulled up before the latrines shaking with laughter at the line of shocked expressions on men's faces. As one of the watchers laconically observed, 'None of those poor buggers should be suffering from constipation.'

Next day Naito erroneously declared that Captain Drower had smallpox and ordered that he be confined in the smallpox isolation tent and that his bed and bedding be burned. Just as a match was about to start the fire, the Japanese corporal distracted Naito's attention and guards carted Drower's belongings back into a hut. Later I saw men leaving a hut like startled hens evacuating a hen house and nearby I saw Naito approaching a man with drawn revolver. Standing in front of the man with his revolver pointed at his navel, Naito asked him, 'How does it feel to know you will die in a few minutes?' The corporal rushed up with a paper message for Naito and during this distraction the distraught man was whisked away to safety.

Someone must have taken on the responsibility of informing Japanese Headquarters in Burma of Lieutenant Naito's behaviour because later a Japanese staff car entered the camp and Naito was forced to hand over his sword and revolver and was escorted to the car under Military Police guard and taken away while we all breathed a sigh of relief. Later a train stopped in front of our camp gates with an empty truck visible opposite the entrance. Then Jap guards dragged out Lieutenant Naito's expensive, beautifully polished wooden trunk; trundling it over and over and kicking it and scuffing its surface they got it eventually into the railway truck. The pair of polished boots received similar treatment as guards took turns in kicking them all the way to the truck and this set the pattern of treatment for all Naito's gear en route to Japan. One prisoner removed a cigar from his mouth and commented drily, 'I don't think the guards liked poor old Naito.'[68]

Another camp would stand out in my memory in Siam because in this camp several men became ill, not because of lack of food, but because they ate too much of one type of food. There was a glut of duck eggs in the district and I would soon become one of the several victims of duck egg poisoning. We found it hard to believe as the Siamese brought loads of eggs into the camp and these were being handed out to us, so many per man. Not knowing that the body can only assimilate the good of three eggs per day, we were stuffing them into ourselves all day. Some men soon started complaining of aches and pains in the arms and legs similar to influenza and I was one of them. The Dutch doctor had knowledge of albumen poisoning and alerted our doctors to what was happening. Fortunately I had a coinciding malarial attack, and with the usual profuse perspiring associated with the attack I was able to get rid of the poison through the pores of my skin.

Lying opposite me in the camp hospital was a man with beriberi; his body taking on the shape of an inflated rubber dummy. The Dutch doctor ordered the man to be given only fried rice and strong coffee. One night the man called for one of the bamboo urine bottles as his body started draining off fluid, and this process was repeated all through that night. In the morning he was a mass of loose, sagging skin.

The dreaded *Kempei Tai* [69] secret police arrived whilst I was in hospital. It soon became obvious, as they made a search of the hospital, that somehow they had learned of our secret wireless; they must have been puzzled as to why they hadn't found it on their previous searches. If our guard George had told them how certain Australians always insisted on carrying his personal luggage out onto the parade ground every time we shifted from each camp and also insisted on helping him carry it to the Jap guard-house in each new camp, they would have guessed where it was. Now, as they entered the hospital a man sat on one of the latrine 'thunder boxes' with one hand holding the tiny wireless underneath him. As a Jap guard pulled the door open, he groaned as if in pain. The guard looked very sympathetic and queried, '*Bioki?*' He looked up at the guard and answered, '*Takusan bioki*'(very sick) and the guard left him. It had been a very close call indeed. [70]

The guards tried to provoke us by calling out, 'Churchill number ten. Tojo number one,' but the Aussies refused to rise to the bait and made a joke out of it, agreeing with them. Then one day whilst we were being counted, the guards probed the English ranks for a reaction to their taunts. A young English soldier shouted, 'Churchill number one!' They punched and kicked him. There was a loud murmur of anger from the ranks and a sergeant screamed out, 'Don't break ranks, they've got a machine gun ready!'

Now the lad was battered to the ground with rifle butts, still shouting, 'Churchill number one!' He lay covered in streaks of blood and the guards drew back, sure that they had silenced him for ever. As I watched, the battered broken lips opened and out of his blood-flecked mouth came a very clear, audible, 'Churchill number one' and his head flopped over to one side. He had triumphed over them. Our sergeant's voice sounded nearby, 'Very brave, very stupid.'

Later I heard the high-pitched scream of an animal and saw a guard pouring boiling water out of a kettle into the eyes of a little captive honey bear. Seeing red flecks before my eyes I rushed towards him until a dozen voices brought sanity back to me by shouting, 'They have a machine gun trained on us, Holman. You'll get us all killed if you don't watch out.' They had found my weak spot and when a guard brought a small dog into our view and then began torturing the poor creature I left the area.[71]

Still recovering from malaria, I went out to work with men helping to carry out the rice basket and buckets of watery soup. Holding on to the end of a bamboo pole from which was suspended the basket full of rice, I slipped and fell whilst crossing a bridge. I had broken the skin on my right shin. This soon turned into an ulcer and that meant I could lose my leg and even my life.

In this camp we had Dr Coates,[72] who was previously a leading surgeon in Australia. We were always desperately short of medicine and men prayed they would not develop appendicitis, for we had no access to a real hospital for any emergency operation. What passed for an operating table here was a crude table with bamboo legs and frame and a top of bamboo slats, which were halved canes of bamboo. This table was out in the open air in order to gain the best possible light.

Our wonderful surgeon, Dr Coates, had four types of anaesthetic: some dentist's novocaine which someone had thoughtfully brought with them to Singapore, some opium tablets, Burmese whisky and cigars. I always lacked the intestinal fortitude to witness one of these amputation operations performed by Coates but I was told the patient received a novocaine needle in the spine, was given opium tablets to swallow with Burmese whisky and finally was given a Burmese cigar to smoke before being held down onto the table. With a surgeon's knife and a butcher's saw borrowed from the Jap cook, Coates then incised the flesh above the ulcerated leg and, quoting passages from Shakespeare, he then sawed the offending leg off. I believe that the man would still have been very conscious of something terrible happening to him, but this was the best that could be done for him.

One morning after partaking of my breakfast rice I headed off for the hot foment section and unwittingly strayed into the operation area. Hearing someone whistling an old song, I looked up to see a group around a crude table on which a man was being held down by four others. Coming towards me was a man holding a shovel in one hand and a man's leg, held by the big toe, in the other. As he walked past me seemingly quite unconcerned, I felt my stomach heave and it was all I could do to keep from vomiting.

My ulcer got worse and at one stage the situation looked very grim as the doctor and orderly scraped around my shin bone, cleaning it and pulling dead tissue from under the bone. One morning as I left I paused behind a hessian screen for some reason, and overheard Dr Chalmers and Pinkey talking. Dr Chalmers said, 'That man has the greatest capacity to resist pain that I have ever seen.' I sneaked away, realising that despite the compliment my leg was in a terrible condition. I didn't hold out any hope of surviving an amputation.

One day Chalmers came around carrying his little surgical gouge spoon for removing pus from ulcers. He was examining each man's ulcer as he came along and sometimes using his little spoon. The men's nerves were in a bad state and it was pitiful to hear their cries of pain as he worked. Unbeknownst to me, there was only a little of the precious iodoform left and the doctor was determining which ulcer would receive it. He looked carefully at me and then my ulcer and turning to the orderly he said, 'There is considerable improvement there. Put iodoform on it; I think we can save that one.' Dr Chalmers and Pinkey must have seen the relieved look on my face for they both grinned as I almost lost control and fainted with relief.

That ulcer eventually healed up and from the bottom of my heart I thanked God, as well as the doctor and orderly who had worked so hard on my leg. When I thanked God I did it more from training than from real faith. I didn't know what the future held in store for me, that I would one day be in actual contact with this Spirit force in all its terrifying reality.

Looking back, I realise it was a great honour to be associated with these medical men. Dr Chalmers was last seen in a lifeboat with Brigadier Varley after their prison ship was torpedoed en route to Japan by an American submarine.

I was hardly out on the line before I was back in again. My left leg had puffed up due to varicose vein trouble and I was ordered by the doctor to lie in bed and not to walk anywhere. Later, a sergeant came along and ordered me to report to the Jap cook-house to help other men to peel and cut up vegetables. This was ironic because our only vegetable was jam melon in a slightly salty, watery stew. I pointed out to the good sergeant that a doctor's order can in no way under army law be circumvented by a commissioned or non-commissioned officer, and he left. In a few minutes I was escorted by the sergeant to a desk, behind which sat Major Kerr. He kept me standing for several minutes whilst Colonel Anderson looked over his shoulder at my badly swollen leg. Kerr said curtly, 'I understand you refused to obey an army command, Holman.'

I replied, 'On the contrary, sir, I sought to obey an army doctor's command to stay in bed.'

'Don't you dare be insolent with me, Holman. I say you should have obeyed your sergeant.'

I looked at him straight in the face and said, 'Then with all due respect, sir, that would make a mockery of army law.'

Anderson's face went red as, holding a handkerchief over his face, he tried hard to suppress a burst of laughter. Controlling himself, he leaned towards Kerr and said in a whisper that my sharp ears managed to catch, 'He's got you over a barrel now, Major.' I thought for a few seconds the irate Major Kerr was about to have a stroke as he snatched up a pen and started writing. Keeping me standing still for a few minutes with Colonel Anderson hovering in the background pretending to study some document, he finally lifted his head and glaring at me barked, 'Dismiss.' After saluting, I returned to my bed. [73]

During those terrible years in the prison camps, we each tried to keep the other chap alive if we possibly could. [74] When I was in one of our rough camp hospitals, I saw a man who was obviously giving up the fight to stay alive and a wonderful orderly who was just as obviously searching for a means of rekindling this man's will to live.

One morning Pinkey Rhodes saw the dying man's white blanket, and noticing his eyes light up I figured the orderly had found a solution to the problem. Nobody knew where this beautiful blanket came from, or how the man had managed to keep it so white, and he appeared to treasure it. Bending down, Pinkey felt the blanket's texture under the watchful gaze of the owner and stated that he wished he owned it.

Realising the patient was still watching him, Pinkey moved alongside another orderly and, giving him a wink, said loudly enough for the sick man to hear, 'This bloke with the white blanket won't eat. He'll be dead in a few days, and then I'll have the blanket.' Sneaking a look out of the corner of his eye, Pinkey saw the man looking with real hostility in his direction.

Later the man sat up and forced a few mouthfuls of rice and stew down his gullet with very great difficulty. Before he took the man's plate away to rinse it, Pinkey bent over and fondled part of the blanket with a look of admiration.

As the days passed, I saw the man grow steadily stronger, until one day the doctor said, 'You're right to go back with your mates.' As he was leaving, the man glared at Pinkey and said, 'Well, I didn't die like you thought I would and you aren't going to get my blanket after all.'

Pinkey chuckled and patting the man on the shoulder, said, 'I never did want that blanket. I just had to give you some reason to keep on living.'

We had one chap in hospital in one of the prison camps who was expected to die any time, so I wasn't surprised when an orderly felt the man's wrist and pronounced him dead. Two volunteers brought a stretcher to carry him off to the morgue hut, and just then the man's left eyelid fluttered. The startled stretcher-bearers reported this to the orderly, who asked them to return in the morning.

The next day the man was again declared dead, but when the bearers went to move him, he gave out a faint moan. They were asked to return again the following day. On the third day, the orderly once more declared the man dead, but before the deceased was taken away, he held a mirror over the supposedly-dead man's mouth. There was a faint vapour mist on the mirror, so the stretcher-bearers were dismissed once again.

The following day, the man's eyes opened and we could see he was trying to ask for water. He was given a spoon of water and later spoonfuls of soup and rice. He recovered, but my work group moved on and I lost contact with him, not knowing whether he survived the railway camps.

After the war, I was standing near one of the steam-train exits at Sydney's Central Station as people rudely pushed and shoved past each other. A man rushed up and shook hands with me. 'Gee, I was hoping to see an ex-POW,' he said. 'Do you remember the man who died three times?'

When I said I did, he burst out excitedly, 'You oughta seen him, Holly, dressed in a porter's uniform and wheeling a bloody great barrow with cases on it right along Moss Vale railway platform. He looks about fourteen stone and fit, and gee, I was happy to know he survived to get back.'

As we parted after a brief conversation, he said, 'I just had to hope I'd meet another ex-POW, because it would have been useless telling any of these civilians. They wouldn't understand.'

On the railway the two large work forces were closing the gap between the Thai and Burma sides, and Mountbatten's forces were in action against the Japanese troops in upper Burma. Pressure was being put on the sick, worn-out prisoners to complete the job and to connect the two lines as quickly as possible for military use. Twenty-four-hour shifts or up to forty-eight-hour shifts would now be worked. For light to see what we were doing, bamboo torches were being used. These consisted of short pieces of bamboo about five feet in length with an open end filled with some inflammable substance.[75]

One night I was at the head of a group of men strung out along the line driving dog spikes into the sleepers. We had worked all day and well into the night, our only rest being when rails were delayed, at which time we would lie in the mud and sleep until they arrived at the railhead and we were kicked up to our feet by the guards.

Down to about six stone in weight, absolutely worn out and bordering on collapse, I started falling back until I sank down, sitting on one rail completely and utterly exhausted. My bar man who had held my torch left it lying on the rail beside me and continued on using his bar to hold up the end of the sleepers whilst men drove in the spikes. Soon they were well up ahead and I knew as I sat there that only the lighted torch would protect me from the ever-present wild animals. What did it matter, I thought, if it was a tiger it would be a quick death. Realising that I was physically unable to carry on I took off my hat and kneeling down, I prayed to God for strength. As I knelt down the rain started falling and my body was chilled, for the nights were cooler as we entered the mountainous region of Siam.

Suddenly, it seemed that someone stood behind me and I felt the tips of ten fingers on my head. They became ten points of warm power entering my body. Suffused with warmth, I saw cold rain cascading off my shoulders and the utter weariness was leaving my body. I felt both fear and exultation and rising to my feet I fervently thanked God, picked up my hammer and walked towards the long line of torches bobbing up and down ahead.

Reaching the last of the line of men, I was treated to angry suspicious looks and asked, 'Where did you get to?' and 'Where were you, Holman?' How do you tell a group of tired, angry men that you had just experienced a miracle, that Jesus had laid his hands on me and poured his power into my poor tired body and restored my strength? Later, as we were lined up and transported back to camp, and before I slept, I knew I would never be the same again. I now knew that there was a God – nobody could take that away from me.

Finally the two forces joined together and the Japanese made a ceremony out of the joining of the rails. One of the big brass drove a supposedly gold spike into the last sleeper and the 'Railway of Death' was completed.[76]

Back in camp we were told we would go to a rest camp. We were soon packed in cattle trucks and headed for a camp known as Tamarkan. Jostled around in the truck I apologised profusely when I realised I had been standing on somebody's foot. Then came a voice I'll never forget saying, 'Well, ah've bin standin' on thet foot for nigh on twenty-three years so ah guess it's orlraht fo' you to stand on it fo' a few minutes.' As we progressed we saw the high bridges and rock cuttings and we were horrified at the terrific cost in human life paid by the Siam force of Australian prisoners.

At Tamarkan I was reunited with brother Jack and we started inquiries about being placed in the same *kumi*, or work group, should another work party be organised in the future. Now we received plenty of food and we started putting on weight.

A fictional film was made after the war about the River Kwai bridge at Tamarkan, which originally was a simple flat wooden pile bridge similar to old bridges on the south coast of New South Wales and nothing remotely resembling the fancy type of bridge used in the film.

Although food and conditions were good at Tamarkan, when the Japs asked for volunteers for a work party Jack and I promptly stepped forward with a large group of men who reasoned, as we had done, that this area and all the railway bridges were now targets for British bombers.[77] Unbeknownst to us, we had just made ourselves slaves of Baron Mitsui, the Japanese owner of many coal mines.

Saigon and Singapore

We were put into railway cattle trucks and were soon crossing the Red River Delta en route to Phnom Penh. The delta ricebowl was an astounding sight as mile after mile, hour after hour we traversed a virtual sea of rice extending as far as we could see right out to the horizon.

When the train stopped on the outskirts of Phnom Penh we disembarked and marched through the town to the Mekong River where we boarded an ancient river steamer which took us to Saigon. The wooden huts in which we were housed were obviously former barracks for Senegalese troops, and although rough, were palaces when compared to our former bamboo huts in Burma.[78]

With the French surrender the remote colony of Indo-China was left out on a limb. To retain any semblance of being free it became diplomatic for the people to declare themselves Vichy French and now it was paying off. The Japanese, being friends with Germany and Italy, had to respect the people of Saigon whether they liked it or not. It was a comical situation and I've no doubt there were French-speaking English spies circulating with impunity. The people of Saigon seemed to make no effort to control their contempt for the Japanese. With German vessels also entering Saigon there was another problem, because the German sailors didn't seem at all fond of their almond-eyed allies. It behove the Japanese to maintain a low profile whilst in Saigon. Under the strain of walking a diplomatic tightrope our Jap camp colonel had become quite paranoid and even distrusted his own cook, with the result that all his meals were cooked by the English cook. Had he learned that this English gentleman who bowed so politely to him when they met was dosing his food with dysentery germs and hiding a secret wireless under bags of rice, he quite easily might have suffered a stroke. I will spare the reader the sordid details of where the cook got the dysentery germs.

Whether I admired his acting ability or whether we just shared a mutual deep hatred for the Japanese I don't know, but the cook and I soon became good friends. He confided in me how twice now the Jap colonel had become very ill with dysentery and 'the blankety blank Jap doctor had saved him both times,' and he couldn't interfere with the doctor's food because he received his from the Jap cook. He would scowl every time he set eyes on the Japanese doctor walking about.

I was walking down the parade ground one day when he called me over to the cook-house. He looked so happy and excited I thought that either the Jap doctor had dropped dead or maybe it was the colonel who had died. He blurted out, 'They've landed in France – Poms, Yanks and Canadians. The Poms and Canadians are on a beach head and established. The poor Yanks got trapped on Omaha beach and the German firepower created heavy losses, but they're right now.' I was now as happy as he was but I tried to look nonchalant as I walked away.

Having heard the news and realising that thousands of nearby Frenchmen were drinking champagne, the colonel looked at the Jap orderly standing patiently at the door with trays of food in his arms. Letting out a roar of anger, he kicked the orderly down the stairs with plates flying everywhere. Next day I saw a French girl slow her pushbike and leaning over, she threw a bag of money in amongst some Australians. A guard rushed at her and lunged at her with rifle and bayonet, missing her person but puncturing the pushbike saddle. Suddenly a large, expensive car pulled up nearby and a well-dressed Frenchman ran to the girl's aid as she toppled over onto the road. The Frenchman glared at the Jap guard and after brushing the girl down and watching her ride away he followed her in the large car. The incident must have been reported to Japanese Headquarters in Saigon because shortly afterwards the colonel had the guard disarmed and handed him over to the guards to kick and punch, which they all seemed happy to do. When they had finished with him, he was put on show at the camp gates to complete his guard duty sitting on a chair, a pathetic battered figure of humanity.

It must have been frustrating for these brave knights of *bushido* to have to treat the resident population of a country with respect. In Singapore and other places the Japanese had full sway and could indulge in cruel practices with impunity.

The colonel must have received a tongue-lashing from a superior officer for when his humble subservient orderly reached his office door again with his night meal, he put one polished leather boot against the man's midriff and sent him flying off the stairway balcony to land on his back in the dirt and plates, cups and food went flying everywhere once again. I really felt sorry for that poor unfortunate young orderly.

The prisoners of war were having a reasonably good time and with proper medicine now being smuggled inside the camp in large quantities plus food and cigars, we were all putting on some weight and learning to laugh at things again. There were work parties going out to work on the wharves and one day a humorous event took place. One of our frustrated guards started venting his ill humour on one of the Australians right alongside a Japanese cargo ship. He had slapped the man across the face when we heard a shout and a Jap seaman came running down the gangplank. Fronting the guard, he punched him on the jaw, knocking him sprawling on the wharf. Turning to the Australian, he shook hands and to our amazement became engaged in friendly conversation. We learned later that the two men had once been shopkeepers in Melbourne and while visiting his parents the Jap had become trapped by the outbreak of war.

We had been loading a beautiful large French ocean liner named *Leconte de Lisle* and doctors and nurses were parading up and down all day long in full view and red crosses were displayed everywhere. The weight of the boxes was very suspicious and it became obvious that they were full of bullets, not bandages or medicine. Frenchmen told us later that she was sunk out at sea. Since becoming prisoners we had sometimes held concerts in the camps with a surprising number of talented people contributing to the entertainment. Unfortunately our two comedians, 'Mr Gallagher and Mr Sheen' fouled things up one night as Sheen asked Gallagher, 'Where is the *Leconte de Lisle*?' and he answered, 'Gone with the Wind.' A Jap guard heard the ship's name mentioned and raised the spy alarm with the camp colonel and later our sorry pair of comedians were telling a cooked-up story through our interpreter of how they only said how hard they had to work when this ship came into port. The colonel finally accepted their story and it served to show us how frustrated and edgy the Japs were in Saigon. We learned to be very careful with our concert items.

Another day I was in a party working near the aerodrome. On the tarmac was a line of twenty-five Zero fighter planes warming their engines ready to take off. Our guard boasted loudly how these were going looking for American planes and then the Zeros all flew off into the blue sky. A short time later we saw six planes coming in to land.

These were the only planes to return and they were so riddled with bullet holes and shrapnel holes it was a wonder they could still fly. The Aussies were openly laughing and one man turned to the frustrated angry guard and said, 'They were looking for Americans? It looks like they found them all right.' The guard lined us up and slapped each man's face, saying, 'I will teach you not to laugh at our air force!'

We had dug slit trenches around the camp and it was full moon, which our air force mates assured us meant we could get a sneak British air raid on the assembled cargo ships at any time. We spent a restless night but by breakfast time we had relaxed, and collected our plates or dixies of rice feeling secure and safe. And that's when they came from where we least expected. Skimming low over the rice paddies with a low range of hills blanketing out the sound of aircraft engines, they rose up over the hills and were over the top of the ships in seconds, releasing their bombs. It was absolute pandemonium with the roar of engines, exploding bombs and the noisy racket of machine gun and anti-aircraft fire, plus the whine of the air raid siren going in Saigon. I never did learn what damage they did or how many ships they sank but as a morale-booster it was terrific, especially for the poor English prisoners whose spirits had been at such a low ebb ever since the surrender.

We had a permanent comedian and morale-booster in our mate Brownie, who in the middle of the raid was pretending his only worry was whether a bomb would hit his dixie of rice, hastily abandoned on his bed space. Scared as we were, we were laughing as he shook his fist and shouted, 'Piss off, you noisy Pommy bastards, you'll end up hitting my flamin' dixie in a minute.'

Our only worry apart from the fear of air raids or suddenly being arrested as spies was the infestation of bugs. I remember one moonlit night hearing brother Jack going 'smack' with his hand and later remarking, 'Gee, that isn't too bad, I managed to squash five all under one hand.' The work parties were more like picnics and often we were taken in trucks right through Saigon, where we would see beautiful French and Eurasian women. The ones that excited us were the Eurasian women who had the ability to dress like the French but with their sloe eyes giving them an air of mystery.

If memory serves me right, one day Jack and I were members of a Japanese work party on the outskirts of Saigon. We had sat down to eat our rice ration. In front of us was a Chinese house made of bamboo, resting on stilts in the centre of a large duck-pond. Leading from the shore to the only door was a long wooden ramp, a gangway between the house and dry land. As we watched, a group of ducks wandered up to the door, entered the house and wandered out again.

'Gee, what sort of filthy people would live in there?' said Jack disgustedly.

As if in answer to his query, a very beautiful young Chinese girl appeared in the doorway, wearing a long silk dress with a split skirt which exposed a lovely shapely leg. She wore slippers covered with some shiny, golden-coloured substance.

Now she walked down the gangway, followed by a dozen pairs of Australian eyes, none missing a step. At the bottom of the gangway she stepped onto the ground and made straight for us with a very exciting walk.

Jack spoke up, 'Now look at that graceful walk, you young blokes. Girls in Australia pay for lessons at deportment classes to learn how to walk like that. They have to walk up and down balancing books on their heads. This girl here must be a model.'

Now she was level with us, and with our eyes poking out of our heads like marbles, we heard her hawking back in her throat as she produced a mouthful of phlegm, and right opposite Jack, she spat it out onto the road. There was complete silence for a few seconds, and then came a disgusted comment from brother Jack, 'Now that's bloomin' well spoiled everything.'

When the guards weren't looking, the French people would grin and give us the 'V' for Victory sign, and the V sign was being chalked on walls all over town and in full view of German ships. I don't think anyone died whilst we were in Saigon and it was a relief from constant burial parties and from the poor English begging us to help them bury railway trolleyloads of dead prisoners as we built the Burma line.

But there is an old saying that all good things come to an end and one day we were warned that we would be moving the following day. We marched to a wharf and the next morning boarded an old river steamer which took us back down the Mekong River to Phnom Penh. I don't know what went on in other men's minds but I had been hoping that the war would end whilst we were still in Saigon. From Phnom Penh we travelled by train in cattle trucks down the peninsula through country plundered and made poor by the Japanese, past crowds of starving people and thin, starved children looking up at us with solemn brown eyes.

After several days of broken travel we arrived back at a vastly different Singapore showing large V for Victory signs painted everywhere, and people held up their fingers giving the victory salute as we passed. We were taken to a camp containing English and Dutch prisoners, known as River Valley Road. As we prepared bed spaces we were told that there was a secret wireless in camp. The news was that in a long valley in Normandy the Allied armies had trapped the proud German divisions that had formerly marched into Paris and it was being called 'the killing ground' as once-arrogant SS forces were being relentlessly slaughtered by mixed Allied troops showing the same lack of mercy as the German storm troopers. In Singapore, people remembered the long lists of those pro-British citizens who had been executed by the Japs for supporting the troops during the Malay campaign. Now new lists were being made of traitors' names, and knives were being sharpened ready to avenge the dead.[79]

The Germans had shown scant mercy with their submarines and they had inflicted terrible losses in both lives and ships but now positions had been reversed and the submarines were like coffins awaiting almost certain burial. One of them was anchored near where our work party was engaged in loading a freighter. As we walked past looking up at the depressed gloomy faces of the German sailors leaning over the sub's railing, one irrepressible Australian blurted out, 'How do you blokes like yer bloody old Hitler now that you are losing the war?' They either didn't understand or were too depressed to care, for they kept heads bowed in contemplation. Our spirits were lifted knowing the war was nearly at an end.

All around the wharves at Singapore were prominently displayed signs telling you not to smoke or telling you not to put foot or hand into the surrounding water as the whole area was teeming with tiger sharks. One of the German submariners who obviously knew what the signs said decided to have a sly smoke behind a large pile of cargo on the wharf. One of our guards mistook him for an Australian and sneaking around the pile of cargo he seized hold of the German and, calling out 'Bukiro!' (you stupid man), he slapped his face very hard. The astounded German then punched the guard and carried him bodily to the edge of the wharf and dumped him over. It was an amused group of Germans on the submarine and chuckling prisoners on the wharf who watched our guards retrieving a dripping wet Jap from the sea.

Later that day a guard did catch an Australian having a smoke. Rushing along the wharf he fronted the man and began slapping his face, meanwhile screaming 'Bukiro!' A big German sailor leaped off the sub down onto the wharf and seizing the Jap guard he lifted him right off the ground with one hand whilst with his other hand he proceeded to slap and backhand the guard's face till the Jap's brain must have become addled. Then he left off and returned to his ship. The Japanese had definitely lost face that day and although our laughter was restrained while these two incidents were taking place, we had a hearty laugh afterwards. These were the incidents we ex-prisoners of war liked to bring up and laugh about after the war and seeing a group of us laughing during a stay in one of our military hospitals, civilians no doubt wondered what we could find to laugh about.

The sheds all along the wharves were called godowns and in one of these godowns large square bales of latex rubber were piled up nearly to the roof. After long storage in the hot building each became bonded to the next and they had to be levered apart with an iron bar. One chap was doing this and as the bale hit the cobblestone floor of the godown we would push it out of the door onto a rope sling from whence it would be hauled aboard a ship. I had lapsed in concentration this day when a chorus of voices screamed, 'Run, Holly, run!' and I took off like the proverbial Bondi tram hearing the huge bale hit the floor and come bouncing after me. Suddenly I tripped and fell face down on the floor, shrinking in anticipation of the bale crushing me to death. I heard loud gales of laughter and looking around I saw it had come to rest right behind my feet. I had run just far enough away.

Feeling shocked and shaken, I retired to the wharf and stood watching the bales being raised up on board the ship. Nearby a Chinese tally clerk jotted down with a pencil the number of bales that had gone aboard the Jap freighter. As he wrote on his pad, a mate of mine mumbled, 'I wonder where all this rubber is going?' With a quick glance at the Jap guard who was well out of hearing distance and looking away from us, the tally clerk said in perfect English, 'To the bottom of the sea, my friend, to the bottom of the sea.' My mate and I went back into the shed very amused. It was obvious that the underground movement was very strong here and ships were being sunk when they left port, as they had in Saigon.

Further along the wharf, Jack was in a group pushing a wharf trolley on rails loaded with naval shells. As the trolley gathered speed Jack and some mates jumped onto the load to hitch a ride. Suddenly somebody yelled out, 'No brakes!' and men dropped off and ran for cover behind piles of cargo around the corners of the godowns and down stairways on the wharf, whilst Jack lay on the top of the shells. The trolley hit the buffer stop and off fell the shells, with Jack rolling along on top of them. When everything was quiet again, heads popped up from everywhere with strained anxious faces.

Next day we were taken into the arsenal, which was a frightening experience in itself and infinitely more so when I saw an aerial bomb fall through the bottom of a case my mate was carrying, to hit the concrete and roll away. Fortunately it had no activating nose cone on it. However, a group the following day was not so fortunate when loading a case of Mills bombs (hand grenades). Someone had almost removed the pin from one of the grenades on purpose with the result that when the case was dumped on the rear of the truck the pin fell out and the resulting explosion blew one man's head off and blew the other man to pieces.

The next day was even more frightening. Five of the biggest planes the world had ever seen, namely the B29 American Superfortress, flew slowly over Singapore. Guards and prisoners alike stood in complete stupefaction gazing upwards at these huge monsters, realising that just a single thousand-pound bomb alone could destroy everything in the area. My gaze switched to a Japanese guard nearby. His eyes bulged out of their sockets and his jaw sagged open. To anyone who had never seen one before, this giant bomber seen up close was truly an awe-inspiring sight. The vibrations of the engines seemed to shake the ground and probably nearly shook the glass out of the windows of buildings as the planes passed overhead.

To his credit, one Japanese Zero pilot did challenge the intruders with a half-hearted attack on one bomber, looking like a sparrow attacking an eagle, but fortunately common sense prevailed and he flew back home, not wishing to become a dead hero.

Our nervous systems had taken a lot of strain over three years of captivity and the sight of these winged monsters with their awesome power to inflict death and destruction was the catalyst to turn fear into hysteria. That night, outside our hut full of slumbering men a cat stalked a rat. This hut was built with two-tiered sleeping platforms and when the rat realised he was being stalked he went for height to escape. Climbing up to the top tier, he proceeded to run across the bodies of sleeping men, hotly pursued by the cat. One of these men was having a nightmare dreaming of seeing huge bombs descending from Fortress bombers and when the fleeing rat dislodged the dixie and spoon from their hanging places and they fell with a loud clatter on his chest, the dream became reality.

'We're being bombed!' he screamed and leaping forward he promptly fell down onto the floor with a crash. The whole hut erupted with the roar of men falling, screaming and frantically trying to escape from doors and windows. Halfway out of a window I heard my brother Jack shouting, 'Calm down, men, there's no bombers. For goodness sake, calm down.' Eventually men did calm down and this was followed by bursts of half-hysterical muffled laughter as men related their reactions and Jap guards shouted out for us to shut up and go to sleep.

Morning brought with it a long line of men on sick parade with all manner of superficial injuries. On parade, Brigadier Varley reprimanded us for our lack of self-control and we looked very foolish as he reminded us that we were supposed to be soldiers.

Later, we had pulled up on the wharf with a long line of ammunition trucks driven by Indians and were preparing to unload all the ammunition onto the wharf when some keen-eyed prisoner reported five distant bombers. We looked at the train alongside us loaded with ammunition and at the godowns full of ammunition and with great trepidation we began unloading at terrific speed. I don't think in world history was there ever a load of ammunition unloaded with such care and yet so fast. We were banging on the cabins of the trucks and screaming at the drivers as five huge B29 bombers circled overhead. The trucks raced along the wharf and pulled up on the outskirts of Singapore as we viewed the giant bombers circling again before returning to India. We were all soaked with perspiration and limp with nervous exhaustion. It was a very frightening experience.

We were scrounging food of any description from the wharves and hiding it in small bags suspended from different parts of our body underneath our clothing. Getting wood for a fire to cook was another problem. The English mob had worked out a sneaky method of obtaining firewood by removing the bottom boards off their solid weatherboard hut. Our huts were not so solid and we weren't connected to electricity wires.

What the Englishmen had failed to notice was that their hut was old and weak and they were making it even weaker. In amongst the Australians a man was dreaming he was back in action and under heavy shellfire. Whether someone removed the last board or there was a sudden gust of wind, I'll never know but about midnight there was a loud bang, a bright flash of light and a shower of sparks as the hut collapsed, pulling away from the electric wires. Men came awake with a violent start and the man having the nightmare screamed out, 'We're being shelled by artillery!' and I could hear the roar of movement of panic-stricken men travelling from hut to hut right down the row.

Half asleep, I rushed to a window, fell out onto the ground and knocked the wind out of my lungs. Lying there frantically struggling to get my breath, I could hear muffled screams coming from the collapsed hut. Then Jack's voice came from the window, 'Bob, where are you?' Sucking in a breath I answered, 'Down here,' followed by Jack's bewildered voice asking, 'What the dickens are you doing down there?' The night was rent with the sounds of absolute pandemonium, screams, moans and groans and above all angry Japanese guards yelling out and brandishing rifles. I heard Jack once again, 'Calm down, men, it's all right, it's only another panic,' and once again, after the power was turned off and the hut lifted off the unfortunate men trapped underneath, men did begin to calm down and even see the funny side of the situation, except the few injured men.

Next morning there was another long line of, fortunately, not very badly injured men on sick parade. Brigadier Varley was in the process of bawling us out again and the air was thick with angry invective when a humane sergeant strode forward saying, 'With all due respect, sir, I must ask for some consideration for these men.' When Varley stood silent he continued, 'They've been through hell, sir, and their nerves are in rags and seeing those bombers was just about the last straw.' Varley then turned and dismissed the parade.

Becoming depressed was a constant danger and our man Brownie was ever on the alert to combat this weakness. If he saw a group of men looking sullen and depressed he would boast, 'Just watch me stir up this bunch,' and in no time at all they would all be busy arguing on some topic together. On his right shoulder blade he had a tattoo of a crocodile with open jaws whilst on the opposite shoulder blade was a tattoo of a little black boy running and he was always asking us, 'Has the crocodile caught that little black boy yet?'

The Jap guards used to point at Brownie and after one of them shouted some words in Japanese the rest would all start laughing. One day it happened in front of our interpreter, who joined in the laughter. Fronting our interpreter, Brownie demanded an explanation and with a humorous twinkle in his eyes, he said, 'Why, Brown, they look at your wispy beard and tanned brown skin and they reckon you look like a skinny old black billygoat.'

Brownie turned and gave the Jap guards a withering look and said, 'That's about all I could expect from a bunch of buck-toothed bachelors' sons like you,' and turning on his heel he walked away in disgust. After the war ended I saw Brown back in Australia in the discharge area with a group of returned men. He had them all laughing.

The Japs started work on building a large dry dock on Singapore and for security our mob was billeted on a small island off Singapore and ferried to and from the workplace in a Jap landing barge each day. Allied prisoners by hand hewed a huge cut into the side of the island big enough to take the *Queen Mary* liner. But the sides of the cutting were not shored up with timber and part of one wall collapsed, killing a group of Dutch prisoners. One of our chaps also died on the island through eating a type of shellfish that was later identified as poisonous by the Dutch. Thus we left behind a lonely grave covered with shells when later we were transported back to our camp.

We were returned to our camp at River Valley Road in Singapore because our slave master in Japan wanted prisoners to work in his coal mines and convoys would be organised to take us there. Before new number tags could be issued, Jack and I conferred with our officers as to the possibility of us remaining together. Fortunately for me a position swap was arranged five minutes before the numbers were handed out.

One man stepped out from Jack's *kumi* and I took his place whilst he took mine in 36 *kumi* and the swap was made. And so moved the hand of fate, with 36 *kumi* being selected among others for the first convoy to Japan. The ships they sailed on would be either torpedoed by American submarines or bombed by B29 bombers operating from China. Brigadier Varley and the good Dr Chalmers were last seen in a lifeboat after their ship had been torpedoed. It was sad to learn that these men who did so much to help others to survive lost their lives at sea.[80]

We remaining prisoners resumed our work around Singapore and the news we heard now was good. As if to confirm the news received from our secret wireless, we were treated to a spectacle viewed from a work site overlooking the harbour one day. Japanese ships started to appear, steaming into Singapore. They were a battered fleet of warships led by a very battered, sinking destroyer, which made straight for a mudbank where it promptly foundered, sinking by the stern amidst loud laughter and cheers from the prisoners. Into the harbour the ships straggled in groups; the Japanese Light Fleet, which had sunk our convoy sloop *Yarra* and her charges, three passenger cargo ships loaded with nurses, women and children. Retribution had begun and the bloodied, smashed decks, funnels twisted and lying askew and gaping holes everywhere were a glorious sight. These ships had been involved in a terrific naval battle.

An incident happened one night in this camp which would have a traumatic psychological effect on me that would continue for years after the war. There was a game mothers played with little children which very likely originated in America and which went, 'Eeny, meeny, miny, mo, catch a nigger by the toe, if he squeals let him go, eeny, meeny, miny, mo.' It sounded to me like a Jap guard reciting the same rhyme one night as I awoke but this guard held aloft a rifle with fixed bayonet and as I watched with stark horrified gaze, at the conclusion of the rhyme he plunged the bayonet down through a sleeping man's body, pinning him to the bamboo slat sleeping platform. The prisoner screamed and Japanese guards rushed up and disarmed their fellow guard and led him off and a stretcher party was formed to carry the dying prisoner away. I lay for hours wondering where he had started reciting his rhyme and thankful that he had passed me.

One day when I was on a work party working out of Singapore, during the day we noticed we had a new guard in amongst the familiar ones. Fortunately none of us mentioned news from the secret wireless or any incidents involving the underground movement on the wharves. Most of our talk was the familiar jokes and banter between mates. When our work shift finished the new guard walked off and into a nearby shed. As we were being counted the new guard emerged from the shed resplendent in the officer's uniform of the dreaded *Kempei Tai*. One careless word and someone could have been put in the *Kempei Tai's* 'amusement parlour' in Singapore, where the sadists would have tortured him to death. We had been very fortunate indeed.

A chap quietly told me of an incident involving a monument being built somewhere in Singapore. Memorials usually stand on a flat concrete base and this base was being made by workers from this camp. One oblong section had not been completed and men stood ready at this point in time to shovel a pile of mixed concrete into the cavity. It was then that a row started between the guard and one of the prisoners. The guard lashed out at the Australian with rifle butt and the Australian responded by hitting the Jap on the head with his shovel, laying him flat on his back. Realising that they were in a 'no win' situation whether the guard lived or died, their eyes focused on the gaping cavity and with one mind they moved quickly, placing the guard down in the cavity and working feverishly to cover him with concrete.

When the relief guard arrived in the guard truck the men were diligently smoothing over the area with wooden floats. The new guard immediately asked the whereabouts of the old guard. Then began a well-rehearsed act put on by the prisoners as their spokesman explained that the guard had gone to the red-light area on Lavender Street to make very quick love to 'Malay woman' and seeing all the grins on the men's faces the guard laughed and looked towards the red-light area. Then he went over to the guard truck to convey this information to the others and they also laughed and the truck went off down the road.

When the guard asked the other men later, each one gave the same story, with some giving obscene gestures for emphasis but which gained faint amusement from the now-worried guard. There was bitter resentment against the Japanese amongst the locals now and one guard wandering about alone would present fair game for any assassin. The work group was brought back to the camp and the matter was closed. I wonder if the cement cracked or if the body was ever even discovered after the war.

I walked down the parade ground, dodging puddles of water left by a recent shower and without realising it I almost blundered into a large tin on a cooking fire. I glanced at the two big muscular Dutchmen standing nearby and then I peeped into the tin. Amongst its bubbling contents I saw a dog's head slowly turning over and over and as I looked, the mouth opened wide, displaying rows of teeth. I reeled back, feeling nauseated and my look of revulsion hadn't gone unnoticed for as I turned I saw our lightweight boxing champion advancing on the Dutchmen and further back another boxer stood with arms folded. I suddenly read the situation with shocking clarity and retreated fast because I remembered the Dutchmen were champion wrestlers.

The boxer kicked the tin off the fire, saying, 'I told you chaps not to cook dog. You are supposed to be white men, not Japanese coolies.' I don't know what actually happened because I was doing what Malayan Command had called a 'strategic withdrawal', which means getting out of the area very fast before you get clobbered. I heard a couple of thumps and when I looked back the two Dutchmen lay on their backs in muddy water.

We had another crisis later and it was a stillborn calf that was the cause of the dispute. We had been issued a cow for meat and it had given birth to a stillborn calf, which our cooks had buried. Then the Dutchmen were caught digging it up and after another fist-fight it was reburied. After a few days the Dutch were again caught digging it up and by this time it had turned green. The Dutch also coaxed cats into the camp, killed them, cooked and ate them in front of a large group of supporting Dutchmen. The Aussies retaliated by pelting stones at the cats and chasing them away from the enticers. It was a very bad situation.

On another occasion, I was amongst a party of prisoners taken to work on the outskirts of Singapore. We sat down to eat our rice ration when a little Malay girl appeared and stood watching us. Now believe me when I say, we knew hunger when we saw it. She was a pathetic little figure in her ragged grubby dress, with spindly thin arms and legs. But what upset us most were the large solemn eyes in that pinched little face that followed our spoonfuls of rice.

One big rough Aussie upped and said, 'Geeze, I can't eat in front of that poor kid. How about each of us gives her a spoonful of rice?'

He beckoned to her and the little girl moved forward, raising the front of her skirt to form a pouch. Into this we each put a spoonful of rice. Then we watched as she walked over to a banana tree, where a leaf had broken off. She emptied the rice onto the big leaf and picked it up to take it to the edge of some bushes. Next she called out softly and soon a tiny Malay woman appeared from the bushes carrying a little boy, both showing the ravages of malnutrition. The three of them commenced to eat the rice from the leaf.

The big Aussie who'd organised our act of charity had tears rolling down his cheeks when he said, 'If I ever get back to Australia, I want to have a daughter and I want her to be just like that little girl.'

I presume Baron Mitsui must have been in urgent need of slaves for his coal mines because another chance was to be taken to get a convoy to Japan. The day arrived and our first shock was when we were ordered aboard a large new passenger cargo ship, the *Awa Maru*. Our next shocks came when we learned we were to be escorted by a large new destroyer and a new-looking aircraft carrier. The rest of the convoy were mostly tankers.[81]

The engines started and soon we were off again. This time Jack and I would face the journey together. We passed an old World War I battleship with towering pagoda mast and massive eighteen-inch guns, looking like some formidable dowager duchess dressed up in all her frills and furbelows, and the cargo ships followed in line astern. I noticed a large hoop attached to the ship and visible from most angles. A small cylinder was suspended in the centre of the hoop on the end of a cord that ran over a pulley wheel and down alongside the ship, where it was tied to a small buoy. I noticed that the cylinder rose or fell inside the hoop but was mostly in the centre. Shorty Bullivant, late of the cruiser *Perth*, explained that it was a convoy speed marker and every ship would try to keep the cylinder in the hoop's centre.

We had a very unwelcome guest aboard in the person of the Storm Trooper and for the health of every prisoner it behove all of us to know when and where he was all of the time. The deck would magically become deserted the second he made a step in our direction. This brutal Korean guard was a legend in the prison camps and the subject of many stories. In one camp he entered, he lined six men up and slapped their faces, explaining, 'We have now been introduced.' Later he would face justice and receive a long gaol sentence for his deeds.

I asked Shorty why we were hugging the coast and he explained that there is usually a shelf of rock jutting out from land, which means that the water is more shallow nearest the land. Then he explained that submarines could only operate in a certain depth of water on account of their visibility to aircraft and their vulnerability to depth charges being dropped. I asked him if there would be American submarines following us and he said yes, and that they would be waiting for just one unguarded moment or lack of vigilance.

Hours later, the destroyer's Aldis lamp flashed out a message and all the ships started zigzagging, signalling the presence of submarines. The Zero pilots flew their planes off the carrier and began a search of the area with all ships on alert. Later, we sailed along with all ships increasing their speed in order to increase our distance from the submarine, or submarines, that had been forced to dive. We realised now the horrible tensions the men of the former convoy would have been put under, and prayed that the terrible fate they had suffered would not happen to us.

Tension seemed to have eased and the convoy began to relax with the Zero fighters now being lowered on the lift of the carrier down to the refuelling deck. As I leaned over the rail, I noticed Shorty carefully monitoring every detail of movement of ships and men. I asked him, 'If you were the captain of the sub, when would you strike?' He marked the position of the destroyer which had forged ahead, leaving us exposed, and then of the carrier, now in a vulnerable position with planes being refuelled, before answering. After another very careful searching look at the sea for torpedo tracks, he said, 'If I was the captain I would be screaming "Fire!" right now.'

I laughed and turned to lean over the rail. I watched the pretty pattern formed by the sea water being churned up by the propeller as our ship turned sharply with the rest of the ships in a zigzag manoeuvre to present a shorter target for probing torpedoes.

Then suddenly there it was, moving through the blue foam: a large black torpedo with little propellers turning, only feet away from the ship. I jerked back and without thinking I yelled out, 'Torpedo!' Immediately I was knocked sprawling by Japanese seamen rushing to mount the stern gun whilst others started rolling depth charges over the stern. As I looked shorewards I noticed a large black rock and then there was a dull booming sound and a high column of foam shot up into the air above the rock. I knew that if our ship had not veered off course I would have been blown as high as that column of foam.

The Storm Trooper now demonstrated to the seamen his power over the prisoners, ordering the few on the rear deck into the baggage hold. We scuttled in like timid sheep threatened by a savage blue heeler. As we listened to the intermittent boom of exploding depth charges, ironically we hoped that the Japs didn't get the submarine that tried to sink us. Back in our bunk area we spent a restless night listening to the steady throb of the ship's engines and expecting our ship to be hit at any minute by torpedoes. But we lived to see the morning again.

After the heavy barrage of depth charges the sub, or subs, had dropped behind and had probably been up on the surface recharging their batteries during the night and just keeping in distant contact with the convoy. Now with the light of morning, Zeros were leaving the carrier and making a wide sweep of the sea, searching for a submarine on the surface. I stood with a small group of men on the rear deck watching the carrier and with the other men I was getting heartily sick of our guard bragging about how clever the Jap pilots were. One chap said drily, 'I would give anything to see one of those slant-eyed bastards fall into the sea.' As if in answer to a prayer, one of the Zero pilots gunned his engine and sped down the flight deck but as he revved his engine and thrust his wing flaps down near the carrier's bows, everything went wrong. We watched with delight as the engine sputtered, the plane lost height and went skimming over the waves to end floating on top of the sea with the pilot crawling out onto a wing. We laughed and cheered gleefully, only to be stood to attention and slapped by the guard for making fun of an honourable Japanese Navy pilot.

Later we watched the water change colour as we entered the Yellow Sea. This phenomenon, I learned from one chap, occurred because the waters of the mighty Huang Ho River – the Yellow River – washed an alkaline clay off the river bank into its stream and carried it out to the river mouth where it mixed with other chemicals in the sea, turning the water a real yellow colour.

Later Shorty informed me we were now approaching the position where the last convoy was sunk. Seeing the worried look on my face, he hastened to reassure me that we were heading into a typhoon and that no American submarine or Fortress bomber can operate during such a storm. He pointed to a threatening mass of storm clouds rapidly appearing in the sky. Jack joined us and together we watched the black clouds cover the sky. We felt the strong wind increase and the *Awa Maru* start to heave as the sea now became rougher and took on a grey-green colour. Shorty had weathered gales before but Jack and I had only read about them in romantic tales of the sea and ships and we agreed that we weren't going to miss this experience, even it if was our last adventure together.

When I tell people how we stood close together clutching wire hawsers in the shelter of the afterdeck housing as waves burst over the ship's side up to our waists, they think I must be mad, but I will treasure the memory always. I will never forget the sound of the wind shrieking through the ship's rigging, the pitching and rolling of the ship and the sight of the other ships emerging from waves covered with foam like a dog emerging from a dip in a river, with water cascading everywhere. I looked up at a green wall of water on our starboard side and shouted,

'How far to the crest of the wave, Shorty?' and he answered 'Sixty foot from the ship's rail.' The aircraft carrier was rolling like a drunken man and one can only guess at the confusion below decks with men trying to hang on to drums rolling about and lash down moving aircraft.

Gradually the storm abated and we three decided to retire inside the ship. Shorty summed it up: 'We are still alive and now we have passed the danger zone.' With morning, the outside scene had altered with the sea now only showing a very even choppiness, and planes were able to leave and land on the carrier at will. Shorty suggested the submarines had withdrawn because we were entering Japanese waters but the patrols would have to be kept up in case one sub captain was more daring than they anticipated.[82]

Japan

It was early January now and the weather had become bitterly cold. We were glad of the English battle dress issued to us before leaving Singapore. We hove in sight of Moji, Japan, with buildings covered with snow and as the *Awa Maru* warped into the wharf, sleety rain was falling on us. The sleet turned to snow and the ship took on an ornamental look with snow hanging on the rigging.

Jack pointed to an English-style church on the hillside, saying, 'There must be Christians here.' After a meal of large-grain hog millet, we were herded down onto the wharf where these Japanese Christians demonstrated how they would love to tear us to pieces.[83] Apparently, Baron Mitsui had ordered that we were to be preserved and taken to his coal mine with our bodies intact, otherwise the Jap guards would not have shielded us. As it was, we were generously spat on and fingernails grazed our faces.

On the wharf an interpreter who boasted of an education at Riverside University in America introduced himself and gave us each a rice flour bun plus some rice. We were then herded onto a train on a narrow-gauge railway with narrow carriages and transported to a mining town called Omuta, on the western side of the southern Japanese island of Kyushu. From there we travelled by truck to a very large camp and our interpreter informed us we were now in a previously American-owned mining camp. Then we were allotted hut rooms and bed areas.[84]

Our morning view of camp showed that it was large indeed and that it contained Australian, American, English and Dutch prisoners of war. We were taken on a short march over to Omuta mine, where we looked around us in astonishment. There were two large entrance tunnels and out of one came a giant conveyor belt loaded with coal running on inverted rollers. The belt took the coal up onto a landing stage where it was emptied into bins with funnel-shaped bottoms. From these coal dropped down into trucks that were shunted along by a locomotive on metre-gauge rails.

The other tunnel was a small train tunnel for transporting miners and coal. If there were any miners in amongst us they must have gasped in amazement, for it would be fifteen or even twenty years before we reached this stage of technology in Australia. The machine sheds had a drop forge and I watched a huge hexagonal nut being made; it measured about two feet across and I kept wondering what size spanner would be used to tighten up this giant engineering nut.

Somehow Jack and I became partially separated again. He was picked in a group that would be on night shift whilst I was in the day-shift crew. We were taken down the air-raid shelters to give us an idea of how we would be spending a lot of time in a confined space.

When I told my workmates after the war how my first trip down a coal mine was a complete foul-up, they laughed, saying, 'We'll believe you, it would have to be!' Unbeknownst to me, my miner's lamp had a faulty connection and when men in front turned a corner my lamp suddenly blacked out. I immediately became lost; in my further rushing around I became more disorientated and eventually I stopped still and listened. Just then I saw a light and yelled out, 'Help!' The Jap mine superintendent came rushing up and started screaming at me and slapping my face, then he led me to my work group. It was for me a terrifying, traumatic experience – and a humiliating one, for it seems the whole mine had been on the alert looking for Number 1440. I faced a barrage of, 'What happened to you, Holman?' or 'Hey, 1440, aren't you the bloke who got lost?' and it took days to live it down. But it seems I wasn't the only one with a lot to learn, as I soon found out.[85]

At the mine assembly point we would hear a Jap call out something and then we were supposed to bow to a little Japanese model house sitting on top of a pole. This house occupant was the Japanese god who is supposed to look after Japanese miners and keep them safe all through their work shift. We mostly treated it as a joke and it was hard not to burst out laughing at some of the humorous comments made by men around me.

One morning a chap near me said he was a Christian and would refuse to bow to a graven image. We quickly realised that this was no joke. One chap explained that it was only a ridiculous little wooden house and suggested that he could still pray to his Christian God. But he seemed blind to all persuasion, until our sergeant came up behind him and said in a low, threatening voice, 'You'll bow, mate, or I'll give you a swift kick in the bum. You are not going to play martyr and jeopardise other men's lives.' When the Jap yelled out, he decided to bow with the rest of us.

We were usually assigned eight men to one Jap miner. If you were lucky you drew a miner who wasn't real bad, but as time went on we learned there were some sadistic monsters among these miners and if you drew a bad one you were in trouble. God must have set angels to watch over Jack and myself, for we seemed to miss the worst of them.

If we thought the Jap guards in Burma were bad we were to find these guards were even more cruel and sadistic. One day it had snowed heavily, with about six inches of snow everywhere. In the Japanese lockup, or torture house, I could hear men being savagely beaten and then two men were pushed into view out in the snow and forced to kneel down. These were American army men, the smaller man being a Canadian, and they appeared to have taken a savage beating, looking battered and bloody as though beaten with pieces of timber.

The next day they were pushed out in full view and again forced to kneel, but this time pieces of sharp-edged timber were forced behind their knees and the guards played jockeys, leaping up and down on their backs, causing the men to scream with pain.

After that, I didn't see them for a while and I thought they must have died. Then I heard that the American doctor had had to amputate the young Canadian's legs. Fortunately his mate was a huge man who worked in the cook-house and he carried him about on his shoulders when he wanted to go anywhere. The cook was seven foot tall and the pair received nicknames from one of Charles Dickens's books: 'Bob Cratchit and Tiny Tim'.[86]

In the mine were endless large chains suspended from big sprockets on the shafts of electric motors and they perpetually dragged a steel trough carrying coal out to the entrance of the shaft and onto the conveyor belt. On one shift, I went to step over a chain and the Japanese miner gave me a great kick in the behind, knocking me sprawling. Losing my temper, I leapt over the chain and, grabbing hold of him, I held him against the wall and shouted, 'I ought to tear you apart, you rotten bastard!' Then I released him and my spine went cold as I realised what could happen to me now. I went through the rest of the shift in a state of severe anxiety, waiting for my number to be called and to be escorted by guards out of the shaft and taken topside to be severely beaten or shot. But I was lucky; the miner decided to do nothing about it.

Next shift I was in Old Ugly's gang and I felt very relieved. Ugly wasn't a bad Jap to work under as long as you didn't stir him up, but today he had been given a raw deal by his boss and given a dangerous shaft to work in and he was nervous.

As soon as I entered the shaft my spine tingled and I sensed something was wrong. Worse was to come as we stopped at the working face. One glance around me and up at the ceiling told me everything I needed to know. The mine ceiling was cracked and fragmenting and the mine timbers were bowing under pressure. Seeing my searching inspection, Ugly screamed at me to start shovelling, but pointing upwards I shouted, 'Ceiling, Dummy.' He screamed back that the ceiling was okay and this dialogue was repeated several times until he smacked my face in anger. I persisted: 'We put in strong timber now or all men dead.'

Shouting, '*Bukiro!*' he chased me along the shaft, pelting coal at me, but knowing I was right he nevertheless ordered us to bring timber in and to prop up the ceiling. We re-timbered, shovelled off what coal was there and then drilled and placed our explosive charges. After that we retreated along the shaft and the charges went off, blowing more coal off the seam face.

On the way back I saw a group of men looking at me with awe-stricken faces. Then I felt something graze my back and land with a crash behind my heels. Looking at the floor, I saw a large, square rock. Then one man said, 'Blimey, did you blokes see that? A bloody great rock peels off and hangs by a hinge waiting until Holly walks safely past and then – Wham! – down it comes!'

We were horrified at how much ceiling rock had come down but we ate our meagre rations and then shovelled the coal onto the endless chain. Glaring at me, Old Ugly ordered more props to be brought in and the ceiling was strengthened again. We blew more coal down off the face and shovelled it away, and now the props were bending and making creaking noises. Our sweat was now not only born of exertion but of fear, for we knew our very lives could be ended at any moment. Suddenly it dawned on us that Ugly had fled; knowing it was near finishing time, he had been too scared to take us out near the entrance in case the Mine Super caught him, but he was making sure he didn't get trapped. Then we heard him shouting, '*Yame!*' and we all scuttled out of that shaft like rats. We had escaped but not long after there was a low roaring sound as the whole ceiling collapsed.

The mess hall in our camp must also have been a concert hall, because it contained a large stage. As we ate our evening meal we were treated to the spectacle of two battered, bloody figures being pushed out onto the stage by Japanese guards. We were told that these two Englishmen had stolen three onions from the Jap stores.[87]

By the time we were entering the camp next day at the end of our shift, the guards had decided to test us. As we stood in line waiting to be dismissed, we heard the Englishmen being beaten to death inside the torture house. Our sergeant walked up and down shouting, 'Don't move, boys, they are trying to provoke you.' When the moans subsided the Jap guard dismissed us and as we walked away we looked at the palms of our hands; they were bloody where our fingernails had cut through the skin.[88]

Although I was now in a temperate climate, I went down with an attack of malaria. The Jap doctor refused to believe it but when the Australian doctor pricked my ear lobe and produced blood on a slide, he was forced to accept my condition and I was allowed off work for a few days on quinine.[89] Meanwhile, in the carpenter's shop an American carpenter was talking to a buddy and feeling very depressed. He pointed to four coffins he had made and said, as a morbid joke, 'I reckon I might end up in one of those.' This was Carson, who was said to be a direct descendant of the famous American frontiersman, Kit Carson.

After sweating profusely during the night, I woke up and decided that I would put the blankets and eiderdown supplied courtesy of Baron Mitsui out in the sun. Keeping an eye on them,[90] I stood in the hut doorway while watching a hut being demolished nearby. This hut had a large timber lintel over a wide, high doorway and young Carson stood underneath it giving orders. I felt weak and dizzy with the effect of quinine or I may have been able to warn Carson. The building swayed and suddenly there was a loud crash and the whole structure collapsed. I could see Carson pinned down by the lintel timber and the unnatural position of his body told me his spine must be broken. Men rushed to lift the timber off Carson and they carried the dying man, dripping blood, and placed him on my eiderdown. He kept moaning, 'Put my legs down. Put my legs down.'

Carson died and his body was placed in one of the four coffins he had made and joked about. I took my eiderdown to one of the long concrete pools full of water beside each hut to be used for fire-fighting. There I tried to soak Carson's blood out, but not having soap it was hopeless.

I think one of the most terrible and pitiful sights of a prison camp is a person whose will has been broken and I have no doubt that some of our poor nurses who were taken prisoner were persecuted and harassed to the point where their mind and spirit just gave up. Just as women were subjected to sexual harassment so it also happened to men; the man shot in Burma for resisting a guard's sexual advances was our first example.

Our hut mate, Tom, was a quiet, intelligent, sensitive man who had air force friends in other huts and, what with me being a loner, I never really got to know him very well. When I heard that a spirit-breaking Jap miner had asked for Tom to be permanently in his gang I knew the die was cast and that there was nothing any of us prisoners could do. Our officers had been taken away from us in Singapore and could no longer shield us.[91] This was a contest of wills and the Jap had the power to destroy Tom as surely as if he just framed some charge and had Tom executed.

Soon the whole hut was in torment as men learned of his daily harassment by the spirit-breaker but Tom never ever complained, bearing his suffering with a quiet, resigned dignity. His mates would ask one another, 'Why doesn't he drop a rock on his foot or put his foot under one of the skip wheels?' We all knew of one of the Americans who got his mate to 'accidentally' crack his arm with a pick, breaking the bone, and there were other suspicious accidents, but Tom would not resort to this type of escape procedure.

After some time, we noticed Tom was becoming trance-like in his actions, as though he had no conscious thought or awareness of the world around him. When he just sat in the mess hut looking at his food and not eating, just staring off into space with dull unseeing eyes, we knew what he was doing. Tom was giving up and losing the will to live. He got thinner and we would wake up to find he had not covered himself with blankets, and soon he developed a terrible congestive cough. One day men in our room came in off work to find Tom gone. We were told he had been taken to our camp hospital and had died of pneumonia soon after admission.

That night I served my period of vigil over Tom's body. Standing in front of his coffin, I wrestled with my conscience, thinking surely there must have been something we could have done to prevent this tragedy. It was a terrible thing to happen to such a kind, sensitive, decent man and tears of frustration rolled down my cheeks.

A Jap guard approached and asked, '*Tomodachi?*' meaning 'friend', and I answered, 'Yes, my *tomodachi*'. The guard replied, '*A so*' and walked away. I hadn't been a very good friend to poor Tom, and I would always feel guilty when remembering him.

There was a young American in the camp who greatly interested me because although his mates avoided him and referred to him as 'our loony case' I couldn't accept their verdict. One day I talked to him and managed to gain his confidence and he had an interesting story to tell. It seems that in America he had been in a group of amateur actors and had been a dismal failure. He never looked like getting any standing ovations and critics said he didn't show any realism or conviction and failed to impress his audience. Years later, here he was in a coal mine working like a slave and the only way out was to be carried out if you wished to be out for any length of time. He couldn't face putting his foot under the wheel of a coal truck or any of the other methods of self-inflicted injury, and he was depressed.

Suddenly it struck him like a thunderbolt. He knew his plan was worth attempting, even if he ultimately failed. He was going to go suddenly insane in this mine. Slipping a piece of soap in his mouth he worked up a mouthful of froth, threw his shovel down and with a vacuous expression on his face he strode past his mates, out into the main shaft. Sitting with his back to the wall he placed a large stick within reach. The mine superintendent came along and stared at him and he stared straight ahead, allowing foam to trickle out of the corners of his mouth and down his chin. The super bent down, shining his lamp on the chap's face, and enquired with the word for sick – 'Bioki?' He went on looking straight ahead with his vacuous expression. The super went down the working shaft and brought back his overseer miner who shouted at the American and kicked him. His only response was to let more foam dribble out of his slack mouth. The miner went to kick him again but he reached out and grasped hold of the stick, whereupon both Japs retreated.

The super now beckoned the mine overseer and making circular motions with his forefinger alongside his head, he indicated that the American was mad. Soon after he was escorted out of the mine by suspicious mates but he kept up the slack mouth routine and by the time he reached the American doctor, they too were sure he had gone mad. Here was the acid test: he drew on past knowledge gained about mental cases and their behaviour and his memory served him well. He passed the American doctor and the Australian doctor. To his inward amazement he had put on an Academy Award performance, and a sympathetic Jap doctor ordered he should be taken back to the camp garden and be shown how to pull out weeds. He laughed when he told me, 'Nobody noticed how eager I was to learn.' That is how this man managed to get his sweet job. He allowed his mental state to improve slowly but not enough for him to be put back down the mine. I promised him I would keep his secret and I did.

As a boy I remember my mother would often tell me not to remove a splinter with a safety pin as you could poison yourself. She said safety pins were made of brass or were dipped in brass. I was feeling very depressed down the mine when my eyes fell on a safety pin in my shirt. With an idea forming in my mind, I started pricking a hole in one hand until I made it bleed. Now I got some filthy slime off a pipe running into the mine and rubbed it into the self-inflicted wound. As I had hoped, several hours later the wound looked red and inflamed. I repeated this the next day and the wound looked worse. By the end of the third shift, my hand was puffed up like a boxing glove.

I showed my hand to the Australian doctor who gasped and didn't seem to know what to do. He sent me to the American doctor who also gasped and sent me to the nearby Australian orderly. 'Hold this kidney bowl under it,' he grunted, 'while I slice into it with a scalpel.' The bowl caught a lot of pus as the scalpel cut into my swollen hand and I had to wait for more to drain out. The orderly grinned and said, 'It will take at least a week before you will work again,' and I grinned back happily. And the orderly reported this diagnosis to the doctor – I had gained some time out of the mine.[92]

One day the air-raid siren went and we rushed out of the hut to look up. I noticed that this plane was very unusual, having two thin fuselages. Our army intelligence man told us, 'It's a Lightning: twin fuselage,' and after posting lookouts at each end of the hut he ran to his room. I followed and watched him unfold a map. Using a pair of compasses he placed one point on Nagasaki and then made a circular sweep. Suddenly he said excitedly, 'Okinawa! The invasion fleet must be assembling at Okinawa. That plane's fuel range would allow him to reach Nagasaki from there.' When I asked for details he said the plane we saw was a reconnaissance plane, which meant one could measure its range and estimate its base; in this case it was likely to be Okinawa. He added that the Americans were probably massing landing forces there. I asked him where they would land and he said, 'My guess is that they will land here, seeing we have shallow bays here at Kyushu.'

My immediate thought was, how is it I seem to end up getting involved in all the action? Now I am going to be in the middle of an invasion.

We had another air-raid warning that night and running into our shelter, we heard the first of several waves of bombers bombing Omuta. The people of the world had by now no doubt heard of the Japanese massacres of civilians and all of the many atrocities committed against helpless wounded soldiers, women, children and even hospitals and nurses. Now the Americans were striking back and as my mother would say, 'Two wrongs don't make a right.'

The tops of the air-raid shelters were covered with mounds of loose earth punctuated here and there with ventilator shafts with a sort of Chinaman's hat cover over them.[93] Growing near one of these ventilator shafts was a small green pumpkin. Even to this day I shudder when I think of it: I must have been terribly hungry or temporarily insane at the time, for I started planning to steal it. It was on the top of the English shelter and near the entrance and I had noticed that nobody liked being near the entrance. I realised I mustn't speak or my Australian accent would be noticed. When the next siren sounded I hung around till all the Englishmen were well down the shelter, then holding my arms upward, I leapt up inside the ventilator and wormed my way till I could reach out of the opening. Straining my muscles I extended my arm in the desired direction and at last I felt my fingers touching the top of the pumpkin. Straining all my upper body muscles I managed to grasp the stalk and after snapping it off the vine I pulled the pumpkin in on top of my head. As the bombing of Omuta continued I slipped downwards and dropped onto the floor of the shelter. Now I pulled my knife out of my pocket and cutting the pumpkin up into little squares I proceeded to eat every bit, seeds, skin and all, leaving only the stalk to be buried.

When the all-clear sounded I walked out towards my hut and suddenly I found myself confronted by a seedy little Englishman. He pointed an accusing finger at me, saying in a whining nasal voice, 'Ah saw yuh pinch poompkin and mark mar words, if there's any trouble aboot it, ah'm goin' to dob you raht in to the Japanese.'

I looked at him with feigned amazement. 'Gor blimey, you wouldn't betray another British soldier?' I asked. I turned away and walked to my hut, but inwardly the cold fingers of fear clutched my heart. The next few hours were mental torment as every time a guard poked his head in the door to check our hut I waited for my number to be called.

As time passed I realised the Japs must now have many other things to worry about and I had survived another crisis period. My assumption turned out to be accurate, for carrier-based planes were bombing all coastal towns.

After the war, back in Australia, I was in Kiama Hospital recuperating from an appendix operation and telling a World War I digger the story about the pumpkin. I had just got to the part where I swallowed the pumpkin skin and all, in square lumps, when a pretty Latvian nurse entered the ward. Pausing to shake an admonitory finger at me she said, 'It no yolly vunder you get bad pendix, Mr Holman. It yolly serve you right for eating raw pumpkin in square lumps.' This was too much for the old digger, who burst out laughing.

After returning from one shift down the mine I found Jack in a very depressed state in the mess hall. When I asked him what was wrong, he told me. It seems Jack's friend, Don Tweedie of the 2/20th Battalion, had been too sick to eat his rice and he had given it to Jack. Then Don reported sick to the guard in charge of those working topside outside the tunnel entrance. The guard asked to see his rice and Don said he'd given it to Jack, whereupon Jack was questioned and admitted eating the rice. Several guards set about hitting Don with rifle butts, knocking him unconscious. He had to be returned to the camp hospital by stretcher whilst they then took Jack over to a paling fence and proceeded to belt him with the palings they tore off the fence. Much later he would joke about this, saying, 'There I was backed up to a post surrounded by broken palings. I thought to myself, I hope these heathens haven't heard of Joan of Arc because if they have I might end up like her any time now.' It seems he felt that were Don to die, he would be responsible.

To relieve Jack's mind I visited Don and found him propped up in bed and bandaged up like an Egyptian mummy in a museum. I could only see one eye and sparks seemed to fly out of it as he snarled, 'Tell Jack these bastards won't stop me from getting back home to Australia.' And Donald Tweedie did get back, as he predicted.

I was lining up to be counted a few days later at the top of the mine when I heard Riverside Joe, the Jap interpreter, calling out, '1440, where are you?'

When I answered he confronted me and said, 'You are three minutes late getting out of the mine. You will be punished.'

I was led to an area in front of the mine guard-house and standing in six inches of snow I saw a little guard coming towards me carrying a stick as big as a pick handle. He proceeded to rain blows on me with the stick. Throughout this ordeal my brain was saying, 'Don't go down or the other guards will kick you,' and I kept on my feet. Then something penetrated my fear-stricken brain and I realised that this little guard was like a boxer pulling his punches and he wasn't hitting any vital areas of my body either. It looked convincing from where the other guards stood watching, and probably sounded convincing the way the little guard grunted and puffed, but I knew he was trying to avoid hurting me as much as he could. Eventually he stopped and I was led back to the main mob and dismissed.

In the morning I could hardly move but somehow I did get moving and forced my bruised, aching body to walk to the mine and do my shift. But I vowed I would kill that interpreter one day.

One day as I shovelled coal on to the endless chain I tried to ease the muscles in my back by making a sort of backward motion, which gave me some relief. Then the Japanese miner saw me and rushing up to me he started demonstrating the orthodox method, frequently using the word *bukiro*, 'stupid man'. When he moved off I started doing it again and very soon after he rushed up to me shouting out, '*Takusan bukiro*', or 'very stupid man'.

Later he appeared with the mine foreman and, making circular motions with a finger alongside his head and then pointing at me, he indicated that I had gone completely bonkers. The foreman pointed to my shovel and beckoned me to follow him out of the shaft. He took me into the main conveyor-belt shaft and I noticed there were small heaps of coal at different points along the way where overhanging lumps of coal had hit roller supports and tumbled onto the floor. He pushed me towards a heavily bearded man who could have been anything from seventy-five to one hundred years of age.

The old man glared at me fiercely while the foreman was there but as soon as he had gone the old man's attitude changed and he smiled at me and indicated I was to shovel the loose coal back on to the conveyor belt. I had miraculously gained the best miner and the best job in the mine. This was the man the Australians had christened 'Santa Claus' because of his flowing white beard, just as the hated interpreter had become known as Riverside Joe because he wore a cap and was a Riverside University educated man. Old Santa didn't seem to fit in here for he was quite obviously an Ainu from the northern island of Hokkaido. I didn't know it then, but looking back I think getting put to work with old Santa may have saved my life. I finished my term in the mine under his supervision. In all my many friendly conversations with him during our meal breaks, I never did learn how many children he had, for he generally dozed off to sleep while reciting all their names.

One day I stood looking through the window of our hut with another chap as our only camp transport vehicle, a decrepit old horse and flat-top wagon, brought in a load of meat. Staring at the heaped-up carcasses, I said, 'Gee, that's good, a great load of carcasses. Oh well, goat meat is as good and clean as deer meat.'

But my companion kept on staring hard at the meat. Finally he asked, 'Since when did goats have toes and toenails?' The significance of this statement finally penetrated my consciousness. Dog meat was going to be our food, or part of our food from now on and my stomach felt squawmish just thinking about it. I reasoned it had come to this with Japan now under blockade. We had already eaten questionable shellfish, octopus, squid, whale meat, horse meat, shark and seaweed, and were thankful to get it, but now dog was on the menu.

Apparently the cooks were anticipating the revulsion we would feel at eating dog. They had decided to make soup out of the carcasses so that we could put a peg on our nose and hopefully gulp it down. I tried to swallow a mouthful of dog soup but the moment I inhaled the smell of it, my stomach heaved and the soup went up and down like a yoyo. Finally, with massive willpower, I forced it down.

One sympathetic onlooker suggested I should try imagining I was in the centre of a beautiful field of tulips. My eyes fell on the little mound of rice and seaweed that I knew I could manage to swallow. 'I'll starve to death before I'll eat dog,' I answered. Later, again looking through the window of the hut I watched a furtive figure wearing a long peaked baseball cap lift the lid off one of the garbage cans outside the cook-house. Placing the lid quietly on the ground he dived one hand inside and removed a dog's skull. He then pulled a spanner out of his pocket and started cracking the skull with the spanner. As I watched with horrified fascination, he poked his finger under the dog's brain and lifting it out, he popped it in his mouth. I turned away, feeling absolutely nauseated at the spectacle. [94]

The Japanese had placed an anti-aircraft crew at all four corners of the camp, apparently to convey the impression that we were a military camp. Now when the Americans came over they would be fired on, and would presumably come back later and erase the whole camp. Some Japanese military head had worked out a neat scheme to have us wiped out.

We were getting raids frequently now and our last one had lasted for hours. When the terrible noise ceased, I turned in the dark to Jack and said, 'Gee, wasn't that one terrific air raid?' Jack's voice answered, 'What air raid?' He had slept through the racket and din of four waves of bombers, bombing for two hours.[95]

In these last months I had been switched to night shift and I was in amongst a party of men returning to camp when I became aware of the sound of aircraft overhead. Looking up into a clear starlit sky, I saw a blue flare signal fired by the leader of a bomber squadron. Then came the familiar shrieking sound of wind through tailfins.

What happened over the next few minutes I would remember for the rest of my life. The whole area of Omuta burst into flames. The Jap guards screamed at us to run for the camp. Overriding every other sound came the screams of people being trapped and burned alive. I remember an incendiary landed at one end of a street and I could hear people running towards us for safety. Then another incendiary cut off their retreat and the screams of those women and children were shocked into my brain for life.

Now bombs were landing all around us as we ran for our lives and now to our dismay we could see half our camp ablaze. We ran through the camp gates and nearly choked trying to breathe in the dense clouds of smoke. Suddenly I remembered my mother telling me that smoke never touches the ground and that there's always a clear area six or eight inches above ground. I lay down and as I did I saw feet and ankles running all around me but I found I could breathe. Then I remembered the rest of Mum's advice, which was run to the nearest hole, just like pigs do, during a fire. Knowing of a hole I ran for it but when I got there I found about thirty other men whose mothers must have given them the same advice.

By this time the smoke was lifting and the damage was becoming visible with several huts, including the hospital, burned down. Multi-coloured flames were visible over Omuta from electric sub-stations with their oil tanks and copper wire creating a series of firework displays.

The Japanese took truckloads of prisoners over to Omuta to bury the dead. We learned later that only two buildings survived the burning: the local hat shop and the town's brothel.

Dreadful things had been happening around this period, some of which we were aware of and others which would have shocked us had we known about them. We were aware of daylight shifts which had been confronted by groups of very angry citizens of Kyushu bearing signs in English saying 'Japan Will Not Surrender' as they brandished pitchforks and other farm implements. We knew something bad had happened on the sixth of August because whatever news that had been received down the mine threw the Japs into confusion. There was continual reference to the war in conversations among Japanese miners but they didn't mention Hiroshima. We always expected a backlash if anything went wrong because when the Japanese received any humiliation (or loss of face, as they expressed it) you could bet some helpless person or poor harmless animal would die. The worst thing we didn't know about was an order sent down the chain of command of every area still under Japanese command, including Hong Kong, Singapore, Malaya, Burma and Thailand, for all Allied prisoners of war (including doctors and nurses) to be executed on a certain date set by the Imperial Japanese Army. In the near future a huge fleet of B29 Superfortress bombers would pass over our camp and drop surrender leaflets over Tokyo in a leaflet raid. I heard Japanese chanting, 'We are like Churchill, we fight, we never surrender.'

After one bombing raid, a Jap officer strode across the parade ground and yelled out '*Kara!*' (Hey you) and about eight men including myself stood still. Motioning for us to follow, he strode off through the camp gates towards the bay. Soon we sighted several large incendiary bombs standing upright, their explosive cones buried in soft mud. The officer made signs indicating we were to lift them out of the mud and carry them to the edge of the slope and let them roll down into the bay. We stood looking at him, as much as to say, 'You've just got to be joking.' He undid the flap over his revolver, removed it, cocked it and pointed the revolver at our group. There was instant movement as we began grappling with the bombs. One man remarked loudly to us, 'You've just got to admit he's got a very persuasive manner about him, hasn't he?' And so we went to work, not understanding why the bombs hadn't gone off or what pressure it would take to set them off.

No baby was ever more gently carried than those bombs and what was unnerving was the distance the officer backed away from us as we handled them. Our wit remarked, 'Real Knight of Bushido, this bloke. Anyone can die bravely as long as it is not going to be him.' And another remarked, 'Well, if we go, at least it will be spectacular. A bloke won't have to wait till he's dead to burn.'

I was talking to Jack on the parade ground when someone said, 'Twelve B29s headed our way and flying very low. Too bloody low,' he added. We looked about in horror, knowing our camp's four ack ack gun crews would at this instant be training their guns on the flight leader.

Suddenly it happened: the guns roared and at least one shell scored a direct hit dead centre on the bomber. The plane exploded and we saw the sun flashing on a million pieces of aluminium floating earthwards. Several parachutes appeared but the men underneath them appeared to hang limp; we could see no movement at all.

Then I saw the sunlight flash on the wings of the Hellcat fighters as they peeled off to attack. 'Run for shelter!' I screamed out to Jack.

We ran past several huts and then, realising we wouldn't make it in time, we both yelled out, 'Get down!' and threw ourselves flat. Planes were aiming for the ack ack gun pits and soon we heard ack ack shells exploding, Japs screaming, bullets ricocheting off concrete and tearing through the huts' iron roofs and glass windows collapsing.

Someone yelled out, 'One down, three to go!' and 'Three down, one more left!' Another wave of Hellcats roared in low with bullets whining all around Jack and myself and we felt the shock of exploding shells around the nearby gunpit, and then suddenly it was over. We lay trembling as silence followed, broken only by the tinkle of small shards of glass falling onto the concrete path below. Then came the voice, 'That's the lot.'

The next day trucks appeared and a ring of sandbagged gun pits was made, spaced around the parade ground with machine guns set up on tripods inside each gun pit. I felt the horrible cold fingers of fear clutching at my stomach, especially as all work parties were kept in camp.

The town of Omuta was no more, and that included the town's air-raid siren, so it was a deep low drone that warned us that bombers were approaching. We moved towards shelters until someone shouted, 'If they're going to bomb us it's no use running. You may as well stand and watch them blow us all to hell.' And so Jack and I stood near a shelter looking up at a stupendous sight. Crossing our immediate visible area of sky were fifty huge B29 bombers. We stood with fingers pushed into our ears to prevent our eardrums bursting as the pressure of the planes' engine vibrations disturbed the air and shook the ground around us as they roared overhead.

By the ninth of August we were still alive and staring down the muzzles of encircling machine guns. The Jap guards had been taunting us by pointing at the guns and running a finger across their throats, indicating we were to be executed.

The morning wore on, then I heard a chap say, 'That's funny, I can hear one B29 bomber. Why would the Yanks send over just one bomber?'

I walked out of the hut to watch this bomber and was joined by others on the parade ground. There were Jap guards near the gates and some activity was taking place, but everybody else just watched the Fortress circling. Someone said, 'He's going to make a bomb run over Nagasaki. The Yanks wouldn't send a B29 to take photographs.'

Then we saw a bright flash and the ground shook underneath us and the long hazy blue peninsula of Nagasaki was enveloped in a red and purple rolling cloud. From out of the centre a column of coloured cloud arose. The cloud column rose high and then spread outwards, forming the shape of a massive mushroom. 'Geeze,' said one chap, 'what sort of a bomb was that?' We turned to our intelligence man, who was standing with two ex-RAAF men and asked, 'Well, you blokes, what sort of bomb was that?' They could only tell us that it must be some sort of giant fire bomb.[96]

Once again we saw Japanese in awed confusion as they had appeared on the sixth of August. There was a lot of traffic in and out of the gates and comings and goings of civilians and army personnel, and then a guard ran around shouting, 'All men! You no drink water! You no drink water!' Drinking water had been the last thing in my mind previously but now I became suddenly thirsty.

One glorious morning I walked out of the hut to look around and soon I beheld a wonderful sight. As I looked up towards the camp gates they were opened and trucks appeared, driving towards the gun pits. Soldiers loaded sandbags, dismantled the machine guns and loaded them onto the trucks and drove off through the gates. Whatever was happening we would not now be herded out onto the parade ground like cattle and slaughtered.

A little later I noticed that I couldn't see a guard anywhere. Deciding to look up towards the gates again, I saw that they were wide open. Outside stood a line of trucks with Jap guards running from the guard-house and boarding the trucks carrying their packs. Within seconds the gates were closed and two Americans took over the guarding of the gates. I rushed to tell Jack and together we walked back and looked at the gates guarded by Americans. Jack said that it must have been the giant fire bomb dropped on Nagasaki on the ninth of August that finally made the Japs decide to give up. We all talked things through and agreed the war must be all over, but having been prisoners for three and a half years, this conclusion was taking time to penetrate our minds. [97]

On the sixteenth of August the American officer who had taken control of the camp escorted the Japanese former camp commander down to the parade ground where, standing on an old wooden box, he addressed us. The war was over, he said, and later we would all be taken back to our homelands. He said he wished us well. We stood listening to this hypocrite prating away without laying a hand on him, and when he finished his speech he walked back up the parade ground, escorted by the American.[98] I suppose subconsciously we had known it was all over ever since the machine guns had been removed, but speaking for myself I was still in a daze.

I walked back to the hut and grabbing my mine belt and cap, I walked down to the toilet and threw them in the trench. With this gesture I was showing my hatred for the mine and its owners and also proving that I was finished with it and the horror and fear it represented. Then I walked back to my hut and sitting there I cried with emotion. It was all over now, and I had survived, and I thanked God.

Jack came over and we talked of home and he said we should not expect to see all the same old faces, for it had been a long time and anything could have happened whilst we were both away.

A chap came in and said, 'We have just made a big POW sign on the parade ground with white shells and we have put each country's flag up on a pole attached to the fence.' Jack and I walked out of the hut to inspect them and just as we arrived a squadron of carrier planes flew over. Seeing our sign and the flags flying, they wheeled about and each separate plane flew low over the flags and waggled their wings in salute, and we waved back. Now the Americans knew who was here.

Next day a transport plane flew over the camp and dropped a parachute dispatch. Men rushed to seize the parcel and open it. Inside was a message to say that the carrier planes had reported finding a prison camp and given our position. It said the pilot of the plane was an Australian with an American crew and they supplied names and addresses and cordially invited any of us to visit them. The message said that food and medical supplies would be dropped and for us to keep clear as canisters sometimes collapsed and stray tins of food could fall free. The water was running in the taps and was probably now coming from an uncontaminated source. We knew nothing yet of atomic fallout.

That night I dreamed I was home. In my dream there was a long table and I saw all my relations who had been alive when I left home, with the exception of one empty chair where one of my brothers-in-law would have been sitting. Later we would learn that he had died of a heart attack. I went and told Jack about this very strange dream.

On the second of September our camp was liberated. The gates were opened and a car full of officers of different nationalities pulled up outside. It soon sounded like the tower of Babel as each man yelled out questions. We learned that at Okinawa there lay at anchor the greatest mass of ships ever to be assembled in the world. A thousand B29 bombers had flown over Tokyo, dropping leaflets begging the Japanese to surrender after an atom bomb had been dropped on Hiroshima. The vibration of sound created by the bomber engines blew glass out of the tall buildings in Tokyo. When the Japs still didn't surrender, the atomic bomb was dropped on Nagasaki, less than forty miles across the shallow bay from our camp.

Someone was calling out 'Letters' and then our name, 'Holman'. Opening our mail, Jack and I learned that our brother-in-law had died but that everyone else was alive and reasonably well.

There was great excitement when the first food-drop occurred. Over came the transport plane dropping parachutes under which were canisters of beautiful food and a dispatch 'chute as well. Inside the parcel was a complete map of the area, showing our camp and the mine. A letter said, 'If you look at the map you will note that this area was to be completely obliterated in a bombing raid set for 15th August.' We all looked at one another and wondered who would have killed us, the Yanks with bombs or the Japs with machine guns.

We started sorting out the food, with perishables to be used first; these were rationed out to each hut. Next other types of food were sorted and distributed around the camp, and then we came to the problem of the khaki-coloured unmarked tins. Someone tossed an opener at me and said, 'See what's in them.' Everyone paused as I punctured a tin in a couple of places and held it up to my mouth. I filled my mouth then, rushing away a few paces, I spat it out on the ground. Pulling a face, I said, 'Urgh, don't touch that stuff, it's vile.'

Somebody asked, 'What is it?'

I gave a personal opinion. 'It tastes like some kind of sour soup to me.' When men began to comment on the growing pile of these tins and ask what was in them, the mob of sorters pointed to me and said, 'Holly tasted it and says it's some kind of sour soup.'

Jack came to my hut and I had a billy of tea made so we sat down and drank real tea with milk and sugar in it and ate biscuits. Jack said,

'I think a lot of blokes are going to get bilious because we haven't eaten food like this for three and a half years.'

The medical supplies presented the biggest problem: we had been out of touch with things for so long that some brands and names proved a bit of a puzzle. To make things worse, bottles had been broken or lost their lids and men had tried to match loose tablets with other tablets in bottles. Of course, amidst all this confusion a bottle of white headache tablets became mixed up with a bottle of identically shaped sleeping tablets, which set the stage for potential human disaster.

There had been a man in my hut who seemed to get a lot of pleasure out of parading around without any trousers on. Up till now no one had made any verbal or physical attack on him, but now we were free men and we ate and drank in our own room. We were squatting down on our beds and stuffing ourselves with food and washing it down with tea or coffee or hot chocolate because the only other liquid was in the khaki tins.

Suddenly our weird mate decided to go on one of his pantless parades around the small room. It was the last straw for the man next to me and his usual good-natured self-control snapped. 'Don't dangle yer dirty dingle-dangles in front of me, mate,' he snarled, 'or I'll flamin' well job yer, fair dinkum I will.' The exhibitionist turned away very upset, and putting his pants on he left and made his way up to the doctor's hut.

We learned later that he had asked for some headache tablets but he must accidentally have been given three sleeping tablets. We grew suspicious after he had slept several hours and when we tried to wake him it was useless. We brought the doctor and he said in a puzzled voice, 'This man is heavily sedated.' When he did wake up he started mumbling away like someone insane and he never ever did seem to get better. Whether you liked him or not, it was a very nasty thing to happen and I have been very, very wary of any type of sedative since then.

The food drops continued and some canisters came undone in midair. One Dutchman was too eager and rushed out of an air-raid shelter only to have a tin of peaches take a curved piece out of one of his feet. A little Japanese lady who lived near our camp and who had survived the incendiary raid and the Hellcat strafing with machine guns, stepped out of a doorway and was immediately demolished by a case of pork and beans. There was a terrible ironic humour involved but even those who laughed would probably in their hearts have felt sorry for anyone suffering such an undignified death after surviving so long.

As I have said before, lids came off bottles and on the ground were dozens of little different-coloured pills. I asked a chap what they were and he said, 'They're only vitamin pills, they won't hurt ya.' To emphasise the point he picked up several coloured pills and popped them in his mouth.

Seeing three little white tablets lying loose, I tried to emulate my mate's casual approach and popping them in my mouth, I swallowed them. Then my eyes focused on a small bottle with no lid and still half full of the same little white tablets. 'Gor blimey, what am I going to do now?' I gasped out.

My mate seized the bottle and read aloud, 'Water Purification Tablets – one tablet per gallon of water. I'd run to a tap and drink three gallons of water very fast,' he advised with a very concerned expression, adding, 'You'll have to dilute them in water now.'

I ran to the nearest tap at the doctor's hut and started swallowing as much water as I could force down, then sat down on a piece of rock to await developments. Strangely, I started to feel better than I had been, except for the discomfort of a highly distended abdomen and a disconcerting sloshing sound every time I moved.

When I eventually got back to my hut I found a state of gastronomical confusion. Some men were out in front of the hut with sallow complexions clutching on to the nearest object to support them whilst they brought up all their breakfast. Inside the hut men slumped over retching violently, while one man with both hands clutching the door jamb for support glared at me and demanded angrily, 'How come you aren't suffering a bilious attack?'

I thought quickly. Remembering the white tablets, I said, 'Maybe it was something that I drank,' and perhaps I was right.

That afternoon, a transport plane disgorged a man who came floating down to earth underneath his parachute to land right on top of our huge pile of khaki cans. As we helped him out of his harness, he introduced himself as a dietitian who had been sent by the United States Air Force to advise us so that we would eat the food wisely and avoid developing bilious attacks.

He paused to point at the huge pile of khaki-coloured cans. 'Don't you guys like beer?' he asked in obvious amazement.

'Beer!' echoed a dozen voices. 'You mean that is a great pile of tinned beer?' Then there came loud shouts of, 'Where is that Holman?' but they were a bit slow off the mark as I had suddenly grasped the situation and beaten a hasty retreat to my room in the hut.

American troops had invaded the area and feeling secure, a mate and I paid a visit to Omuta mine. We were looking for the interpreter and if I found him I intended to remind him about the beating I had received and to clobber him good and hard. But we couldn't find him. We were puzzled, for we just couldn't see any of the bad ones as the shifts came up out of the mine. We met other men with scores to settle but they too searched in vain – Riverside and his bad boys had vanished.

We came to the brothel and found the scene very disgusting. Japanese girls covered with filthy inflamed sores on their legs were being openly fondled by visiting American troops. As my mate commented, it seemed that, 'Yanks would sleep with anything.' Further up the road we found the hat shop and as we looked, several Australians emerged from the doorway. They wore black bowler hats and carried walking sticks under their arms as swagger canes whilst their usual clothes were in rags, which added to the ridiculous spectacle they presented. As they proceeded down past the brothel they sang, 'I'm Burlington Bertie, I rise at ten-thirty, I'm Burlington Bertie from Bow.' My mate and I stopped to laugh as they paraded past.

We now decided to visit the Chinese camp that had housed the men captured when the Hong Kong garrison was overwhelmed by the Japanese. When we came in sight of the camp we were rather taken aback at the sight of two neatly dressed Chinese soldiers standing each side of the gates holding British Lee Enfield rifles. I said to my mate, 'We may have to get permission to get inside this place.'

As if in answer, these two wonderful human beings both came to attention with a clicking of heels and gave us a full British 'present arms'. Recovering, we both stood and saluted. Inside the camp we saw a Chinese major and after we had saluted him he congratulated us on our survival and invited us to sit at a table. We were given mugs of steaming hot coffee and biscuits and we discussed local happenings, including the generosity of the Americans with the food-drops.

The subject of souvenirs cropped up and brought an enigmatic smile to the major's face. He said, 'My men seem to have acquired a few samurai swords to take back home.' I was thinking along the same lines as my mate – Japanese officers and sergeants do not hand over their swords easily and we were wondering how they were acquired. He reminded me of Colonel Anderson – both men made you think of tempered steel. He spoke the same faultless English and was every inch a British soldier.

After we had shaken hands and wished each other a good future, we left the camp. I think my companion summed things up very well later.

'Gor blimey, did you see that bloke's eyes?' he asked. 'Fair dinkum, he sent shivers up my spine. I think I would rather be his friend than an enemy.'

Weeks passed by and we picked up in health, but this was still Japan and we were still in a camp where terrible atrocities had been committed and we were constantly reminded of them as we looked around us. We were told that decontamination procedures had been taking place in Nagasaki, from where we would eventually have to leave when the time came.

At last the day that we hadn't even dared to dream of arrived. On the fifteenth of September we passed through those terrible gates for the last time. We were transported to Omuta railway station, where we boarded the train that would take us on the long horseshoe loop around the shallow bay and out onto the Nagasaki peninsula.

Entering the Nagasaki area the train barely crawled, either because of bad track or because the driver wished us to get a good view of the desolation. We saw white squares or oblongs of ash where once buildings had stood way out to the bordering hills. There was no sign of life anywhere as far as the eye could see. Not a tree, bush, bird or blade of green grass. There was an eerie silence and the air was full of a pungent odour as from a crematorium chimney, and indeed that is what this place was.

We passed what had obviously been an assembly factory of some kind. There were regular lines of human bones spaced a short distance apart. The bones looked dried and parched, like the bones of somebody found in a hot desert. The fierce heat from the bomb had stripped the flesh off the bodies and the skeletons had dropped into little piles with skulls topping each pile amidst the ash.

At Nagasaki station Jack and I stood looking at the ruins around us. It looked as though some giant had seized the massive steel girders of

200

the station and twisted them into knots. The area was now swarming with Americans dressed in white uniforms. Doctors, nurses, welfare workers, orderlies, Red Cross workers and naval officers. Prefab buildings had been erected with showers, decontamination areas and a field dressing centre.

Groups of Japanese survivors stood about, awaiting attention for atomic ash wounds. Surprisingly, some of them spoke good English and one man showed me where a piece of ash had landed on his thick head of hair, burning a hole through the hair and then through the skin, exposing the skull bone. Another had been looking at Japanese warships in the harbour when the bomb dropped. He said there was a flash and then not a ship remained. These people had some horrible injuries caused by the effects of this bomb and we were all visibly shocked at what we saw.

We were then given a glimpse of American efficiency as, like dolls on a conveyor belt, we dropped our clothes, walked forward under the showers and were then sprayed, dusted with a powder, checked with a Geiger counter and finally each fitted with an American rookie enlistment uniform with forage cap. After passing down the line, we ended up with some American welfare ladies handing out doughnuts and coffee. This was our first glimpse of white women for three and a half years and it seemed to us as though they had dusted their faces with some sort of white powder, they looked so white.

There was a big new aircraft carrier in the harbour and a lovely large white hospital ship. Jack was sick with malaria and was looking longingly at the beautiful hospital ship. He asked whether there would be a doctor on the carrier and if so whether he would have quinine, and was assured he would be all right on the carrier. A patrol boat took us out in groups to the carrier, the USS *Cape Gloucester*, and once aboard Jack received quinine.

On that ship we were treated to absolute kindness and courtesy from the crew, who went out of their way to do anything to make us comfortable. We all had stretchers to sleep on, on the aircraft deck just below the flight deck.

The great motors started and I asked Jack if he was going up with me onto the flight deck to see Japan fade into the distance, but he said he just wanted us to be taken away from the horrible place as quickly as possible. I stood with a group of men looking out over the desolation of Nagasaki and I understood how Jack felt, for there was a terrible depressing atmosphere about the place.

The motors throbbed and the coastline of Japan faded into smoky blue and as I descended onto the aircraft deck they seemed to be saying, 'Going home, going home.'

That night under a beautiful starlit sky we sat on the flight deck and watched a film. The projectionist was set up in the 40mm ack ack gun bay opposite the flat side of the carrier's superstructure and control tower. The flat surface provided an excellent outdoor film screen. Jack said that it was the best picture theatre that he had ever been to. If I remember correctly, the film was *It Happened One Night*, starring Claudette Colbert and Clark Gable, and we thoroughly enjoyed it.

Late in the afternoon the next day we arrived at Okinawa, where Jack and I saw a spectacle that would remain indelibly imprinted on our minds. Our carrier had slackened speed and was now barely moving as we sailed right into the centre of a narrow sea lane through the middle of the greatest armada of ships ever assembled in any one place in the history of the world. We had two huge American battleships either side of us and as has always happened with army and navy men, the friendly humorous banter went on between the crews of the ships with the ex-prisoners contributing their two shillings' worth. Jack and I marvelled at the massive armament on these ships. Just one shell from one of the guns would have had the capability of knocking flat a whole row of buildings.

That night was a spectacle not to be forgotten as every ship was lit up with their normal lights plus the red and green riding lights extending right out to the far horizon, and we had a grandstand view.

Now we had time to think about what we'd seen in Nagasaki. It had shocked us to think that any supposedly Christian country could even think of using a terrible weapon like the atom bomb, but now as we surveyed the alternative, we shuddered. We both realised that if you looked on the situation from the perspective of points on a map, America had totally destroyed two little dots on a very large map of Japan with a great mass of dots denoting cities. But when you stopped to think of a thousand B29 bombers dropping 1000-pound bombs on women and little children, the results would be horrible. Then there were these great monsters creating havoc with their heavy explosive shells and the carriers with their incendiary bombing aircraft. As we stood on the flight deck of the aircraft carrier looking over this great mass of ships spreading out as far across the sea as the human eye could gaze, we were shocked. It occurred to us that should the Japanese have continued their stubborn refusal to surrender they would have been massacred. To save a large nation the Japanese had surrendered and it seemed that to prevent loss of life they should have done so much earlier than they had. Jack was very depressed and kept saying, 'This means the end of the world when they have atom bombs.'

After the war I heard loud-mouthed politicians ranting away and they usually had all the facts wrong. People would question me and I would answer, 'Did you want them to use the invasion fleet? Did you really want to see Japan wiped out?'[99]

Next morning our shipload of ex-prisoners was transferred onto the Liberty ship SS *Hiram Bingham*. The Liberty ships were built in the famous Kaiser shipyards. They had been built quickly with the new welding process that did away with the time-consuming riveted plate method of ship construction. What they lacked in appearance or size was compensated for by the astonishing speed with which they were produced. These were no glamour ships like the sleek new *Cape Gloucester* which we had just travelled on, and their crew was merchant marine, not navy. The men weren't as soft and flabby either as the *Gloucester* crew, whose chefs turned out roast turkey dinners and food usually found only in high-class Australian hotels. But although the Liberty men were rougher, we still received the utmost courtesy and consideration and we enjoyed our trip down to Manila.

As this ship, the *Bingham*, nosed slowly and cautiously into Manila harbour we could see the half-sunken wrecks of bombed ships all around us. The captain of the *Bingham* must have been a clever man to negotiate a path into the anchorage.

Later we travelled along a road quite literally lined with food, mile upon mile, in the form of large wooden crates stamped with a description of the army rations inside. We looked in astonishment at this sight, evidence of the huge resources of the United States and the war efforts of their people.

We were taken into a large camp and told we would be well fed in an effort to put some flesh over our bones before we were to return to our home countries. This wasn't hard to take. Welfare workers provided us with snacks of doughnuts and coffee in between meals and we were all issued with slouch hats. I became angry later at the piggish behaviour of some of the Englishmen who showed deplorable manners, snatching and grabbing at food in front of the obviously disgusted American ladies. They probably saw the slouch hats and thought they were seeing Australians and I felt like snatching the hats off their heads. The Australians, on the other hand, were very well behaved and showed appreciation.

We saw an outdoor film taken by Russian cameramen of the war on the Russian front when the great Russian offensive began, and I have never ever seen war film sequences in my life that could match those in this film, with ground shots and aerial shots of dramatic content and quality. The opening sequence shows a massive army ready for battle, stretching for at least twenty miles on a field of thick snow. The huge artillery pieces are in a long line fading off into the distance and the artillery officers stare at the faces of their watches. As the minute hand reaches the appointed time, the officers' hands sweep down and hundreds of gun barrels leap forward, lumbering across the snow whilst overhead clouds of fighter planes fly across to strafe the German troops. This scene had us glued to our chairs as we saw war fought on a massive scale.

Later scenes showed the whole German army in an inglorious retreat with Germans falling under wheels of trucks and being run over and German tanks squashing their own troops in panicked retreat. It soon became obvious that brave cameramen must also have lost their lives to produce this film, but the footage showed the people in Russia the fruits of their work and sacrifice in the humiliating defeat of the enemy. There were peals of nervous laughter as men reacted to the noises of war, ducking behind seats and dropping to the ground.

We did put on weight and in the short period we were in Manila we enjoyed our stay with all credit going to the Americans, who were wonderful hosts. Then we were told that we would be taken once more to board a ship for the last leg of our journey home to Australia.

After arriving at the wharf, we boarded an English carrier named *The Speaker*. The first thing we noticed was the lack of the easygoing relationship seen on the American carrier with no saluting of officers as they made their inspections. Here it was different: men sprang to attention at sight of an officer and there were no flabby fat men around either. We realised why as mealtime came around and we received a bowl of stew and a piece of bread, our diet from now on. I became angry as some men cried out, 'Good old stew,' as though the Americans had fed us on dry bread and water instead of beautiful delicious food. But I hadn't realised they were getting into practice for when they fronted the pub bar and joined in guzzling beer with their anti-American mates in Australia. That Americans had kept Australia free and saved these men's sisters from Japanese brothels would soon all be forgotten as they languished in safety and freedom in Australia. Our freedom had cost a heavy toll in young American lives.

I'm sure most of us would have wanted the captain just to sail right in between Sydney Heads and let us get our feet down on Australian soil but no, English spit and polish had to be observed. The ship stopped off the coast and the captain ordered all hands to the painter's locker and seeing that the quicker *The Speaker* was painted the sooner we would see Sydney, hundreds of ex-prisoners of war volunteered to assist in sprucing up the ship.

That was a very quickly painted aircraft carrier. We had a brief bit of excitement as a school of large sharks had ideas of snapping off a few legs dangling from lowered planks but the Pommy cook put a stop to that. Whilst a mate enticed the sharks to break the surface after meat dangled on the end of a rope, he shot them through the head with a Lee Enfield .303-calibre rifle.

Eventually the ship was painted and with the ship's band playing 'Cock O' The Walk' we sailed through the Heads in bright sunshine, escorted by a great multitude of small craft of all descriptions. With ships' sirens blasting from everywhere around us it was a beautiful welcome home. We warped into the wharf, where we were told we would be transported by bus to Ingleburn army camp, where we would meet relatives and be taken home.

We stood on the flight deck looking down at the wharf and the street behind the wharf. And Jack was looking with a rapt expression at a group of little children playing with a ball as children were doing all over the world. Suddenly he noticed me alongside him. Pointing to the children he burst out with, 'The world is going to go on! Look, kids playing with a ball!'

'Yes, Jack,' I said. 'It's all over now and we made it back to Australia.' Then we walked down onto Australian soil and boarded the buses.

At Ingleburn we were surrounded by family, and stealing glances at other men who were undergoing the same emotional bewilderment as ourselves. I think my Aunty Maude summed it up; I heard her talking to another of our relations: 'Did you see their eyes?' she said, and added, 'They have seen some terrible sights.'

And she was right, for later all Jap prisoners could pick out one another even in a crowd. It would take a long time before that strained look would fade from our eyes. We had returned with a different set of values and we would never ever quite fit into civilian society in our lifetime.

Editor's Epilogue

'Yea, though I walk through the valley of the shadow of death...'
They built an embankment through the valley of death, they chipped
bloodied cuttings through its rocks. Over cholera streams they put up
bridges and cut clearings in malarial forests to bury their mates with
rough wooden crosses at their heads. They promised never to forget
them and when they finally made it home, they did not. They promised
to bear witness to the great crimes perpetrated, and they did that too.
Colonel John Williams, the officer who had crawled through the mud
to be with his men in the cholera huts, came out of the valley. He flew to
Tokyo after the war and on behalf of his fellow POWs was a determined
force in the establishment of the war crime tribunals.

The gold nugget of the railway doctors, Bertie Coates, resumed
his surgical practice in Melbourne after the war, was made a fellow
of the Royal College of Surgeons in London, and in 1955 became
Sir Albert Coates. When the guns fell silent, Rowley Richards
carried on doing what he knew best, ministering to people in need
of medical attention. He became a Knight of the Most Venerable

Order of St John of Jerusalem and was awarded a string of medical fellowships.

Bill Drower, the Pommie officer loved and respected by Aussie POWs, recovered from his near-death experience at Kanchanaburi camp. He joined the British diplomatic service and it was said of him when he passed away in Somerset in 2007 that he represented everything that was best in the character of an Englishman. Colonel Anderson, VC returned to his former life as a grazier in New South Wales and for many years served as a federal member of parliament in Canberra. Roy Whitecross applied his sharp intelligence to an economics degree at Sydney University and became assistant registrar of that place of learning. Pinkey Rhodes, the medical orderly who had picked clean countless stinking tropical ulcers to save men's lives, made it home to Sydney and lives here still. Jim Armstrong, in whose gentle arms so many were soothed through final hours of suffering on the Railway of Death, returned to his loving family and resumed a life of raising chooks.

Both Jack and Robert Holman found their way back down the coast of Illawarra to the bright sea-light of Werri Beach. Jack never married, and they reckon he didn't need to, as he had already raised his dead father's family. He carried on with his carpentry and looked after his mother during the years of her infirmity, right up until her end in the Blue Mountains. Jack always had his music, and when he moved back to Werri Beach he started a band, the Melody Makers, playing gigs in Kiama and up Kangaroo Valley. In the band Jack played any instrument needed: piano, banjo, drums, ukulele, trombone or violin, and occasionally Robert joined in on the vibraphone.

There was an irony in Robert's post-war occupation when he joined the fettling gang on the railway that runs up and down the Illawarra coast. But after all, he would tell people, working on a railway track was something he knew how to do. Robert settled down at Werri Beach, married and had four children. Sadly, the marriage ended in divorce when the family was still young.

Jack built his house on a hill above the ocean at Gerringong. He went blind in his later years, but shunned a place in a care home. The old soldier made his way around his house by following string tied strategically from room to room. From the house Jack could hear the surf where, well into his sixties, he rode the waves. They say it was common at Werri Beach to catch sight of old Jack on his bicycle, surfboard under his arm, heading for the ocean.

There is a salt-encrusted wooden shed just above the high-water mark at Werri Beach. In this, the local surf lifesaving club, Robert gave drawing classes. He was unschooled in art, but his maxim was, 'Give the people something to do'. It was a lesson learnt in the depression years of his youth and the dragging days of the POW camps.

Robert built his house at Werri Beach and the concrete sculptures he fashioned during his bouts of creative impulse still line the driveway. Neither Jack nor Robert had a car, but most days around lunchtime Jack would ride his bicycle down to Robert's place for a bite to eat and a yarn with his brother. There they would sip at cups of tea and philosophise on the way of it all.

An ex-POW from Queensland related how he had reunions with his mates from the Burma Railway, when they all met up in the wards of the Brisbane psychiatric hospital. Most families of ex-POWs know such stories, for hospitals of one sort or another played a big part in the ensuing years and post-traumatic stress manifested itself in many ways. In one of his notes, Robert Holman describes bouts of 'suppressed aggression' and how he went through a time of wandering around Sydney looking to get into fights. The numbing refuge of alcohol was turned to by many an ex-POW, though not by Robert Holman, as he never allowed it into his life.

There is nothing in Robert Holman's writing that shows he ever forgave the IJA for what had been done to him, and many other POWs felt the same, thus taking a heavy burden with them to the end of their days. For many the issue was a closed shop, one they could only truly share with fellow POWs, for the ex-POWs were connected by bonds of extraordinary experience. They had experienced emotions and seen such things, high and low, that it was nigh on impossible to share with anyone but one of their fellows. Even amongst themselves there was reluctance to return to memories of the dark days, and for many resolution was never achieved.

In this unrequited anguish of the surviving POWs, one sees the evil that denial does. For all the great benefits of General MacArthur's post-war reconstruction policies, a regrettable trait of denial on the matter of IJA war crimes grew out of the new story inculcated by post-war Japan. With MacArthur effectively burying the issue and the build-up to the Korean War taking priority, the IJA story became one of faults on both sides, and that somehow Japan had been forced into doing what it did in World War II. The cover-up process and denial mindset took hold, in stark contrast to the revelations and expiation of guilt experienced by the German nation. Emperor Hirohito had set that denial in motion with his broadcast speech of 15 August 1945, when he said that in Japan's unleashing of the Pacific War, it was 'far from our thought either to infringe upon the sovereignty of other nations or to embark upon territorial aggrandisement', even when the whole wide world knew the opposite to be the truth.

One of the casualties of denial is forgiveness, for it is a hard virtue to exercise when it is not sought. There is tragedy in this omission, for like mercy, the bestowal of forgiveness is a blessing on both the taker and the giver. Robert Holman, and so many other ex-POWs, were never asked for forgiveness and as a result never received that blessing of forgiving.

Some former prisoners of the IJA found it in their hearts to forgive, regardless of the confutations of their former abusers, putting into practice the POW code of 'forgive but do not forget'. A few lucky former prisoners were sought out by those who wanted absolution, and then it was possible to achieve the double blessing. In his book *The Railway Man*, Eric Lomax gives a lyrical description of reunion with his tormentor, Nagase Takashi, who with his fellow *Kempei Tai* agents tortured Lomax close to death in Thailand in 1943. Takashi-san made the approach to his former victim through an intermediary and when the two men met in Japan, nearly fifty years after the event, Lomax told Nagase he could never forget the torture, but that Nagase had his 'total forgiveness'.

Operatives within any institution of enforcement retain a sliver of free will to behave humanely. In that narrow opportunity some choose to exercise it and some do not, but all are ultimately accountable for their conduct. When hard moral choices are there to be made, as Eric Lomax's torturer testified, the consequences are with them forever. The extremities experienced on the Railway of Death remind us there are moral choices to be made at every level of life, and hopefully that when we make them, we try to do the right thing by others as well as ourselves. This is straightforward stuff, the sort of homilies our grandparents tell us when we are starting out in life – like treating others as we wish to be treated ourselves, understanding that the strong must protect the weak, learning to love our fellow creatures on this earth, and respecting the virtue of mercy.

As in the great majority of the POW camps of Japan's wartime empire, there was a darkness governing the camps on the Railway of Death. But even a cynical mind perceives that the prisoner's light shone through the darkness.

We are now far removed from the times and places where the IJA played out its atrocities, and its philosophies of human devaluation have long been consigned to vaults of shame. Nevertheless, in writing about the IJA's victims, it remains impossible to set down a dispassionate account, for, as the Galilean said, 'the words the mouth utters come from the overflowing of the heart'. So indeed let us not forget, and in our journey of remembrance let us walk lightly, for with every step along those paths of ash we are crossing holy ground. May their souls rest in peace.

Notes

1. The Holmans were Methodists and were not consumers of alcohol or tobacco, thus Robert's grandfather's nicotine levels were as notorious as their claimed life-saving properties. Robert remained a non-smoking abstainer from alcohol all his days.

2. The Holman boys spent a lot of time with their paternal grandparents, who lived nearby in Georges River Road, Croydon Park. Next door on Georges River Road were Robert's Aunt Caroline and Uncle Jim Murch. Their son Arthur was seventeen years older than Robert and was by then an up-and-coming artist, soon to win an artist's travelling scholarship, which would take him away to Europe. It was Robert's glazier father, Harry Holman, who inadvertently put his nephew Arthur's artistic destiny in motion. Up at the top end of town, naked models were visible through the windows of the Royal Art Society School in Pitt Street, so Harry was summoned to install frosted glass windows. Job done, he picked up the school prospectus and gave it to Arthur. As a result the young man enrolled at the RAS school and spent the next seven years there, learning to be a professional artist. After a life before the easel, Arthur Murch

died in 1989, by then an Archibald Prize winner and widely recognised as one of Australia's finest painters.

3. The Holman paternal grandparents loomed large in the lives of Jack and Robert. Grandfather Luke Holman, known to them as Nandad, had emigrated from England to Brisbane in 1883, with his wife Ellen and their two infant children, Harry and Caroline. He established himself as a builder in Brisbane, but in 1893 the building industry was hit hard and clients' bad debts forced Luke Holman to close up shop and move to Sydney. In Sydney his business was that of a carrier for building companies and hardware stores, for which purpose he owned a dray and some draught horses, all kept at the back of his Georges River Road house. Old Luke had built the house himself and though he had installed electrical outlets throughout, it was said he refused to have the house connected to the mains because he was scared of electricity's supernatural powers.

4. Luke Holman put his grit into the Holman boys' lives and they always loved to recount stories of Nandad's doings. As adults, when they set themselves up with parcels of land on the Illawarra coast, Robert and Jack considered it a matter of course that their homes be built with their own hands, just as their grandfather had done before them. Wielding hammers and drills, as they went about their work the brothers would repeat tales of Nandad's adventures in carpentry.

5. Robert's maternal grandfather, Nicholas Lean, was a Sydney brick-maker of Welsh origin. On a dark night in 1890, he fell fatally into a brick-pit while searching for a misplaced hammer.

6. The son of a Yorkshire blacksmith, Reverend Samuel Marsden sailed out to Australia in 1793 to take up the position of assistant to the chaplain of New South Wales. From his Parramatta home, Marsden became a much-respected missionary to the Maoris of New Zealand in the early decades of the nineteenth

century. On top of his Anglican clerical duties, Marsden was a prominent farmer, second only to Macarthur in the early development of Australian wool exports. He was appointed as magistrate and superintendent of government affairs at Parramatta, contemporaneously with his clerical duties. Marsden's term as magistrate was 'stamped with severity', earning him his place in Australian history as 'the flogging parson'.

7. Master mason David Lennox was a Scot who had worked for many years with Telford, Britain's greatest bridge-builder, before coming to Australia in 1832. The following year, he became the superintendent of bridges in Sydney. The ANU's *Australian Dictionary of Biography* says David Lennox was a kindly taskmaster, 'who sought mitigation of the sentences of convicts who gave good service and seldom had trouble with any of the hundreds of prisoners employed on his projects'. Apparently he was retiring by temperament but demonstrated 'quiet determination when his plans were opposed by others: for example when Bourke in 1835 advocated a more elaborate design for Lennox Bridge, Parramatta'.

8. For some time Australia had been receiving ever-worsening economic news from the wider world, and with the New York stock exchange collapse of 1929, the Great Depression came down. Australia's dependence on commodity exports to the United Kingdom meant it would be hard hit and by 1932 almost 32 per cent of Australians were out of work. In Canberra the ruling Labor party split and fell from office. As a result of the split, a left-wing splinter party popularly known as Lang Labor was formed under the leadership of Jack Lang, who had become premier of New South Wales in 1930. He was dismissed as premier in May 1932, but in March of the same year he officiated at the opening of Sydney's iconic Harbour Bridge – the famous disruption to the tape-cutting ceremony reflecting the strife of those difficult days.

9. With Britain's declaration of war on Germany on 3 September 1939, rallying to the defence of the British Empire, Australia too went to war. Those early war months are often called the Phoney War, a time of soft-pedalling when the war seemed very far from Australia. But there was nothing unreal at the time about the Nazi occupation of Poland, Denmark and Norway, or their move on Holland and Belgium. The whole map of Europe was changing and that would hold life-changing implications for Australians.

In Canberra, throughout 1940 the government stood firm behind Churchill's war priorities for the defence of Britain and the fight for control of the Middle East and North Africa. Thus it was that in January 1940, the Australian army's 6th Division set sail for the Middle East and the grimly heroic destiny awaiting them in Tobruk.

Japan was not yet at war with the Allies and the Dutch East Indies was still intact, but Japan's aggressive intentions had been amply displayed in recent years by its invasion of China. Concern was rising in Australia about the nation's ability to defend itself against a Japanese attack. Singapore was still seen as the bastion of the British Empire's Asia-Pacific defence, but cracks in British and Australian accord were emerging. In October 1940, a defence conference in Singapore, attended by representatives of the British, Indian, Australian and New Zealand military, identified alarming deficiencies in Singapore's capabilities. Thereafter, relations between Canberra and London became increasingly terse, with Australia increasingly calling for the transfer of military resources from the Mediterranean theatre to Singapore.

10. With the way the world was turning, men like Jack Holman saw their duty as clear as a bell. Jack was thirty years old, healthy and believed in the obligation to defend his homeland. War was the last thing he needed in his life, for he had the great personal responsibility of the welfare of his mother and family to consider; but Jack knew that as a soldier he could direct his army pay to his mother. And so by the middle of 1940, Jack was an enlisted man, serving in the

8th Division of the Australian Imperial Force (AIF). With completion of military training in Parramatta and Tamworth under his belt, on 2 February 1941 Jack boarded the *Queen Mary*. Now converted to its wartime role as a troopship, the *Queen Mary* set sail in convoy towards Singapore, for the 8th Division was bound for the defence of the Malayan peninsula. Jim Holman was to spend the remainder of the war in Australia, serving as RAAF ground crew with responsibilities for engine maintenance on Fairey bombers and Wirraways.

11. On 7 December 1941, the Japanese struck Pearl Harbor and simultaneously launched their invasion of the Malayan Peninsula. Reeling from these blows, Australians found themselves suddenly at war in the Pacific and the spectre of Australia's invasion by a fierce foreign foe loomed as a distinct possibility. Immediate calls were made for the AIF's 8th Division in Malaya to be reinforced and Robert Holman was swept up in the process, being posted to the 8th Division's 2/19th Battalion, with news of imminent departure for Malaya.

12. As the Australian coastline faded from view, *Aquitania* ploughed on with her cargo of seasick soldiers, for whom a world of terrible uncertainty was drawing near. On the same day Robert Holman was sailing out of the Sydney Heads, off the coast of Malaya Japanese torpedo bombers sank the vital British battleships *Prince of Wales* and *Repulse*. Churchill was advised of the sinkings of these prized capital ships by a phone-call, and said in his memoirs he was thankful to be alone at the time, for in all the war he never received a more direct shock. Following on from the destruction of the American Fleet at Pearl Harbor, the sinking of the two British battleships meant that for the first time in history, in all the great maritime ways of the Indian and Pacific oceans, it was Japan that ruled the waves.

13. The Australian official war history, Lionel Wigmore's *The Japanese Thrust*, describes the background of the men who went absent without leave in

Fremantle. They were largely of the 2/4th Australian Machine Gun Battalion (942 all ranks), a battalion formed in Western Australia in 1940. After training they were posted to Darwin in October 1941 and then boarded *Aquitania* in Port Moresby to be carried to Singapore via Sydney and Fremantle. Upon arriving in Fremantle on 15 January 1942, the men were back in their home port. 'No leave was granted but most of the unit became absent without leave, and 94 had not returned when the ships sailed for Singapore,' Wigmore notes.

14. Siam is the name by which the nation of Thailand was known until 1949.

15. Lieutenant General Arthur Percival has shouldered much of the blame for the Allies' loss of Malaya and Singapore to the Japanese in January and February 1942. With the passage of time, historians have come to place most of the blame upon successive British governments' short-changing of the Singapore naval base, concluding that whoever had commanded the Allies in Singapore in 1941–42 would have been fighting a losing battle. In Percival's defence, it should also be noted that he was required to take overriding orders from the commander-in-chief for the Far East theatre. At the time of the Japanese attack on Malaya on 8 December 1941, the commander-in-chief was Air Chief Marshal Brooke-Popham, who by 27 December 1941 had been replaced by Lieutenant General Sir Henry Pownall, who was himself superseded with the arrival in Singapore on 7 January 1942 of General Archibald Wavell as the newly-appointed supreme commander of the Far East theatre.

16. The Japanese attack on Malaya began on 8 December 1941, through Japanese amphibious landings in southern Thailand and at Kota Bahru on the north-east coast of Malaya. The British forces based in Singapore had a strategy (Operation Matador) for repelling a Japanese invasion along this very route, but at the last minute there was vacillation and the strategy was never implemented. Over the next seven weeks, what followed was essentially a rout. Soldiers of the

British, Indian and Australian armies fought fierce battles down the Malayan Peninsula, always resulting in retreat further south. The rampant Imperial Japanese Army (IJA) pursued a breathtaking campaign of aggressive frontal assaults, combined with improvised out-flanking manoeuvres, harrying the enemy through jungle, swamp and endless rubber plantations, driving them all the way to the causeway-crossing of the island 'fortress' of Singapore.

Initially it was the British and Indian troops in Malaya who mounted the defence against the Japanese. Fighting rearguard actions from the failed defence of Kota Bahru, to the lost battle of Jitra, there were brave but futile stands made at Perak River and Kempar, followed by surrender at Slim River and withdrawal from Kuala Lumpur. The battle for Malaya was lost from day to day and a great humiliating tide of British military and civilian vehicles filled the highway heading south to Singapore.

As the IJA advanced, increasingly vitriolic communications were penned between the prime ministers of Australia and Britain. For Prime Minister Curtin it was a case of I-told-you-so, as he called for all possible military reinforcements to be sent to Malaya. Churchill's responses conveyed the view that the game was up for Malaya from the terrible December day the *Prince of Wales* and the *Repulse* went to the bottom of the South China Sea. For Churchill thereafter, the 'fortress' of Singapore and its immediate hinterland were where the stand would have to be made.

17. Major General Gordon Bennett (his promotion to the rank of Lieutenant General occurred after his return to Australia) was at the time the commander of the 8th Division of the AIF in Malaya.

18. It is incorrect to say General Bennett advised the 8th Division reinforcements to return to Australia rather than proceed on to Singapore. In David Day's *The Politics of War*, it is shown how as late as December 1941, General Bennett was assuring the Australian government that Singapore could be defended

successfully 'provided he was sent sufficient reinforcements. The government responded to these encouraging signals by ... dispatching a further 1800 ill-fated and half-trained men to Singapore.'

Relations between Canberra and London had by now become caustic. As the loss of Malaya was resolving into reality and Singapore's demise seemed a logical sequel, Churchill was considering an evacuation of Singapore. The attack on Pearl Harbor had brought the Americans into the war and Churchill, now confident of eventual victory, was prepared to carry unfortunate losses in the interim. But for the Australian government, Singapore still represented a bastion of last defence. The belief remained that without this long-vaunted Singaporean 'fortress', the prospect of an invasion of Australia by imperial Japan loomed large. On 23 January, the Australian war cabinet sent a vitriolic cable of protest to Churchill, saying any evacuation of Singapore would be an 'inexcusable betrayal'. Australia's frayed nerves were understandable, for the Japanese were at the time overrunning Rabaul in New Guinea, thereby putting their bombers within striking range of Queensland.

The British war cabinet was sufficiently goaded by the Australian position that it diverted the British 18th Division, then crossing the Indian Ocean, to the defence of Singapore. The direct result of this diversion was that, with hardly a shot fired after their arrival in Singapore, the 18th Division would spend the rest of the war in captivity. Churchill had wanted them in Burma for ongoing battle with the Japanese.

Then on 24 January, in the climactic last week of the Malayan campaign, Australia's reinforcements arrived in Singapore. *The Japanese Thrust* describes this late arrival as a blunder, an Australian blunder. The fault lay in the fact that most of these reinforcements were untrained, raw recruits who were being sent forward to back up the 8th Division at a time when the fighting men of the division were preoccupied in battle. Robert Holman was one of those raw recruits.

19. When the conflict descended to southern Malaya, Singapore's immediate hinterland was at stake. It was then that the Australian forces, champing at the bit, were given the opportunity to fight. Allied command handed control for this phase of the battle to the AIF's Major General Gordon Bennett and the Australians went to war.

First came the dramatic success of the Gemas ambush of 14 January 1942, described by Robert Holman in his memoirs. During this time, Jack Holman became engulfed in front-line action in his capacity as an infantryman and stretcher-bearer, and it is from Jack's accounts, given over ensuing years, that his brother recounts those last fighting days in Malaya. For a more accurate description of the AIF's battles in Malaya, see Lionel Wigmore's *The Japanese Thrust*.

Next came the Battle of Muar, where the Aussies were involved in a torrid series of fire-fights, all the while buying valuable time for others to continue their withdrawal south to Singapore. At the estuary town of Muar on the south-west coast, an area considered vital to the defence of Singapore, the 45th Indian Brigade proved no match for the Imperial Guards Division, the elite troops of the IJA.

By 16 January, General Bennett had little choice but to send in his reserve Australian battalion to reinforce the Muar front. This was the 2/29th under Lieutenant Colonel Robertson, along with a troop of the 2/4th Australian Anti-Tank Regiment. From an original brigade strength of 4,000, only some 500 Australians and 400 Indians escaped the IJA onslaught at Muar. General Nishimura, the officer commanding the IJA troops engaged in the ensuing battle, described the experience for the Japanese as 'severe and sanguinary'.

Robert's undying bitterness about what the Japanese did at Muar comes from the first-hand evidence of escapees. After Colonel Anderson's decision to leave the wounded behind, terrible acts were carried out by the invading Japanese force. Australia's official war history records that the wounded, some 110 Australians and forty Indians, were herded together and subjected to abject cruelty and mocking degradation, before being bludgeoned, bayoneted, shot and burnt to death. Then on the outskirts of Parit Sulong, 200 Australian and Indian wounded prisoners of war were taken to a riverside and executed by the method seemingly most enjoyed by the IJA, beheading. The bestiality of Muar was a harbinger of what lay in store for those destined to become prisoners of the IJA.

With the conclusion of the Battle of Muar on 23 January, the defence of Malaya was numbered in days. Fighting bloody rearguard action, the beaten British, Indian and Australian troops fell back to the tip of the peninsula at Johore Bahru. By 31 January, withdrawal to Singapore was complete and the causeway across the narrows of the Johore Strait was blown up.

20. After this briefest of visits to the Malayan mainland, Robert Holman was back on the 'fortress' island of Singapore. There, along with 85,000 British, Indian, Malayan and Australian troops, he awaited the first shots of the Battle of Singapore.

If governments repeat an imaginary construct frequently enough, they can convince themselves of its existence. In London and Canberra the word 'fortress' had been appended to Singapore with such confidence for so long, prevailing politicians believed such to be the case. Singapore could have been one – it was after all an island, and a ring of fortifications could have been built around its foreshores to create a citadel. But it was not a citadel, for the landward defence of the island was always expected to take place on the Malayan mainland, and no effort had been made to build significant fortifications along the northern coastline of the 'fortress'. Churchill later admonished himself for not having asked the question of his military advisers that would have revealed this fatal flaw. He said the possibility of Singapore not having well-established landward defences no more entered his mind than the idea of 'a battleship being launched without a bottom'.

Back in October 1940, when the Singapore military conference was held, it was made clear there were insufficient military resources in Malaya and Singapore to defend against a major attack by Japan. The main deficiency highlighted was in the number of fighter aircraft and bombers available to mount the response to such an attack, and this was emphatically rammed home when the attack came. But for all this military forethought, the conference did not result in Singapore being transformed into the kind of military bastion the governments of Britain and Australia believed it to be. The Japanese suffered no such delusion. Thanks to on-the-ground inspections by Japanese civilians and fifth-column collaborators, the IJA was satisfied as to the vulnerability of Singapore's northern foreshore.

In January 1942, with Malaya lost and the enemy commanding the surrounding sea and air, Lieutenant General Percival set out his orders for the Battle of Singapore. The north-eastern side of the island was to be defended by the British and Indian forces under Lieutenant General Heath, the south by the Malayan Infantry and Straits Settlements Volunteer Force under Major General Simmons, and the north-west by the Australians, bolstered by a newly-arrived Indian brigade, under the command of Australia's Major General Gordon Bennett.

Percival's superiors had made it very clear to him there must be no thought of surrender and that every British, Indian, Malayan and Australian unit must fight it out to the end. Percival must have been struggling for inspiration when he issued his statement to steel the Singaporean public for the battle ahead. 'With firm resolve and fixed determination we shall win through,' he said. And in this most un-Agincourt of addresses, Percival still referred to his vulnerable charge as 'our island fortress'.

21. During the first week of February while the IJA prepared itself for an amphibious assault on Singapore, Japanese artillery and air force bombers pulverised the island. On 8 February the barrage intensified and that night the IJA carried out its crossing of the Johore Strait. With the Japanese barrage having concentrated on Bennett's north-west sector, it followed on that this

was where the invading forces would land, but Allied command seems not to have grasped this fact until the enemy's amphibious landings were actually effected. With the Battle of Singapore now under way, it was quickly apparent that communication on the island was woefully inadequate, and a thick fog of war descended on the defenders.

22. This cryptic reference to the execution of an English officer during the Battle of Singapore is in all probability the case of the traitor Heenan. Although the details were hushed up by the authorities at the time, the story was passed amongst the enlisted men as a grim piece of hearsay. The traitor was Captain Patrick Heenan of the 16th Punjab Regiment, Indian Army. Born out of wedlock in New Zealand, Heenan had been brought up in Burma and England. A disliked man at his regiment, he was turned by the Japanese and proved particularly useful to them by being posted as an air liaison officer in northern Malaya in time for the Japanese invasion at the end of 1941.

Heenan was caught sending radio messages to the Japanese, helping guide in their air attacks. He was arrested on 10 December, taken to Singapore and court-martialled. Two days before the surrender of Singapore, the traitor was taken down to Keppel Harbour by military police, shot in the head and dumped in the sea.

23. Some 50,000 of the Allied prisoners captured in Malaya or turned over with the surrender of Singapore were Indian nationals serving in the British Indian Army. The Japanese separated them from other Allied prisoners and held them in a camp at Farrar Park. Here they were harangued to defect to the enemy by agents of Chandra Bose's Axis-sponsored Indian National Army. They were told the Japanese would help them drive the British Raj from India, so that their act of defection would in fact be enlistment to the cause of India's liberation. The offer was seductive and some regiments went over en masse. Others resisted and were tortured or executed for their defiance: the Gurkhas, for

example, remained loyal to a man. But in all, more than half the Indian prisoners of Singapore became turncoats, marching off with the Indian National Army to its eventual destruction in Burma.

24. Robert Holman's unstinting admiration for General Gordon Bennett, the commander of Australia's 8th Division in Malaya, is significant, for it represents the view of a humble foot-soldier who fought under Bennett's command, albeit for only a month. Perhaps it is in the light of Bennett's post-war fall from grace that Robert Holman goes out of his way to show solidarity with his old commander. His statement that all Australian troops admired Bennett is impossible to defend, for in Australian military history this soldier remains a most controversial figure. Bennett demonstrated personal bravery and outstanding leadership in World War I, becoming a brigadier at the tender age of twenty-nine. He was a member of the Australian militia, rather than the regular army, and was publicly critical of Australia's military preparedness in the years between the two world wars. Possessed of a prickly, aggressive temperament and disliked by many in the Australian officer corps, the general was passed over in the early command appointments of World War II.

Appointed to head up the 8th Division in Malaya, Bennett arrived in Malaya in February 1941 and soon demonstrated his poor regard for British officers. To the significant detriment of the Malayan campaign, his relationship with Lieutenant General Percival, the Allied commanding officer in Malaya and Singapore, was a distinctly unhappy one. During the campaign, Bennett constantly derided the British commander and was possessed with what has been described as 'an overconfident cynicism'. When the time came for him to apply his generalship in southern Malaya and Singapore, like those he so freely derided, Bennett was found wanting.

At the capitulation of Singapore, with surrender procedures still under way, Bennett relinquished his command of the 8th Division 'without competent authority', and escaped by launch to Sumatra. There he obtained air transport back to Australia, his purported purpose being to convey the valuable knowledge he had accumulated in Malaya relating to Japanese military tactics. Bennett met with a cool reception back in Australia, where he was told his escape was ill advised. Prime Minister Curtin absolved him, but shortly after the war a judicial commissioner was appointed to examine whether Bennett had done the right thing in relinquishing his post in Singapore. The commissioner's finding was that Bennett was not justified in doing so.

The *Australian Dictionary of Biography* says that Bennett claimed he had learned how to defeat the Japanese, but had been let down by the British and Indian troops. 'Yet, he had proved no more proficient than other commanders in Malaya and his tactics were outdated. Just as important to him was his wish to lead the Australian army, a consuming aspiration which had been sharpened by not being given an early command. His prejudice against regular officers and his ambition clouded his professional judgement at the most important point in his career. When his most cherished goals were in tatters, he convinced himself that blame for his failure lay with others.'

25. The incident Robert Holman describes occurred on 10 February 1942, the day Wavell visited Singapore for the last time. General Sir Archibald Wavell was at that time based in Java. A month earlier he had been appointed supreme commander of American, British, Dutch and Australian forces in South-east Asia and north-west Australia. In spite of heavy fighting nearby, Wavell had insisted on visiting Bennett and his officers. Alerted to the presence of high-ranking officers, Japanese aircraft attacked the headquarters, and as the official war record puts it, 'casualties resulted, but the generals were unharmed'.

26. On Singapore, the pattern of the Malayan campaign was repeated – fierce hand-to-hand fighting, out-flanking manoeuvres by the IJA, and day-by-day retreats by the British, Indian and Australian forces. On the south-west coast of

Singapore, the Malayan regiments put up a gallant defence and were decimated in the process.

What remained of Singapore's RAF presence now withdrew to airfields in Sumatra and the sky was surrendered to the invaders. Within days of coming ashore the Japanese had captured the western half of the island. Next, Bukit Timah, with its giant depots of food and munitions in the centre of the island, fell to them. Prior to Bukit Timah's capture, the great reserves of petrol held in the area were set alight, rather than let them fall into enemy hands. The oil burned for two days, setting up a pall of black smoke that billowed over Singapore like a banner of impending defeat.

From Churchill to Wavell, and then from Percival to his troops, went the command that the battle must be fought to the bitter end. At this stage, whatever the consequences for civilians and troops alike, there was to be no question of surrender. Every unit was to be brought into close contact with the enemy and they were to fight it out to the finish.

27. As Singapore's defences crumbled, under conditions of widespread confusion and conflicting orders, the distinction between desertion and escape became somewhat blurred. The 'bayonet point' desertion to which Robert Holman refers is a case in point. Undoubtedly he is referring to the men who forced their way onto the Blue Star liner, *Empire Star*. This is probably the most widely cited example of desertion by Australian soldiers during the fall of Singapore, and while there is basis to the story, the popular versions of it are well wide of the truth. The men were part of the dockside melee trying to board the ship, and, being soldiers, were armed. But there is no evidence of guns or bayonets being used to get aboard, or that women and children were pushed aside in the process. There were plenty of other escaping troops on *Empire Star*, but the forceful group was singled out by the ship's captain as deserters and he radioed ahead, so that on arrival in Java, the men in question were placed under arrest. After six days' detention, army investigations were complete and the men were

released without charge (cf *Fabulous Furphies – 10 Great Myths from Australia's Past* by Edward Docker and Lynette Silver).

28. Under aerial bombardment, thatch-roofed structures were particularly vulnerable. Such was the situation of the Indian Base Hospital at Tyersall, below Robert Holman's position on Tanglin Hill, which burnt to the ground, killing some 700 inmates in the process. The 'English' hospital he mentions is the Alexandra Hospital, on the left flank of Tanglin Hill, a British military hospital into which Japanese troops pursued fleeing Indian soldiers. They shot a British officer who came out of the hospital waving a Red Cross flag at them. Japanese soldiers then set about bayoneting occupants of the hospital: doctors, nurses, patients in their beds, and as Robert Holman records, even a patient on an operating table.

29. At the back of Tanglin Hill lay the battered city of Singapore. In these last desperate days, General Percival had withdrawn his forces into a last-stand arc dug in along the city's northern limits. To the south of the city lay the sea and the perils of the Malacca Strait. For a million people huddled in a siege city some three miles wide, into which the invader's bombardment was constantly falling, Singapore had become a dubious refuge of last resort. Explosions rent the city as bombs descended from the drone of Japanese planes and shells whined in from heavy batteries on the mainland. The dockyards were being demolished, on orders from London, the great floating dock scuttled, big guns dismantled and dockyard staff evacuated, and now the great depot fires of Bukit Timah were joined by the ignited oil supplies of the naval dockyard. Burning for days, the giant smoke plumes of these conflagrations cast black backdrops over the city.

Air-raid sirens howled, but with absolute control of the skies over Singapore, Japanese aircraft were free to let down their cargoes of TNT. Out in the harbour, fleeing ships loaded with women and children were blown to smithereens, while all over the falling city, pock-marking explosions signalled a multitude of personal tragedies. Survivors were digging the dead and dying from the rubble. They sat weeping by broken children, cradling loved ones in their final moments, full of fear at what lay ahead. Roads were blocked by bewildered people, by collapsed buildings, burning cars, blasted masonry, mangled girders, tangles of electric and phone cabling. Trolley-buses and trucks were tipped on their sides, next to bomb craters erupting from concrete and tar. Flames engulfed vehicles strafed by Japanese dive-bombers, they licked from the windows of burning buildings; but with no water in the hydrants, the fires raged unchecked.

In the streets of the city nowhere was safe, for Japanese snipers had infiltrated and were taking pot-shots at random targets. Last-minute identification of fifth columnists in league with the invading force was under way and many were now being executed in retribution, some by army firing squads, others by summary justice. The city's sewerage system was virtually defunct as water supplies dwindled to a halt. Pestilence was looming.

Refugees from the mainland, driven down by the advancing enemy, dossed down in the besieged city wherever they could find shelter. Exhausted servicemen in from the routs of Malaya and now Singapore slept in their vehicles wherever they stopped. Morale-shattered soldiers of many nationalities milled around: stragglers, deserters, looters drunk on purloined liquor, others just lost in battle fatigue and shell-shock. Military police and officers moved ineffectively amongst them, doing what little they could to shore up the collapse of civil order.

At the wharves, where last desperate attempts were being made to escape, private cars clogged the approaches, abandoned by their fleeing owners. Ordered to destroy property that might be useful to the invaders, servicemen tipped vehicles, munitions, even bullion, into the sea. People goaded by fright presented tickets and passes to jostle aboard vessels that would carry many of them to nautical disaster in the Malacca Strait. All along the waterfront, escape boats were being requisitioned by soldiers – some under orders, some not.

Bob Miller, an Australian coxswain on loan to the Royal Navy, was serving on a gunboat that had spent the previous month up and down the west coast of Malaya, picking stranded Allied troops from the mangroves, grim battle-hammered men from the running battles of the Malayan retreat. In interview, he vividly recalled those days of Singapore's collapse, like the morning Wavell sent out the order of the day. Broadcast from loudspeakers on vehicles moving around the waterfront, the order was repeated over and over again, 'No surrender, no retreat. Officers shall die with their men at their posts.'

By day, the men of Bob Miller's gunboat were on the wharves dodging the attacks of Japanese planes, as they helped women and children onto the last boats out and consigned passengers' luggage and their motor cars to the depths of the harbour. He had to turn men away from the boats, though some forced their way on to join what were in most cases doomed voyages. Bob recalls helping load the Yangtze River gunboats HMS *Dragonfly* and HMS *Grasshopper* with women and children and later seeing them sunk in the Malacca Strait. No one will ever know exactly, but old hands say up to 8,000 fleeing people, many of them women and children, lost their lives in the waters between Singapore and Sumatra. Not content with the sinking of fleeing craft, survivors were machine-gunned in the water by the all-conquering Japanese forces.

While still engaged on duties on the Singapore waterfront, Bob Miller saw Royal Marines who'd survived the sinking of the *Repulse* and *Prince of Wales* doing what they could to guard the perimeters of the docks. He said that without them the boats at the wharves would have been overrun by the multinational mob. His own gunboat had to pull away from the wharves at night to deter deserters from commandeering the vessel.

A survivor of the fall of Singapore described the aroma of it all as 'a pervasive smell of decay, ordure, anxiety: the smell of defeat'.

30. General Tomoyuki Yamashita had command of the IJA's 25th Army from November 1941 and as such led the invasion of Malaya and Singapore. These military successes earned him the sobriquet 'The Tiger of Malaya'.

31. Aware of impending catastrophe for Singapore's civilian population, and faced with an inevitable end to this military struggle, be it gallant fight-to-the-finish or shame-faced capitulation, from his base in Java, Wavell gave Percival 'discretion to cease resistance'. On reflection, it must be very hard for any general to say the word 'surrender'. In his order of the day to Allied troops, citing loss of requisite 'sinews of war', Percival said that it was 'necessary to give up the struggle'. And so on 15 February 1942, it fell to him to personally march under a white flag to General Yamashita's headquarters and enter into an unconditional surrender.

32. Defeat is an orphan and as those tens of thousands of idle men sat around Changi gnawing at the bones of their humiliation, the finger of blame was pointed in many directions. While the average Australian judged General Percival as weak and out-of-touch, many of the British prisoners blamed General Bennett's abrasive character for the lack of cohesion at the top. The Australians were vilified by many British for a collapse of discipline when the defence of Singapore was imploding; while the Australians who had fought some of the toughest battles of the Malayan campaign blamed downfall on poor decisions by British generals and the unreliability of untrained British and Indian regiments on their flanks.

    The Malayan Volunteers, many of them rubber planters and commercial men, were particularly bitter about the inaction of Singapore's governor, Sir Shenton Thomas, whom they held responsible for the slow evacuation of women and children when ships were available to do so. They pilloried Percival for Singapore's lack of preparedness for attack from the mainland – 'building defences was bad for morale' he had famously remarked. Two days after the fall, seeking to explain the debacle, General Wavell blamed 'the lack of vigour in our peacetime training, the cumbrousness of our tactics and equipment, and the real difficulty of finding an answer to the skilful and bold tactics of the Japanese'.

In the end, the battle for Malaya and Singapore had been lost in Canberra and London. For Churchill, with the resources available to him at the time, North Africa and the Middle East had to take priority over Singapore. Pearl Harbor changed everything, but by then it was too late to save Malaya, and hence Singapore. Once the Americans were committed to war, Churchill could accept short-term losses like Singapore, secure in the knowledge that in the long term they would be won back. Therefore when the fight for Malaya got under way, no British battleships would come to replace the *Repulse* and *Prince of Wales* and no more air-force fighters and bombers would be sacrificed to bolster inadequate Allied squadrons. By conceding the Japanese control of the sea and the air, the struggle to defend Malaya and Singapore was all but over.

33. After the order to surrender, the Australians, now without the hastily departed General Bennett, had assembled at Tanglin Barracks and on 17 February marched across the island to its north-east tip. On this tip was situated the British army barracks of Changi, which, with effect from the capitulation, had become a giant tropical POW camp. The Australians were billeted at the adjacent Selarang Barracks, while the British and Dutch were allocated Roberts and Kitchener Barracks further out towards where Changi pointed towards the South China Sea.

After the mental and physical exhaustion of battle, and compared with the camps to which many of these POWs were bound, Changi was an odd sort of haven. The 'Changi Hilton' the POWs named the place, in contrast to the squalor of the standard IJA prison camps. In Changi, Allied officers remained responsible for the men in their charge and those prisoners who remained in the main camp area of Changi until the end of the war hardly ever saw a Japanese soldier.

But Changi's 'delights' were only relative to the darkness that ruled those other camps. Over 60,000 men had to settle into Changi as best they could, one-third of them Australians. Hunger followed hard on the heels of the reality of their incarceration, the three telling deprivations of Changi being a diet of woeful deficiency, the severance of contact with loved ones at home, and a seemingly endless absence of freedom.

34. Upon conquering the city, the Japanese renamed Singapore Syonan-to, 'the light of the south'. Its beam of victory was thrown all the way to Tokyo, where, in high celebration, Emperor Hirohito mounted his white horse and rode out to salute the victorious crowd gathered at the gates of the Imperial Palace.

With the Japanese now in Singapore, the true nature of Japan's Greater East Asia Co-Prosperity Sphere was demonstrated by what is now called the Sook Ching Massacre. The invaders called it 'the purge of Chinese', by which the Kempei Tai, the despised military police of the IJA, set up screening centres for Chinese. Those who emerged from a screening centre stamped with a triangle were herded off to the waterfront to be dispatched as bullet-ridden corpses.

To further educate the populace, the new Japanese administration set severed Chinese heads on pikes, this mediaeval barbarity becoming a common roadside feature of Syonan-to. Conservative estimates show somewhere between 25,000 and 50,000 Chinese civilians of Singapore and Malaya lost their lives in the Sook Ching Massacre.

35. Robert Holman makes no mention of a famous Changi event of which he was a part. In March 1942, all Changi prisoners were ordered out for a massive parade, lining the roads of the sprawling camp, four and five ranks deep. They were unwitting extras in a propaganda stunt of epic proportions. General Yamashita and his staff appeared in open-topped cars, immaculately dressed, swords at their sides, cruising slowly by the long parade. As Yamashita surveyed

the assembly of his 50,000 prisoners, he took the salute of Allied officers from his passing car. Driving before him was a flat-bed truck, mounted with the cameras of a film crew, recording for cinema audiences across Asia these potent images of Japanese ascendancy. General Yamashita let it be known that the British commanders had been 'out-generalled, outwitted, and outfought'. And so they had. In these dark days, no one could deny the Japanese military their triumphalism, for they had delivered the British Empire its greatest ever defeat.

36. The Geneva Convention relating to the treatment of prisoners of war states that no work which prisoners are called upon to perform shall have direct connection with the operations of the war. For the Japanese victors, this provision was a nicety at a time when they had at their behest in Changi such a fine workforce of able-bodied men. There were airfields to be built in support of the war effort in Burma, and, more importantly, they had come up with a grand scheme to supply that theatre of war. It was after all a vital theatre, one that was expected to result in Imperial Nippon conquering India. From occupied Thailand, the Imperial Japanese Army would build a railway to Burma, through cholera-ridden ravines, over jungle-clad mountain passes, to carry supplies and troops to the battlefront. For labour, they would use their prisoners of war.

The nature of this mad scheme – for its madness would in time be revealed – was kept from the prisoners at Changi. All they were told was that work parties were being organised for projects in overseas locations. The Changi buzz was that it was all part of a prisoner-exchange scheme and that they would be bound for Timor, neutral Portuguese territory where the swaps would take place.

In early May, the Japanese ordered that 3,000 Australians be selected for the work parties. Encouraged by the rumours, and after three months of captivity bored by the repetition of Changi days, there was no shortage of men willing to go. A brigade was formed under the leadership of Brigadier

Varley, organised into a battle formation of three battalions with 1,000 men in each.

At dawn on 14 May 1942 the brigade left Changi, bound for points unknown. At first they were detained all day under the tropical sun on the Singapore docks. Here many had forebodings of what lay ahead, as regular bashings of the sunburnt Australians by over-eager Japanese guards punctuated the intense heat of that long day. In the evening they boarded two rusty, rat-infested coastal vessels, 2,000 of them on the larger vessel, the remainder on the other. The night was spent tied up at the sweltering dock. Conditions on board were appalling, with men cooped below in battery chicken conditions, so that when the boats got under way in the morning, dysentery was already rampant. These two vessels, the *Toyohashi Maru* and the *Celebes Maru*, were early examples of the infamous Japanese hellships, unmarked Japanese freighters that transferred Allied POWs to labour camps, in conditions resulting in over 10,000 POW deaths.

37. On 17 May, the boats anchored off-shore at Belawang, the port of Medan in northern Sumatra. The next day they were joined there by three other ships, one of which carried Dutch prisoners of war. The little convoy set off north, under the escort of a small Japanese minelayer. At sea again, the rising stench of vomit was added to that of the involuntary bowel movements of the diarrhoea and dysentery-ridden men. On the *Celebes Maru*, amongst the stacked platforms on which 1,000 prisoners huddled and jostled, temperatures soared alarmingly in the fetid hold. Perspiration from the top platforms fell through to those below, to join with that of the next rung, and fall like sour rain upon those on the bottom-most level.

38. Robert's precarious position on the toilet roof is all the more bizarre when you consider the words of Dr Rowley Richards, who was also on board the *Toyohashi Maru*. In his book *A Doctor's War*, Dr Richards writes that because of the outbreak of diarrhoea and dysentery amongst the men, there was a

constant need for the latrines. This need meant that 'at least the men in the holds had an opportunity for a breath of fresh air up on deck. With only two five-hole latrines slung over the side of the ship to cater for all of us, the queues were permanent.'

39. Among the men, the mana of Colonel Charles Anderson, VC was high. He had done more than enough to prove he was a leader of men at the Battle of Muar. Born in South Africa, he had served in the King's African Rifles during the Great War and had been a farmer in East Africa before moving to Australia to become a New South Wales grazier. Anderson was as demanding of his own men as he was tough on the enemy.

40. Roy Whitecross was also aboard *Toyohashi Maru*, and in his book *Slaves of the Son of Heaven* gives a perceptive description of the interpreter Captain William Drower. 'He was tall and awkwardly angular ... unmistakably English. He was constantly in the company of Japanese officers and privates and from his six feet three inches height he had to bend down to hear what they said. On first impressions, the majority of us disliked him – disliked his apparently affected speech, the fact that he came from Malaya Command, and his close contact with the Japanese.' First impressions are so often wrong and it would not be long before the men of A Force gave thanks that Bill Drower was in their number.

41. Dr Rowley Richards was a young medical graduate of Sydney University with a bit of experience at Sydney's St Vincents and Mater hospitals. In the estimation of the men, it was early days for him, but in the days that lay ahead, his name would earn its place among the immortals.

42. On 20 May the convoy reached the southern tip of Burma and stopped at Kawthoung, then known as Point Victoria. Here a thousand men of A Force

disembarked under the command of Major Charles Green, for reasons unknown at the time, but for what turned out to be a three-month stint rebuilding the Point Victoria airstrip.

In a privately published war diary by Charles Watson, one of those disembarked at Victoria Point, there is this description of the work on the airstrip. 'At last our work has been allocated. Prior to leaving the 'drome the British mined it, and the craters left by discharged mines are to be filled in and the mines that failed to discharge are to be dug out. In addition, the runway is to be extended by fifty yards. Although the Japs were not signatories to the Hague Convention [sic] we decided to protest. The guards flew into us with pick handles and rifle butts, and the guards on the hill turned their machine guns on us as if to fire. It was probably the shortest strike in history.'

43. They had been landed at Simbin, still a day's march from their destination of Tavoy, and were billeted in the local mill. Roy Whitecross describes the scene at Simbin as 'a tumbled-down rice mill and a few poverty-stricken native hovels, the whole scene set in a sea of stinking mud and slush'. Dr Richards remembers that night being spent 'attempting to sleep on top of rice bags in the company of weevils, fleas and rats'.

The sleepless night was followed by early breakfast, one cup of bug-filled rice for each man, and the long march to Tavoy. Roy Whitecross calls Dr Richards the hero of that march, telling of how, 'carrying a large pack of medical supplies, he walked up and down the straggling column giving aid to the men who collapsed. He must have covered about twice the distance marched by any other man.'

44. When Robert Holman says 'we spent the night' in the hangar, he might have said 'what remained of the night'. From Simbin the Australians had marched through an afternoon deluge and continuing evening rain before entering the town of Tavoy, whence they stomped on to the Japanese camp. There the

weary men sat down in the rain and worked out they'd covered 20 miles in a bit over twelve hours. Sometime before midnight they were given a plate of rice and pork, their first meal since departing Simbin.

Then it was back to marching, another six kilometres through torrential rain to their destination, the Tavoy aerodrome. At the aerodrome's empty hangar, they were organised into small groups and stood in the rain for several more hours of interminable Japanese head-counts, and head-beatings for any exhausted man who had the temerity to sit down. These beatings, it was noted, were delivered by the scabbard of the Japanese officer in charge, Captain Chiina of the Imperial Guards. Eventually the Japanese soldiers were satisfied with their numbering and the prisoners moved into the hangar.

Dr Richards says, 'The ground inside the hangar was covered in large jagged rocks; it was impossible to clear a smooth surface on which we could lie. Most of us were so physically shattered we fell asleep regardless of the sharp edges jutting into our rain-soaked skin. I was wakened the following morning by the sound of more heavy rain belting loudly on the tin roof.' Then Dr Richards set about tending to the head wounds of those who'd suffered Chiina's casual wrath the night before. So began life at Tavoy aerodrome.

45. The Australian executed at Victoria Point was 25-year-old Robert Goulden, shot by a Japanese firing squad for attempting escape. There were also reports that Dutch POWs at Mergui had suffered the same fate and that three hungry young Australians who went over the wire there in search of food had been executed.

46. Escape was such a desperate option in this place, for the escapees' choices were environments of mangrove foreshores and jungle-covered hills, or agricultural areas populated by communities keen to reap the rewards posted by the IJA for POWs on the run. In a continent where an escaping white man stuck out like a sore thumb, it was a forlorn choice to make. Nevertheless, in the months

and years ahead, the execution of would-be escapees was to become a dismal feature of life in the POW camps.

At Tavoy, the eight executed men, led by Warrant Officer Quittendon of Windsor, Victoria and Sergeant Danaher of Ascot Vale, Victoria, had attempted an escape at night, but were captured by noon the following day. Accompanied by Captain Drower, Brigadier Varley argued strenuously for the men's lives, pointing to the Geneva Convention's prohibition on prisoner executions, but Captain Chiina was unmoved. Varley put his own life under threat by telling the Japanese officer that if he carried out the execution, Varley would see to it that Chiina would be tried for murder when the war was over.

Some apologists for the IJA's treatment of POWs, internees and conquered civilian populations say Japan had not ratified the provisions of the Geneva Convention at the time of World War II and therefore was not bound by its provisions. That may be a politically correct argument, but it is a morally vacuous one, condoning by default all manner of state war crimes. The convention was designed exactly to outlaw the aspects of barbarity the IJA practised.

47. Despite the hard physical labour and the IJA's savage beatings of the prisoners, the Tavoy interlude was one of relatively passable conditions for the men. Dietary improvement resulting from Ali Baba's ox-cart supplies made it so, along with the tolerable living conditions of what had once been an RAF camp. In the early days at Tavoy, the lingering effects of the hellships were still upon them, with ongoing deaths from dysentery; but Dr Richards had been happy to see his daily sick-parade numbers fall from 40 per cent of the men in June to 10 per cent by September. To this young doctor it was as plain as day: 'The better the health of the men, the more physical work they were able to perform. It seemed logical that our keepers might also see the benefit of keeping us fed and clean – but in the days to come we would realise that logic had nothing to do with whether men lived or died.'

48. After four months of toil, the prisoners' work on the airstrip at Tavoy was complete and they were barged and then tramp-steamered north, in both cases in conditions of appalling sanitation, heat and overcrowding. On 1 October 1942, the Australians arrived at the Burmese coastal city of Moulmein, where the prisoners were crammed into goods wagons and hauled by a locomotive to their new home, the POW camp of Thanbyuzayat.

49. As an example of the mental state of those caught up in the prevailing Japanese imperial-militaristic cult, Colonel Nagatomo's speech is worth revisiting. It was translated into English and given to prisoners on paper, so that they might consider it well. Here are some of the colonel's illustrious words:

> It is a great pleasure for me to see you at this place as I am appointed Chief of War Prisoners camp in obedience to the Imperial Command issued by His Majesty the Emperor ... His Majesty the Emperor has been deeply anxious about the War Prisoners and has ordered us to enable opening up of War Prisoner camps at almost all the places in the southern countries. The Imperial thoughts are inestimable and the Imperial favours infinite, and as such you should weep with gratitude at the greatness of them and should correct or mend the misleading and improper anti-Japanese ideas.

Nagatomo went on to say that it was not just to His Majesty that the assembled rabble should be grateful, there was also the military to thank.

> At the time of such shortages of materials, your lives are preserved by the military and all of you must reward them with your labour. By the hand of the Nippon army, railways works to connect Thailand and Burma have started to the great interest of the world. There are deep jungles where no man comes to clear them by cutting the trees. There are countless difficulties and sufferings, but you shall have the honour and you should shed tears of gratitude to join in this great work which was never done before and you should do your best efforts. I shall check and investigate carefully for your non-attention.

The complete text of Nagatomo's speech is reproduced on pp. 93–95 of Charles Watson's unpublished memoir, 'Tears of Gratitude'.

50. Now the men were organised into work groups of fifty men, *kumi* as the Japanese called these groups. Each *kumi* was to be led by a *kumicho*, the latter being an Allied officer of lieutenant rank; while captains would be given responsibility for two *kumi* and be known as *hancho*. Each prisoner was given a piece of wood with his number engraved on it and henceforth that was to be his identity. Parades were now to be known as *tenko*, and when one was called, the men had to number off in Japanese, citing the number from their piece of wood.

The railway they were to build would in different circumstances have been something to admire. With the IJA's maritime supply lines to Burma overly long and exposed, in June 1942 imperial orders were made for the construction of a railway between Thailand and Burma. From Thanbyuzayat it was to run for over 400 kilometres through the mountains of Burma, cross the border at Three Pagodas Pass and run down the jungle-banked rivers of southern Thailand to the existing railway at Ban Pong.

It would be necessary to construct nearly 700 bridges, shift three million cubic metres of rock and build some four million cubic metres of earthworks to carry the railway. Instead of the estimated five to six years required for the project, with scant consideration for the resulting toll on human lives, the railway was to be completed in just sixteen months.

Then and now, at any level of humanitarian consideration, the chief flaw in the IJA's grand plan was that rather than using machinery to achieve this giant engineering feat, they would instead apply the bone, muscle and sinews of prisoners of war and press-ganged labourers from the conquered territories. This approach had worked for the building of the Pyramids and so it could be made to work for the IJA in the twentieth century. By the time the last spike was driven in October 1943, to the 'great interest of the world', the IJA's railroad was seen to have recorded the historic tally of about one worker's corpse for every one of the 100,000-odd sleepers laid on the Railway of Death.

51. With construction of the railway now on, the establishment of camps further down the line began. It was decided that Brigadier Varley would remain in Thanbyuzayat with a few staff, carrying out administration and supervising the thousands of other Allied prisoners who would be passing through the base camp on their way to the railway construction. A small hospital was also maintained at Thanbyuzayat.

Led by Colonel Anderson, VC, the first contingent, numbering some 600 men, set off on an eighteen-kilometre march, amongst them Dr Richards, Roy Whitecross and Robert Holman. They entered a scruffy camp previously occupied by coolies, at a place called Hlepauk. Whitecross recounts the camp as a collection of dilapidated bamboo huts with scrappy thatch, set between a road and stream beyond which rose a small jungle-clad hill. 'Above that first hill and stretching as far as one could see, was a chain of high peaks.'

52. The words of the chant 'Itchi, ni, san, si, go' are the Japanese numerals from one to five.

53. With the effects of malnutrition setting in, all prisoners now had a distinctly sallow, bony look. Clothing had worn out or been traded away for food, so many of the men wore nothing but a piece of cloth tied over their private parts. They called this minimal garment a 'jap-nappy'. On their feet they wore what little remained of their army boots or camp-made clogs fashioned from wood, webbing and wire.

54. At daily sick parades, Dr Richards was now inspecting an average of 200 men a day, most of them suffering from beriberi, malaria, dengue fever and tropical

ulcers. Cases of pellagra were also appearing, like beriberi, due to a deficiency of vitamin B. Causing swollen tongues and inflamed mouth, pellagra made eating painful and walking difficult, for it resulted in dry, cracked scrotums and an intense itch in the groin. The dermatitis and diarrhoea that came with pellagra could extend to dementia and death. The camp kitchen double-boiled the rice ration so that it became a thin gruel that could pass with slightly less agony across the lesions in the men's mouths and throats.

Tropical ulcers were rampant because the victims' metabolisms were weakened by malnutrition. The ulcers could steadily rot a man's leg, as if a beast had taken a toxic bite from it, creating pus-filled craters the size of saucers, exposing tendons and bones to view. For those tending to the ulcers, the stench of the pus and dying tissue was repulsive. Meanwhile, the victim suffered not just the atrocious smell of himself rotting, but the intense pain and itching that went with it.

With hardly any medicine to dispense, a new technique for treating these ulcers had to be devised. Dr Richards felt the prevailing practice of gouging and scraping was too invasive and he devised his own treatment. It was based on the principle of not destroying any healthy or granulating tissue surrounding the ulcers. So many men owed the retention of their legs to this new treatment that Dr Richards's description of it should be repeated:

> Along with my orderlies, I placed hot foments on the hard scabs of the ulcers to soften them up, then, ever so gently, we used forceps to remove all the dead tissue. It was a painstaking and time-consuming process. We treated three or four men simultaneously, running backwards and forwards between our patients at timed intervals. In total we spent about half an hour treating each ulcer, which we then covered with bandages — improvised from torn sheets, shorts, shirts, mosquito nets and even blankets, all sterilised in boiling water. Then we left the bandages on for four to seven days, to prevent damage to the granulating tissue and ensure minimal handling.

The success of this technique meant no ulcer patients treated by Dr Richards and his team of orderlies went to the next step of amputation. Elsewhere along the railway and in the myriad of fetid Japanese POW camps in the conquered Asian territories, in criminally primitive conditions desperate doctors sawed limbs from ulcer patients to save them from gangrenous death.

55. In November 1942, 200 Korean guards arrived in the railway camps. With its profusion of POW camps around Asia, the IJA had decided to recruit Koreans for what was regarded as the rather demeaning task of guarding the prisoners. Thereby Japanese troops were freed up to continue their war of aggression. Some sources say these Koreans were forced into IJA service, others that they volunteered; whatever the truth, with just a few exceptions the POW consensus was that the new guards were poor examples of humanity. Even with the healing passage of time and from the perspective of a whole new century, in the considered medical opinion of Dr Richards, the Korean guards were 'fundamentally sadistic, bad bastards'.

It was not an easy time to be Korean. Annexed by Japan in 1910 as a colony, Korea and its culture was thereafter forced into assimilation with Japanese culture. From 1938 the Korean language was forbidden at all levels of the Korean education system, and young Koreans were made to worship Emperor Hirohito at Shinto shrines in an all-out effort to convert them to the imperial-militaristic cult of Japan. Korean names were nipponised, to the effect that all the guards on the railway had Japanese rather than Korean names. Not that these names registered with the prisoners, for they bestowed monikers on each of their guards according to his character or looks. There was the depraved, low-brained Boofhead; the fat, no-necked Maggot; Jeep with his explosive temper; the 'vicious little dwarf' Mickey Mouse, possessed of a colossal vanity; the Bull, who bashed without pretext; and the edgy runt Greenpants who tried so hard to be like the Japanese.

Roy Whitecross says the broad-shouldered Storm Trooper was 'the daddy of them all ... If he did not bash at least one prisoner every half hour when he was on duty, we knew he must be sick.' He proceeded to bash the doctors, the stretcher-bearers, the sick; all were fair targets for his wrath, all were expendable. For an error by one of their men, the Storm Trooper led a bashing of Colonel Anderson, Captain Drower, Sergeant Lynch and Sergeant Maher that savaged them beyond unconsciousness and resulted in the death of Jim Lynch.

All POW diaries of days on the railway describe the ferocity of the bashings by the Korean guards or their Japanese superiors. Face-slappings, kicks and cane beatings were a daily occurrence around the camps, hardly meriting mention. But when the guards really put their minds to it, punishments were extended bashings and torture sessions sometimes lasting days and resulting in serious injury or death.

The days of reckoning would come for the Korean guards and many would be put on post-war trial for their crimes. Some would hang as a result. Tainted as war criminals and branded in Korea as Japanese collaborators, they found it hard to go home and many had to settle for third-class lives in Japan for the remainder of their days.

On the railway, the Japanese treated their Korean subjects like scum. This very fact might have led the Koreans to feelings of empathy with the plight of the prisoners – after all, for anyone placed in a position of coercive authority, there is ever the option of fulfilling duty in a humane manner. But the great majority of the Korean guards, admittedly under duress and with the approval of their Japanese overlords, chose instead to brutalise the ailing prisoners on the Railway of Death.

56. The Korean guard in question was named Tomoto. Dr Richards found out early that the Korean guards were not to be trifled with, that they were 'brutal by nature as well as by orders'. When he was told by one of these guards to order sick men to go and work on the railway, men who were down with malarial fevers, dysentery and beriberi, Dr Richards refused. The guard concerned was

Tomoto, who carried the nickname of Peanut, because he was nuts and was said to possess a brain the size of a pea. On this occasion, Tomoto set upon the doctor with a bamboo cane, beating him around the head and shoulders for long enough to leave him a mess of bloodied lacerations.

In December 1942, Peanut Tomoto committed a heinous crime that went unpunished by the Japanese authorities and haunted the POWs long after its protagonist slipped into oblivion. For Tomoto's crime made the prisoners face up to the depressing reality of their powerlessness and the fact that justice had flown far from them. It had been noticed among the men that Peanut Tomoto was obsessed with sex. In his broken English, he liked to provoke the prisoners with incessant talk of the 'jiggy-jig' the Japanese would be having with Australian girls once they invaded Australia. But it was also made obvious to the prisoners that Tomoto's sexual interest extended to men.

At an evening *tenko*, they discovered Sergeant Ronnie O'Donnell was missing. Colonel Anderson mounted a search and O'Donnell's body was found. He'd been shot in the chest, front-on at close quarters, and two bullets had been pumped into his head as he lay on the ground. Next it was discovered that Tomoto admitted to the shooting and was now telling the Japanese camp commandant that O'Donnell had been trying to escape. Those who knew O'Donnell assured Colonel Anderson that escape was the last thing on the sergeant's mind, and given the gunshot evidence of the killing and the fact that Tomoto had taken so long to report it, cold-blooded murder was the obvious judgment. Most concluded Peanut Tomoto had been after sexual favours, and not getting them, had vented his rage with his gun.

Colonel Anderson demanded justice and the Korean was sent to Thanbyuzayat for the case to be investigated. Eventually word came back to Hlepauk camp that Colonel Nagatomo had exonerated the guard and believed that O'Donnell had been correctly shot while attempting to escape. Peanut Tomoto went back to his guard duties in another camp.

57. In his role as interpreter, Captain Bill Drower earned the undying respect and affection of prisoners up and down the line. As the medium of communication in many a malevolent moment, he was the great defuser. But Bill Drower would have to take many a severe beating to do this job for the men. His last IJA punishment, suffered near the end of the war, very nearly killed Drower. He was mediating in an incident at Kanchanaburi camp in Thailand when the psychotic chemist, Captain Noguchi, and his camp assistant, Lieutenant Tagasaki, lost it. They turned on Drower with their sword sticks, giving him the mother of all beatings. After the beating, he was made to stand for three days in front of the guard-house, following which ordeal Captain Drower was thrown into a soggy pit where for a further three days he was given no food or water. Starvation rations commenced thereafter – two rice balls a day and two daily rations of water. With Drower on death's threshold by week seven, the Japanese finally agreed he could receive food from the prison cook-house and be moved from his filthy pit to a detention cell. After more than eleven weeks of this murderous persecution, Captain Drower was released, his mind wandering, his body in a pitiable state from malaria and the blackwater fever that ravaged him. In spite of the IJA's efforts, Bill Drower survived the war.

58. The medical orderlies were the unsung heroes of the railway. Up and down the various camps they worked day-in, day-out, tending to the sick and dying. In Anderson Force the orderlies were led by Sergeant Jim Armstrong and Corporal Pinkey Rhodes, and all men treated by this pair remembered them as saints among saints.

59. In early January 1943, Anderson Force moved to Tan Yin camp a further seventeen kilometres up the track. Tan Yin saw an improvement in conditions after the dilapidated huts of Hlepauk, partly because Williams Force had been there for a fortnight and had got the place in order. There was no river at Tan Yin, so water had to be drawn from wells.

Williams Force was led by Lieutenant Colonel John Williams and was made up of men of the 2/2nd Pioneer Battalion of the AIF and the survivors of the sinking of HMAS *Perth*. The Pioneers were veterans of the Middle East campaigns and the lost battle for Java. Williams was starved and tortured for a month by the despised *Kempei Tai* in Batavia; a Sydney engineer, he hated the Japanese and let them know it.

60. Anderson Force and Williams Force were now combined into one force known as Number One Mobile Force, numbering over 1,400 men. In March they were moved to Kunknitkway camp and then to Anarkwan camp. As they progressed deeper into the Burmese mountains, a pattern was emerging: even more strenuous labouring hours demanded of the prisoners, coupled with greater violence bestowed on the men by the guards, together with a worsening of already meagre rations and a sharp decline in men's health due to the ongoing effects of beriberi, malaria and dysentery.

The wet season set in, bogging camps, tracks and work sites in muddy muck. There would be no time to settle down anywhere, for over these next eight months the struggling force would be based in ten different jungle camps. The IJA engineers demanded a new level of effort from the wasted bodies of their labour force, regardless of cost to human life. It was a mindset of criminal madness; and if that description sounds extreme, consider the fate of two Japanese surveyors summoned to account for their incompetence when two sections of the railway did not align according to the survey plans. A British officer, Captain Butterworth, and a group of prisoners at Takanun camp were treated to the spectacle of the errant surveyors being made to kneel and having their heads removed by the swords of their IJA companions. Rather than this being a solemn ceremony, the Japanese onlookers clapped and laughed as the surveyors' heads went rolling.

61. Any POW account that makes mention of the surviving sailors of HMAS *Perth* speaks of them with affectionate respect, as if they were a special group of

men. These tars had seen battle in the Mediterranean in the defence of Greece and Crete, before joining battles off the coast of Java. On 1 March 1942, in a gallant, gun-blazing finale that dispatched a Japanese minesweeper and four troop transport ships, the *Perth* sank to the bottom of the Sunda Strait. Of the 683 men of the ship's company, two-thirds were killed on her final day.

62. There were some prisoners on the railway who thought officers were a waste of space, but they usually changed that opinion when they got a glimpse of camps where leadership was absent. Being part of a disciplined force, staffed with selfless doctors and orderlies, greatly improved chances of survival when compared with fellow workers up the track.

For the Asian labourers on the railway, the people the Japanese called *romusha*, there was no organised leadership but for callous IJA guards. The labourers had no access to medical treatment until June 1943, when an ill-provided team of Allied medical officers from Changi was dispatched to provide belated medical supervision. For the most part, labourers such as those found by A Force in such distressed conditions at Taunzan camp, were left to fend for themselves in subhuman conditions.

Where the *romusha* did receive IJA attention, it was that of brutal compulsion. The war diary of POW Dr Robert Hardie, published as *The Burma-Siam Railway*, has a chilling entry on 29 January 1944. 'More authenticated accounts of savagery to coolies by Jap guards, crucifixion, drowning, blinding and other atrocities.' Dr Hardie goes on to report the other IJA treatment methods for Asian labourers suffering from cholera: live burials, dumping of sick men in the jungle and 'at Kinsaiyok men are sometimes compelled at the point of the bayonet to brain coolie cholera cases with a hammer'.

Though written records from the *romusha* themselves are scarce, there are many witness accounts of the Asian labourers' camps from their fellow sufferers, the POWs. These tell of men in tattered rags huddled together in the wet, all in the grip of dysentery and cholera, without medical aid of any kind. In his book *One Fourteenth of an Elephant,* Ian Denys Peek relates how as a British POW on the railway, he was assigned to duty in a bare-handed burial party for the *romusha,* spending many days putting Tamil corpses into shallow graves. Peek describes the start of such days. The Tamil labourers would point out the place where men with cholera had been sent into the bush beyond their camp, but they were not prepared to go anywhere near the area themselves. Peek held no grudge against the labourers for standing off.

> After a moment's glance at the scene in front of us, none of us can blame them one little bit. The ground is dotted with shrubs and hacked trees; probably everything that will burn has been taken for cooking fires. Lying all over the place are bodies – stretched out flat on their backs, faces in the mud, collapsed into the bushes, leaning against tree stumps, twisted in the contortions of a painful death, eyes shut, eyes staring, teeth bared, limbs sticking out stiffly. Dozens of them, and these are just last night's victims.

The *romusha* came from the conquered territories of the so-called Greater East Asia Co-Prosperity Sphere. Nowhere was the hypocrisy of Japan's imperial-militaristic cult more evident than in the sweet-worded trickery and violent compulsion by which these labourers were press-ganged onto the Railway of Death. *Romusha* were collected from all over South-east Asia to build the railway and the network of airstrips and roads required to support the IJA's war in Burma. The *romusha* are estimated to have totalled 300,000, of which number it is conservatively estimated over 80,000 were slain by disease, malnutrition and brutal exploitation. Virtually all contemporary accounts verify that these democidal statistics arose directly from the IJA's wilful neglect and astounding maltreatment of the *romusha.*

63. In his book *A Doctor's War,* Dr Richards records the arrival at this camp, Taunzan. He too was deeply shocked by the scene; piles of rotting rubbish and stinking human faeces covered the ground. A storm of flies moved over decomposing corpses of scores of Burmese workers, many of them bloated, causing the

arriving men to retch involuntarily. In order to forestall further spread of disease, the Australians set to work immediately burying the Burmese bodies. In the rudimentary cemetery set up at the edge of the camp, the Australians counted up to 200 other graves of labourers. Outraged as they were by this further evidence of the ongoing IJA genocide, there was no time for the Australians to consider the ledger of guilt, for the survival of the living now came under new threat. In alarming numbers, Burmese workers were continuing to die horrible deaths at Taunzan, and the fear that cholera might be hovering somewhere around turned to acceptance by the Australians that it was now amongst them.

This macabre camp haunted all who experienced it. In *Slaves of the Son of Heaven,* Roy Whitecross describes his sleeping hut at Taunzan, wherein he found the emaciated body of a Burmese labourer. 'From the gaunt skull the whites of the eyes looked sightlessly into space. The open mouth was twisted awry as though the agony, cruelty, starvation and utter destitution that made up this poor creature's existence had not been relieved even by death.'

Rectal smears were taken of the guards and prisoners and cholera was confirmed as present. One of the Japanese engineers contracted the disease and quickly died, underlining the fact that the cholera germ had no prejudices when it came to prisoners and guards. This knowledge galvanised the Japanese into cooperation. Dr Richards set up an isolation hospital, staffed by volunteer orderlies from Anderson and Williams forces, and the Japanese authorities provided quicklime and phenol to improve camp sanitation standards. Before too long, booster cholera vaccine was sent up the line to Taunzan.

Cholera is a disease of traumatic dehydration, so at Taunzan's makeshift hospital the POWs improvised equipment out of parts salvaged from Japanese trucks to administer saline solution to the dehydrating men. In spite of all that was done for them, cholera claimed its victims one by one; for the cholera germ can kill a man in hours, with dehydration occurring from uncontrollable vomiting and the constant emission of 'rice-water stools'.

With the strict medical controls imposed on Taunzan camp, death was restricted to scores of POWs rather than hundreds. Meanwhile, up and down the line, over a hundred men were now dying of cholera every day. In the numbing detachment imposed by statistics, it is easy to pass over the truth that each one of those deaths was a personal tragedy, a life forgone and unfulfilled – each death meaning the abandonment of grieving mates left to struggle on through the IJA nightmare. And each of those deaths was an act of ultimate bereavement for loved ones at home: parents, siblings, wives and lovers, still unaware of their loss, for years would have to pass before they could receive the bitter news.

At least in Taunzan's little hospital, men died in the loving arms of their comrades, the volunteer orderlies, experiencing the grace of altruism even as they slipped the bonds of a troubled world. The isolation unit Dr Richards set up for the cholera-afflicted was strictly off-limits to all but him and the volunteer orderlies who bunked down with the sick men. But the young doctor would turn a blind eye when he saw one of two figures creeping on their bellies through the long grass towards the isolation unit. He knew who the furtive figures were: either Padre Smith or Colonel Williams, going through to share hope and companionship with the dying men.

64. It was this film crew's visit to Anarkwan camp that resulted in a celebrated act of defiance by Colonel John Williams. The Japanese wanted to film an Australian bugler, but the bugler was out on the railway with one of the work gangs and Colonel Williams was held responsible. As punishment he was made to stand bare-headed for 26 hours outside the guard-house in the blazing sun and tropical rain, collecting blows and kicks from passing guards. His obstinate defiance throughout this punishment gave great heart to all who witnessed it.

65. This camp of death is probably Apparon, eighty kilometres up the line from Thanbyuzayat (hence its alternative name, '80 Kilo Camp'). At Apparon, the POWs were allocated muck-filled cowsheds as sleeping accommodation and

with the incessant monsoonal rain, the camp floated in a muddy jungle clearing on an accumulation of bovine and human excrement. The latter had been layered onto the ground by the camp's previous occupants, *romusha* debauched by dysentery and cholera. The stench was nauseating and Dr Richards says they were made to live 'like neglected livestock'.

Further deterioration in their desperate conditions came when the bridge down the line was washed away and supplies of meat and rice couldn't get through. This was an ongoing problem and when meagre meat rations did make it through, they were green and full of maggots. Colonel Williams recorded that with food so scarce, it was decided maggots were protein and that they were to be boiled up with the rotten meat.

Roy Whitecross says he saw nothing but rice and white beans for food during the month he was at Apparon. Sick with malaria and diarrhoea, it was nearly the end of him. He describes the dismal rain falling unceasingly and the sad burial groups making their way past his hut day by day to the shallow graves, the muffled sound of the graveside bugle and the bedraggled men returning, some of them so emaciated they had to be carried back. Though he hated the sound of the bugle for what it represented at Apparon, Roy could still write, 'Many Williams Force men died in 80 Kilo Camp, most of them naval men from HMAS *Perth*, and the bright notes of the naval reveille would come in sorry contrast with the sodden, sombre surroundings'.

66. Robert Holman's reference to the plight of F Force begs explanation of the fate of this body of men. They were the last big POW force sent out from Changi to work on the railway's construction. In Changi they'd been hoodwinked by IJA assurances they were sending prisoners to health camps for recuperation, so some 7,000 POWs had climbed into the freight trucks in Singapore in high and adventurous spirit. They were sent north in seven rail shipments, quickly losing their optimism as they were crammed inside closed freight cars in health-destructive conditions. After five days of this sad journey, already sick, filthy,

and exhausted, they were greeted at Ban Pong by guards who bestowed savage beatings on officers and men alike.

From Ban Pong they were forced to march for close on 300 kilometres under heavy tropical rain, through fetid swamps and boot-sucking jungle tracks up into the mountains of western Thailand. Stragglers and sick were beaten about by Korean guards, or put out of their misery by the Thai bandits who trailed the marching columns. In their bedraggled state, hounded by storms of sandflies, the prisoners swallowed starvation rations and, with no shelter but the sky, lay down in the mud to catch a few hours' sleep. On reaching their destination near Three Pagodas Pass, where the mountains announce the Burmese border, F Force was divided into a series of camps around Sonkurai and Nike. Those who had not already met them on the trek from Ban Pong were now introduced to the railway's life-sapping spectres — beriberi, dysentery, malaria, pellagra and cholera.

Next they were familiarised with the whips of the IJA engineers, whom POWs remember as the worst of the worst. Obsessed with their glorious imperial quest, the completion of a soon-to-be-redundant stretch of jungle railway, the engineers overrode any regular IJA officers who might evince a touch of mercy for the stumbling labour force. If a Korean guard or POW officer impeded the engineers' insatiable demand for more and more labour from their sick and dying subjects, such objections were crushed violently. In the end, the cultist zeal of those IJA engineers drove tens of thousands of young men to gruesomely unjust deaths.

There was no release from the menace of the clammy grip in which F Force was caught. Beyond the reach of sane administration, with supply lines washed away and engineers screaming for more work, faster work, longer and longer hours of work, with every tropical disease available invading their innards, brutal beatings for the slightest transgression, rations fouled with rat faeces and alive with maggots, many POWs reached the end of hope and endurance. At No. 2 Sonkurai camp nearly 1,200 POWs died — three out of every four men who stumbled through its gates. When cholera scythed through the camp's hovels, there were no niceties to death. Bug-eyed and cramping, a man could be gone in a day, sprayed by the vomit and excreta of those spooned up against him in the huts of death, his last view of the world that of skeletal corpses stacked at the open door, and in the yard the sound of bamboo crackling as cremation fires burned around the clock.

Stan Arneil was one of the Australian survivors of F Force and his diary of the ordeal is contained in the epic journey of his memoir, *One Man's War.* Here are some extracts from Stan Arneil's testimony.

> *This horrible itch kept me awake half the night and I think I am fighting a losing battle against two would-be ulcers on my right foot ... Sorry to record that last night I spent a bad time sitting up almost all night, trying to prevent myself from vomiting. My stomach has been tying itself up in knots all day and the ulcers won't let up one minute ... I walked through the hospital today: the stench in the ulcer ward would turn the strongest stomach. The ulcer cases cannot get up to wash and they, like the whole camp, are infested with horrible grey body lice ... I have been intensely depressed all day by a couple of visits to the horrible ulcer ward and cannot shake off the feeling of hopelessness it has given me. Men are dying for the want of simple things ... Feet worse, one ulcer is down to the bone. Great pain to walk now ... They have begun to amputate limbs because of ulcers ... Today a chap lay on a bamboo stretcher under a primitive shelter of attap leaves and had his arm amputated. The open latrines were twenty yards away and two orderlies had to keep waving branches to shoo the flies away.*

Those entries in Stan's diary are from September 1943, but by October he is knocked up in the grimness of the ulcer ward himself, alongside two of his long-time mates from Australia, Doug Blanshard and Stinney Reinhard:

> *It is hard to keep alive the will to live. I can hang on myself but others are falling under the strain every day. Have been in hospital since yesterday*

afternoon and so far have not been able to sleep a wink. Seven men to a bay last night meant that if one man turned over the other six did the same. … Men are dying like flies now and the itch is sending most of us half silly … Stinney is in a very bad way.

And then, 'Stinney died last night in awful circumstances. God rest his poor soul, he died hard.'

Of F Force 3,600 were British POWs and 3,400 were Australians. Sixty per cent of these British prisoners were slain by the Railway of Death, while for the Australians the figure was 30 per cent. Why the discrepancy? The more one reads of the vileness of conditions to which these men were condemned – learning of the best and worst of leadership provided, of differing ability to adapt to extremes of hardship, or just of the presence of a dogged retention of the will to live – the more one is left to conclude that different cultural attitudes to sanitation and hygiene were what caused that tragic one-in-two variance of mortality.

An ability to adapt was certainly critical to keeping men alive, but if an individual lost the lantern of hope, the game was up for him. And in the rank injustice of the circumstances brought upon them, it was an easy thing to lose. Malayan Volunteer Ian Denys Peeks witnessed it like this:

We all suffered physically and spiritually, and those of us who survived were in no way more deserving to live, we were just a bit luckier. Death came bearing a dismal shroud of utter loneliness, which sealed off dying men from all those they had loved and who had loved them, warmed only by the intense compassion of those few friends who were with them at the time. We must never forget them, or allow them to pass from their people's memories.

67. War has many tragic ironies, one of the saddest of which goes by the cruel euphemism 'friendly fire'. In Burma, Thanbyuzayat camp was repeatedly bombed by Allied planes, resulting in the deaths of many POWs and wounding of many more, including Brigadier Varley. Requests that Red Cross signs be laid

out in Thanbyuzayat and the other POW camps to warn off bombers were denied, so that when Thanbyuzayat camp was finally abandoned, its cemetery held many a victim of friendly fire.

On the Thailand side of the railway, at the Tamarkan camp, next to the famed bridge across the River Kwai, and at the camp at the rail junction of Nong Pladuk, the IJA deliberately housed the POWs where they were cheek-by-jowl with Allied bombing targets. As a result the death toll of POWs was even higher there. Being subjected to bombing by your own planes was 'a refinement of mental torture', says Rohan Rivett in his book *Behind Bamboo*. Because of the strategic marshalling yards at Nong Pladuk, at one stage of the war nightly Allied bombings and strafings were experienced and Rivett records the experience: 'We now entered upon a period of constant alerts and anxiety. It is doubtful whether anything imposed so great a strain on the sick men, lying helplessly in the hospital huts, as this hourly apprehension of attack by their own planes.' Somewhere near 800 POWs were seriously wounded or killed by Allied bombing in the Thailand railway camps.

68. Kunknitkway camp was memorable for many of the prisoners, because it was where Lieutenant Naito joined them. Naito had been second in charge to Colonel Nagatomo in Thanbyuzayat, where he was known to have presided over the execution of prisoners, three Dutch and one Australian. He was older than most of the Japanese officers in Burma, a former banker and an educated man, and it was said he'd been through many bloody IJA campaigns in China. But by the time he got to Burma, Naito was a confirmed alcoholic with delusional mental problems. One day Colonel Nagatomo had enough of his deputy and gave him a full-on IJA beating, before kicking him down the stairs of the Thanbyuzayat headquarters. On arrival at his new charge, the jungle camp of Kunknitkway, Lieutenant Naito was prone on a wire mattress, still bloodied from his beating. His first order as camp commandant was for the 'boy doctor' Rowley Richards, to come and attend to his cuts and bruises.

Naito's reign as a commandant made an indelible impression on those who survived it. In drunken rages, with pistol drawn, he would sneak through the camp at night looking for people to punish. On one such hunt, he shot an Australian sergeant-major who was on his way to the camp urinal. Naito insisted the Australian had been attempting escape and there was no way to deny the commandant's brandy-crazed judgment. Whenever a bout of Naito's alcoholic madness came upon them, the camp would be put into a state of nervous tension. Naito exercised a mania for midnight parades. These nocturnal communings, lit by flaming torches to hold back the jungle night, usually featured bayonet drills accompanied by the mass expression of blood-curdling screams. Repression was Naito's delight, and he brought it down with psychotic relish on prisoners and guards alike, so much so that in the end it gave the POWs cause for wry amusement. As the days of Naito's undiscriminating malevolence unwound, the guards found little ways to express their hatred of the dipsomaniac commandant.

69. The *Kempei Tai* were the military police of the Imperial Japanese Army. Their notorious brutality in pre-war Korea was well established and they were feared in Japan itself under the police state conditions then prevailing. They had special responsibilities for the IJA's prison camps during World War II, in which their peculiar enthusiasms for torture and cruelty were revealed to Allied POWs. The abhorrent crimes of this force were legion, and it is postulated that until the words *Kempei Tai* carry the same dread, disgust and censure as does mention of the Nazi's Gestapo, the story of World War II is incomplete. The *Kempei Tai* were disbanded after Japan's surrender in 1945.

70. As to what was happening in the world beyond the steaming vegetal mass of their jungle prison, the men's imaginations were nourished by rumours and radio. Wild rumours were spawned from all sorts of portents: the movements of Japanese troops, the temper of guards, and the sifting and resifting of

propaganda reports. Every rumour related vitally to the final haunting questions of – would they ever be freed and, if so, when would that day come?

From tiny, hidden radio sets, a secret camp team would be given snippets of news about the progress of the war, which, following designated channels, would then be passed by word-of-mouth to prisoners. Great care had to be taken that prisoners never let their captors know they knew more than they were telling, for the consequences could be dire. Through the secret radio sets, the prisoners heard the depressing news of Darwin's bombing, but later came more cheering reports that hinted the tide might be turning. News of the great naval battles of the Coral Sea and Midway filtered in; and then from Papua New Guinea an uplifting breakthrough – in early September 1942, news of the Australian army turning back 2,500 Japanese tank-supported troops at Milne Bay – the first land defeat inflicted on the Japanese in the war.

With the penalty of possession being death, radios were more than mediums of information – each hidden set was a talisman of defiance. In one of the Thailand railway camps, lieutenants Jack Hawley and Stanley Armitage suffered the ultimate penalty when they and a group of British officers were found in possession of a radio. These two men were beaten to death with pick handles by a squad of Japanese NCOs and Korean guards, under the supervision of the drunken camp commandant Lieutenant Komi at Kanchanaburi camp. In Eric Lomax's book *The Railway Man*, there is the description of a Dutch doctor counting the number of blows the defenceless Hawley and Armitage received from the Japanese clubs – 400 in all. He then witnessed these *bushido* soldiers dumping the broken bodies of the two officers into a deep latrine in the Japanese section of the camp.

71. One of the peculiarities widely observed of the railway guards and the soldiers of the IJA was a proclivity towards cruelty to animals. For Robert Holman, with his enduring love for wildlife and domestic animals, this was particularly hard to take, but many POW accounts make mention of this strange feature of

prison-camp life. They tell of soldiers shooting dogs to wound rather than kill them, of guards skewering kittens on bayonets and tossing them to each other from bayonet to bayonet, and of the POWs' pet chameleons and monkeys having to be put out of their misery when guards mutilated them. The prisoners were never sure whether it was innate sadism at play, or whether the guards employed the animals' suffering to further torment their prisoners.

72. Up and down the railway there was a home truth known as Coates's dictum. It was that the route-map home was inscribed on the bottom of each prisoner's dixie. Dixies were the prisoners' metal food containers and Dr Coates's point was that however gut-turning or rotten a ration might be, however unappetising the daily dose of unsalted rice, the men would only survive if they ate every scrap of nourishment that came their way. Coates worked tirelessly to save men's lives, even as he recovered from severe tropical typhus – for a month the typhus had his pulse rate at over 120, with a body temperature of up to 105 degrees Fahrenheit. Between July and November 1943 alone, he carried out 115 limb amputations on men who would have died had he not been there.

Fellow former POW Dr Rowley Richards says 'Bertie' Coates was the greatest of them all, a brilliant Melbourne surgeon, always modest and always an inspiration to the younger doctors struggling to make sense of the diseased nightmare in which they were stuck. A man of elevated willpower, having served at Gallipoli and the battlefields of France in the First World War, Lieutenant Colonel Coates knew the horror of war's consequence. Yet in 1942, when he was offered evacuation upon the surrender of Sumatra, he chose instead to stay with his men and the incarceration he knew was coming.

73. With virtually no medical supplies at hand, usually the best form of treatment the doctors could give was preventative, by way of ensuring the men got a day of rest and recuperation. Sick parades were the means of achieving this, by assigning men to light duty, no duty or a hospital bed. But the Japanese

demanded a specified number of men for work on the railroad each day, so at sick parade it was a case of working out who could best cope with a day's toil under the hot tropical sun.

74. All POW accounts of the Railway of Death make mention of the bonds of mateship and compassion that sustained Australian prisoners or eased them through their final days. Mateship carried men through illness, starvation and brutality. Trapped in a quagmire of vine-choked forest, of trackless mud and sordid disease, they had been delivered to a desolate place governed by the cruellest of thoughts and deeds, but their mates bore it with them. With everything taken from them, they still had each other. They say that when the will to live began faltering, or your fevered grip on sanity weakened, it was your mates who pulled you back from the brink, who reminded you with humour and sentimental stories of who you really were, and how one day you'd find a way back home to Australia.

75. By the beginning of 1943, things were going badly for the Japanese on the south-western extremities of their occupied territories. The Americans were making headway against them in the Solomon Islands and Australian troops had turned the tide in Papua New Guinea. The American navy was now revitalised and its submarines were making their presence felt on Axis shipping. The toll on Japanese shipping, coupled with the mounting likelihood of an Allied counterattack in north-west Burma, put frenzied pressure on the need to complete the Railway of Death. And so in February 1943, the railway construction entered a period described by the IJA as the 'hastening'. It would last until the railway's completion in October and be known by the prisoners as the time of *Speedo*. During the hastening, thousands upon thousands of men were harried to their deaths to the sound of IJA engineers and Korean guards screaming, '*Speedo! Speedo!*'

That monsoon rains would deluge the work between May and September, that supply lines would be washed out and disease deplete their labour force to a shuffling horde wounded in mind and body, was of secondary importance to the IJA. Labourers were an expendable commodity.

Roy Whitecross remembers the onset of the hastening and a heavy day of moving camp. He writes:

In charge of the move was the Storm Trooper ... the camp rang with his screams of 'Speedo! Speedo!' ... Most of us could escape from his stick and seldom received more than one blow. The unfortunate ones were those acting as stretcher-bearers for the numerous hospital cases. The only track to the railway line ran beside the screaming Korean and while the stretcher-bearers carefully picked their way down the muddy, slippery bank they were unmercifully beaten about the heads and shoulders.

At Nike camp the IJA engineers behaved so savagely that even the Korean guards were appalled. Such was the sickness in camp arising from the execrable diet and conditions of the hastening that there were insufficient men to work to the engineers' ambitions. So they ordered those still capable of walking to carry the sick on stretchers out to the work sites, then forced these feeble men to crack rocks from their stretchers.

At Hintok, the *Speedo!* policy resulted in hazardous work conditions at the Pack of Cards Bridge. They called it that because it fell down three times. Using primitive tools and green timber cut from the surrounding forest, the prisoners were made to construct a bridge nearly 400 metres long and twenty-five metres high, in the space of seventeen days. While the IJA gloried in their bridge, the prisoners buried their dead, for thirty-one of them fell to their deaths during the bridge construction, while a further twenty-nine bridge-builders were beaten to death by the IJA hasteners.

The hastening brought awful times to the men of H Force, who, with hammers and chisels, cut through Hellfire Pass. Out in the rain in rags of rotting clothing, by day and night on empty stomachs they laboured, hauling out rock-rubble basketful by basketful, trudging back and forth in a seemingly endless round of brain-cracking Sisyphean labours. They worked eighteen-hour shifts for six weeks without break. In the nocturnal mists and rain, their work was illuminated by pale orange flames and the black smoke of diesel fires that swirled about the ghostly host of jerking skeletons struggling through Hellfire Pass. There, for the slightest imagined transgression, exhausted, staggering men suffered terrible beatings from Japanese engineers and Korean guards, their emaciated mates piggy-backing them away to live for another day or to slip their earthly bonds. An estimated 68 prisoners were beaten to death at Hellfire Pass.

76. In the middle of October 1943, hauled by a steam engine, a party of Japanese generals and colonels travelled up the line in *attap*-roofed flatcars. They alighted at the point 157 kilometres from Thanbyuzayat where the two railway tracks had lately converged. As the film cameras of a propaganda unit rolled, two Japanese colonels drove in the final spikes to signal the completion of the Railway of Death. Happy Japanese soldiers stood by for the cameras, shouting their *banzai-banzais* to the Emperor.

The following month, Colonel Nagatomo visited camps along the line to pontificate his valedictory address and deliver a letter of condolence to the spirits of deceased POWs. Once again, his addresses were transcribed into English for the men to read. They found his words engendered only revulsion. 'I have done my utmost to discharge my duties conscientiously, taking responsibility for you all as your commander ...' A Dutch officer in one of the camps rebuffed him in front of the assembled men and demanded to know where all the Red Cross parcels and personal mail were that the IJA had been withholding from prisoners.

'We have achieved this epochal and brilliant feat,' said the triumphant colonel. 'Happily let us celebrate this memorable day by having a very pleasant and cheerful time to everyone's heart's content.' The prisoners turned their gaze to cemeteries of dead comrades and to their assembled company, pop-eyed, knobble-kneed, with gaunt hips and ribs jutting through ragged apparel.

Nagatomo addressed the dead POWs. 'Now you have passed on to the other world, owing to the unavoidable diseases and indiscriminate bombing, I cannot see you in this world anymore. Visualising your situation and that of your relatives and families, I cannot help shedding tears sympathising with your unfortunate circumstances.'

Denial was to be an ongoing feature of the forthcoming Japanese capitulation, all the way up to the post-Hiroshima assessments by Emperor Hirohito himself. In his broadcast to the people of Japan announcing his country's complete and utter defeat, Hirohito suggested the trend of the war was 'not necessarily to Japan's advantage'.

Rohan Rivett stood there listening to Nagatomo's words and felt they were 'one of the most nauseating displays of Japanese hypocrisy that we were ever called upon to witness'. In assigning prisoners' deaths to 'unavoidable diseases and indiscriminate bombing', the Japanese colonel had omitted mention of the chief cause of the atrocity of the Railway of Death – the negligent administration and institutionalised sadism of the Imperial Japanese Army. Medicines, food and justice were available in Thailand and Burma – that they were not delivered to starving and dying men was due at best to the IJA's utter incompetence, and at worst to its deliberate savagery. POWs and *romusha* were put to pitiless deaths in their tens of thousands as a direct consequence of this brutish negligence.

Neither did the pompous Nagatomo make mention of the IJA's disturbed policy of torturing prisoners, summary executions and brutal beatings that blew so many innocent souls away. The evidence of the IJA's sadism is extensive: the beheadings, the bayonetings, the live burials, the deliberate starvations, the crucifixions, the vivisections, the range of fatal water tortures – the list goes on.

Somewhere near 100,000 people lost their lives on the construction of the IJA's railway, setting in stone the record of one dead man for every sleeper laid. For the families of the fallen, there was not just the never-ending sorrow of premature loss, but the subsequent knowledge of the futility of it all. As the war worked its way to an inevitable conclusion, Allied bombers blew to splinters the bridges and causeways assembled at the cost of their loved ones' lives. Termites went to work on what remained of the woodwork, and in the end, most of the rails of the IJA's 'epochal and brilliant feat' were removed by the government of Thailand for use elsewhere.

77. Thanks to Tamarkan's fastidious disciplinary standards set down during the construction of the two adjacent bridges, it was known as the cleanest camp on the line. Credit for that goes to Colonel Toosey of the 135th Hertfordshire Yeomanry Regiment, a universally respected soldier, quite unlike the character masquerading as him in the movie the *Bridge on the River Kwai*. With the completion of the railway, in spite of the Tamarkan camp being cheek-by-jowl with two strategic bridges – or perhaps because of this – the IJA ordered the camp to be expanded. It would now hold most of the POWs lugged from the railway's jungle camps and its hospital was expanded accordingly. As a result of its precarious position, many prisoners were to lose their lives to the bitterly ironic bombs of Allied raids.

By the time the survivors of Anderson and Williams Force reached Tamarkan, Colonel Toosey had been moved on to work on other camps in Thailand. But his legacy remained. His rear party, made up of mainly British servicemen and a few Australians, were still there, and Dr Richards says, 'their generosity and kindness were more than we could possibly have hoped for'. These were men who knew what the new arrivals had been subjected to, for all through 1943, sick POWs had been coming down the line to Tamarkan from the jungle camps. They arrived in windowless cattle trucks, up to forty men stacked in foetid metal containers, some dead on arrival, the rest in very bad shape. Of the arrivals, Colonel Toosey recorded, 'As a typical example I can remember one man who was so thin he could be lifted easily in one arm. His hair was growing down his back and was full of maggots. His clothing consisted of a ragged pair of shorts, soaked with dysentery excreta. He was lousy, and covered with flies all the time. He was so weak he was unable to lift his hand to brush away the flies which clustered in his eyes and on the sore places of his body.' There would be time enough for outrage: what was required of Toosey and his men was palliative action, and they moved smartly to it. (Toosey's observations are quoted on page 68 of Brian MacArthur's *Surviving The Sword.*)

The men of Anderson Force spent the first three months of 1944 recuperating at Tamarkan, until the announcement of the selection of 900 men to go to Japan. Of those who chose to go from Tamarkan and other camps in Thailand, only the young and relatively fit were selected by the Japanese medical officers. To some it seemed a rash decision to leave the relative sanctuary of Tamarkan, but others reasoned it was better to get away from whatever the Japanese had planned for those who remained. They had first-hand knowledge of the poor quality of IJA behaviour in Thailand and all had suffered from the awful tropical diseases of the railway. Thus, Tamarkan saw the break-up of Anderson Force, though many of the men would remain together in the six new *kumi*, each of these numbering 150 prisoners bound for undisclosed tasks in Japan. The Holman brothers were bound for Japan, and so too Brigadier Varley, Dr Richards and Roy Whitecross. But it was farewell to Jim Armstrong and Pinkey Rhodes, the orderlies who had kept so many of them alive on the railway, for they were not on the Japan list.

78. After France's capitulation to Germany in June 1940, a French puppet government was established south-west of Paris in the city of Vichy. Thereafter, for most of its chequered existence, Vichy France retained tenuous control over most of France's overseas possessions, including the prized territories of Indo-China. The latter came under the avaricious gaze of Tokyo, for the French territories were pivotal to the interests of the IJA in blocking supply lines into southern China. In September 1940, Vichy France had agreed to Japan establishing bases in Indo-China, which were then used as jumping-off points for the upcoming invasion of Malaya.

In early 1944, Robert Holman and his POW companions found themselves loitering in Saigon, with the shaky accord between Japan and the Vichy French still in place. The Senegalese troops Robert Holman refers to were the *Tirailleurs Senegalais*, colonial troops recruited from the French possessions of Central and West Africa.

In taking the POWs to Saigon, the Japanese intention was for their human chattels to embark on cargo boats for the trip north to Japan. But as it happened, American submarine activity and Allied bombing of Axis shipping made the embarkation from Saigon impractical. As a result, some POWs bound for Japan were to see the war out in Saigon, while others like Robert Holman, after a few months' sojourn in Saigon, were sent south to Singapore for trans-shipment north.

79. By the time the men arrived back in Singapore towards the end of June 1944, they'd lost most of the good effects of Saigon. The six-day train ride from Phnom Penh on starvation rations, tightly packed into windowless goods trucks, had seen to that. The dormant diseases of Burma and Thailand returned to ravage them and it would take weeks in Singapore for scrounged food and medicine to get the prisoners back to a semblance of health. Instead of returning to Changi, the Japan-bound prisoners were put into camps at River Valley Road and the offshore island of Pulau Damarlaut, where scant rations and guard brutality resembled the bad days of Burma.

In his book *The Blue Haze*, Les Hall recalls how the returning prisoners were shocked by the state of Singapore. 'Gone were the teeming crowds and crowded docks ... the downtrodden looks on the faces of the residents indicated the savagery of Nipponese control of the once busy city ... it was no longer Singapore – it was a dismal, lifeless place where misery held top billing.' Syonan-to, imperial Japan's shining light in the south, had been reduced to a dull rag-lamp, and the Greater East Asia Co-Prosperity Sphere had proved to be what everyone suspected it was from the outset, a fancy name for the asset-stripping of occupied lands. Food was scarce, inflation rampant and memories of the savage Sook Ching Massacre haunted Singapore's waterfront.

80. *Rakuyo Maru's* convoy was struck by American submarines 350 kilometres off the South China coast, with the loss of an escort destroyer, an accompanying oil tanker and the vessel *Kachidoki Maru* with its cargo of 1,000 British POWs. After *Rakuyo Maru* was hit, the rubber in its hold helped keep the ship afloat for twelve hours and seeing this, prisoners who'd abandoned ship on impact subsequently swam back to the doomed hulk. These men clambered up to join the calmer heads who had yet to abandon ship, and began to assemble makeshift rafts and scrounge what they could for the dire days ahead. Some of these men were those who had survived the sinking of HMAS *Perth,* against all odds, nearly three years before. What bitter irony, after all the festering IJA prison camps, that these men were bound for the water again.

The attack on the convoy occurred before dawn on 12 September 1944, but it wasn't until dusk that two convoy frigates returned to pick up survivors. These warships only allowed Japanese on board, flicking back into the water any Allied prisoners who made it up their net-ladders. As night approached the frigates departed, leaving the Allied prisoners to their watery fate. Seeing the Japanese lifeboats now drifting empty, some of the POWs swam over and claimed them, then paddled around in the failing light picking prisoners from the brine.

In all there were twelve lifeboats filled to the gunnels with men, with the other survivors bobbing about in the water, hanging onto anything that floated. The corpses of the drowned men were regretfully pushed away, as the oil slick of the doomed tanker spread its foul carpet over the surrounding sea. The occupants of one of the lifeboats decided to leave the depressing scene and sail east to the Philippines. They were never heard of again. The remainder drifted west, the wind and sea taking them slowly towards China.

On the morning of their third day adrift, the scattered lifeboats were approached by a Japanese frigate and two corvettes. From the direction of where a group of seven lifeboats manned by Brigadier Varley, Dr Chalmers and over 200 men were last seen, came the sound of naval gunfire and long suffering ended for those POWs as they sank to watery graves.

Now the frigate approached the remaining four lifeboats, on board one of which was Dr Rowley Richards. To his surprise they were taken on board and put in a huddle on the foredeck, a group of 136 severely sunburnt, starving, dehydrated, exhausted men. The next day they arrived in Hainan in southern China and were transferred to an oil tanker, on board which were the British POW survivors of the *Kachidoki Maru*. There were about 500 of them, the other 500 of their number having gone down with the ship. These men were in a very bad way, as they had spent 24 hours swimming in an oil slick and most were burnt or blinded.

For Dr Richards, the oil tanker gathering was a Dantesque nightmare at the very edge of mental and physical tolerance. He records that in spite of the macabre sight and smell of all this burnt human flesh, the Japanese refused to provide medical supplies or any form of assistance except for a bucket and a length of rope.

> In the absence of fresh water we had to use sea water to try and wipe oil from their eyes, skin and matted hair. Their skin looked as if it had melted, blisters erupting in patches. There was anguish on the face of each of these men. The decks of the tanker were steel and hot as hell. Little could be done until after sunset; their burned eyes and skin could barely tolerate our touch beneath the sun. With their disfigured faces and scorched bodies, these men were the living dead. The stench of their burned skin was ghastly. I reached my physical limit of tolerance at about ten to fifteen minute intervals, when I would have to move away to vomit and breathe in some fresh air for a minute or two before being able to return to the men.

The survivors of this group of prisoners were subsequently delivered to Japan in the hold of a whaling ship.

Some of the prisoners of the *Rakuyo Maru* who never made it to the lifeboats had better luck. Oil-slicked human flotsam, they just drifted around the South China Sea, until quite incredibly, between 13 and 17 September, American submarines plucked them from the ocean. In all, the Americans rescued 159 of their unintended victims, seven of whom had but a short taste of freedom, dying before landfall could be made. When the living were safely repatriated, it was this group of dogged survivors who were the first to tell the outside world of what really happened on the Railway of Death.

81. While Robert and Jack Holman laboured on in Singapore, in the month of October 1944 away to the north-east the largest sea battle of the Pacific War took place in Leyte Gulf in the Philippines. With the island of Leyte secured by US forces and the rest of the Philippines falling into Allied hands in ensuing months, Japan's links to the oil resources of its conquered South-east Asian territories were virtually severed; and with little naval or air-force cover now available, the chances of convoys making it through unscathed from Singapore to Japan became negligible.

But Japan was desperate for oil, so a convoy of oil tankers was assembled in Singapore in December to undertake the perilous voyage north. Accompanying them would be the vessel *Awa Maru*, which would carry Japanese civilians in its forward hold and the last shipment of POWs out of Singapore in its aft hold.

When the 600 prisoners boarded the *Awa Maru* on 16 December, they were forced into a hold in which they found three platform levels with just four feet of headroom between each tier. Guards posted at the doorway controlled when men were allowed on deck, with this proving to be a daylight privilege, all men being confined to the suffocating hold at night. For the next ten days, the men sweltered on the *Awa Maru* waiting for the ship to leave Singapore.

Roy Whitecross describes conditions in the hold, when for the first two hours on board the hold doorway was locked and the 600 men were left to cook within. Storm Trooper, the same infamous bully of the Burma camps, supervised this mass confinement with blows from his rifle butt.

> On the low platforms the men were jammed tightly with their knees under their chins, and in the open space below the hatch we were standing so close together that no one could move. Out on deck the temperature was about 85 degrees; we could only guess what it was inside ... As men collapsed they were passed out to the doorway ... in such a tightly packed mass, it was impossible for anyone to lift an unconscious man onto his shoulder and walk out with him, so we had to pass them from one to the other until they reached the door. In doing this many of them were dropped, as men found it impossible to grip the wet, slippery bodies with their own wet hands.

On 26 December the convoy finally left Singapore, hugging the coast by day and often anchoring in sheltered harbours at night. Passing Saigon, the prisoners gauged the success of Allied bombing by the many masts of sunken vessels protruding from the water and assessed their own slim chances of avoiding the bombs and torpedoes of 'friendly fire'.

82. As the *Awa Maru* approached Japan, a celebratory meal of pink rice was passed around. It was the normal meagre ration, but was coloured by a few drops of synthetic cochineal, symbolising poverty of circumstance as much as safe deliverance. Against the odds the convoy had made it through unscathed, thanks to that intervening storm and America's concurrent preoccupation with the liberation of the Philippines. From the steamy heat of Singapore, the POWs were now delivered into Japan's coldest winter in forty years. The *Awa Maru* entered the Shimonoseki Strait and on 15 January 1945 tied up at the port of Moji on Kyushu Island's northern shore. The prisoners who had for so long enjoyed the 'favours infinite' of the living god, the 'inestimable' Hirohito, were about to set foot on his hallowed land.

83. Men from the *Rakuyo Maru* suffered similar treatment when they were marched through Tokyo, shuffling barefoot and with only blankets wrapped around their shoulders. 'Men were so weak and bone-thin they could barely stand upright,' wrote Dr Richards. 'Many had lost control over their bowels and their blankets and skin were stained with defecation. Some of the locals seemed stunned by our condition, their mouths agape; others chose to jeer and laugh loudly as we passed them by. This was almost too much for any man to endure ... listening to the sound of fellow humans laughing at our suffering remains one of the lowest moments of my life.'

    With the *Awa Maru's* arrival in Japan, the POWs saw the last of their Korean guards. From now until the end of the war the responsibility for bashing the enfeebled prisoners lay with the IJA and its *Kempei Tai*. The men were now divided into three groups of 200, and sent off to different destinations. The group containing Roy Whitecross and the Holman brothers was taken by train to the industrial city of Omuta, on Kyushu's western shores.

84. They arrived at Omuta, shivering in the frigid dark, several hours before dawn. As they passed through the fortified gates of their new home, snow was falling and the POWs saw guards gathered around a charcoal brazier. Around the camp, pallid pools of electric light illuminated a wooden enclosing wall, twice the height of a man, festooned with three strands of electrified wire.

    Known as Fukuoka Branch Camp No. 17, the place they'd arrived at was one of the largest POW camps in Japan, housing around 1,800 prisoners in long lines of wooden huts. Within the camp walls there was a big mess hall, a hospital of sorts and rudimentary communal baths. Then there was accommodation for the IJA and a guard-house. The latter they learnt had a punishment sweat box, a 1.2 m x 1.2 m metal box into which prisoners could be stuffed as an alternative to the guard-house cells where temperatures hung around freezing point.

    The Australians were ushered in from the snow and fed cabbage soup

273

in the mess hall. Here, for the first time since the fall of Singapore, they ate at tables and chairs. At the break of dawn an Australian officer, Lieutenant Howell, entered the mess hall and gave the new arrivals a briefing.

Howell told them there were American, Dutch, British and Australian prisoners in the camp. The British worked in a zinc foundry, while the Dutch laboured on the adjacent wharves, coaling ships. A group of Americans had cornered all the cushy jobs in the camp, with the remainder of them joining the Aussies slaving in a nearby coal mine.

Down in the mine they would work in shifts around the clock, with each shift lasting twelve hours. They were supposed to get a thirty-minute break underground in which to consume what passed for rations, but they should consider themselves lucky if they got twenty minutes. For every ten days worked underground, they'd get a day off, during which day they should be prepared for constant mental and physical harassment by the IJA guards.

Next they learnt they were to be given haircuts by a camp barber. The rule was they must keep their hair at all times shorter than half an inch (1.3 cm). Anyone not obeying this rule would receive a severe bashing from the guards. Of course, the same punishment would be meted out to anyone who omitted to salute a guard. They must be prepared for endless numberings-off at all phases of their working day and would learn that numbering-off at the mine-head at 4 am in light clothing with snow falling at their feet had to be endured without complaint.

Towards the end of the briefing, IJA guards arrived in the mess hall to commence an intense search of the prisoners' scant belongings, in the course of which the guards confiscated anything of remaining worth to the POWs: pens, watches, tools, paper and string. Lieutenant Howell advised the men to surrender any hidden items, as the guards occasionally made surprise searches in the huts, and when they did, 'If they find anything, heaven help you'.

When the search finally ended, a Japanese officer got up onto a mess table and divided the men into groups of six, making each group swear on their honour not to escape. After that they were issued with clothing – a long pair of underpants, a shirt and a British army greatcoat – and were taken to the communal bath-house for their first bath in a very long time.

When they finally got to their allocated huts, it seemed unbelievable. Mitsui had originally constructed these structures as the labour lines for civilian employees. They were basic but clean, and what looked like warm bedding issue had been laid on for each prisoner. After all they'd been through, it seemed they'd finally arrived on Easy Street. They would soon learn otherwise.

85. In *Slaves of the Son of Heaven*, Roy Whitecross describes his first visit down the Omuta mine. His curiosity for a new experience was immediately dampened at the mine-head by the sight of a Japanese miner being carried out with a broken arm and two broken legs. The Australians crammed into little trucks that drew them down a long, dank tunnel, with their heads ducked and elbows firmly at their sides. Fifteen hundred feet under the ground, they were offloaded into a stone-strewn tunnel. This was their new work environment.

> In the cavern beyond, twenty American prisoners were working a long wall. In the confined space the roar of machinery and the clank of the scraper-chain made speech all but impossible. The coal dust hung in the air like a black fog, dimming our miners' lamps and making the whole scene more unrealistic. The men were dirty beyond description. Coal dust is oily and clings to the skin. The whole scene had a nightmarish quality.

The men came out of the mine with coal dust worked into their skin and every orifice. They smelt bad. There was no water supply underground other than water pouring through cracks in shaft ceilings. Neither were there latrines, only fouled sections of the mine floor used by the diarrhoea-ridden men. Underground, sweating at the coal-face, conditions were hot; but when they got into the main shaft to exit the mine, a cold wind hit them. They weren't allowed to take their greatcoats to the mine, so for the first months of 1945 the prisoners shivered their way through the mine-head *tenko* before marching back to camp for their communal bath. The bath sounded good, but coal dust was ingrained in them, and they never really got clean at Omuta.

86. There were other amputations arising from the effects of IJA punishments. A report by the senior American doctor of the Omuta camp, Dr Thomas Hewlett, states that a young 'Australian soldier named David Runge, was forced to kneel in front of the guard-house for thirty-six hours. During the period he developed gangrene of both feet; bilateral amputation was carried out on March 10th, 1945.' When Lieutenant Howell had observed that Runge's barefoot feet were freezing to the floor of the *aeso*, the guard-house cells, he protested to the camp commandant, Captain Fukuhara, who was unmoved by Howell's plea. Runge's crime was that he'd been overheard advising other prisoners that they shouldn't work too hard at first, since the important thing was to keep working without stopping throughout your entire twelve-hour shift. After the Australian's feet were amputated, a group of IJA guards was seen giggling and playing around with the severed body parts.

Even those hardened to the brutal violence of the guards on the Railway of Death were stunned by the sadism at Omuta. Roy Whitecross recalls that

> ... the guards seized an American for having in his possession a torn scrap of Japanese newspaper. It was Hubbard, the kindly Yank who had lent me his mirror the day after Fukuhara had flogged me. If Hubbard had been found carrying a bomb, the Japanese could not have made more of a fuss. He was bashed by the entire guard and thrown into the aeso. Next day, three Kempei corporals came to the camp. They beat Hubbard to death with their rifle butts. For four days Hubbard's screams echoed across the subdued camp — until merciful death claimed him at last.

Dr Hewlett reports that, 'one prisoner of the A detail was executed for attempting to learn to read Japanese. He was utilized as the target for a bayonet drill by the guard detail. His body when examined showed over seventy-five stab wounds.' Stabbing was an approved IJA method of punishment, demonstrated up and down the realm of Japan's territories from Tarawa in the east to Rangoon in the west. Omuta was no exception and in May 1944, US serviceman Noah Heard was caught stealing from the camp's Red Cross stores. Red Cross parcels, sent from America to help sustain the POWs, were not distributed to them, but were enjoyed as ration supplements by the Japanese guards and the Democrat clique (see note 91). Heard was thus stealing what was rightfully his own property. For this 'crime', Heard was tied to a post and used for IJA bayonet practice. The American officers were forced to stand by and watch Heard being stabbed to death.

87. Dr Hewlett's report on Fukuoka Branch Camp No. 17 states that, 'Early in the course of starvation, hunger is overwhelming and the theft of food by such a person is not a criminal act. Corporal Pavlokos was starved to death in the guard-house for stealing food. It took sixty-two days to accomplish this execution; benefit of trial was denied.' Corporal Pavlokos of the US Marines won the Silver Star for bravery in the defence of Corregidor. In Omuta he got on the wrong side of Lieutenant Little (see note 91) and was turned over to the IJA guards for trading in food.

88. US army staff sergeant, Frank Stecklein, wrote a post-war affidavit that gives a clear picture of the camp's guard-house punishments. 'On 13th May, 1945, I was in charge of a detail working near Red Cross boxes in the Japanese store. I refused to let the men steal but later one of them gave me a can of salmon, with which I was caught.' Taken to the Japanese camp commandant with three other members of his detail, Stecklein was punched in the face by the commandant and kicked many times on the shins. The prisoners were then stripped of their upper clothing and repeatedly beaten across the back and shoulders until they were lacerated and bleeding.

> We were then taken and made to kneel down outside the guard-house. Small
> rocks were placed beneath our knees and then pieces of timber placed under

our shins, so that the whole weight of our bodies rested on a few sharp jagged points of rock. We were only a few feet from the guards and any movement on our part to try and relax our legs was immediately punished by kicks and punches. We were not allowed to sleep at any time during the four days of our detention. When our eyes closed from sheer fatigue we were immediately kicked into wakefulness.

Four times each day, the kneeling prisoners were bashed with a pole swung like a baseball bat. During the night the guards amused themselves by pouring buckets of icy water over the prisoners and taking turns to punch, kick or strike them with their rifle butts. These nights were spent topless, the prisoners being left to shiver through frequent heavy falls of rain. In the morning when the relieving guard took over, the bashings began with new ferocity, one notorious guard specialising in a cat o' nine tails kind of strap. 'I thought he would never stop,' wrote Stecklein. 'I begged for mercy but he kept on and on.'

One night in Stecklein's *aeso* ordeal, one of the guards 'decided to relieve his boredom by practising ju-jitsu. He flung me over his shoulder about six times onto the rough ground, besides subjecting me to several painful holds. About midnight a guard urinated in our faces. We were now given short heavy sticks and made to beat each other over the head. This continual beating was one of the worst features of our torture.' On the morning of the fourth day, the men were given their first sustenance since their punishment began – a drink of dirty water, from a trough in which cement had been mixed. After more beating in the camp commandant's office that morning, the men were made to sign a declaration promising never again to cause the Japanese authorities trouble. By midday, hardly able to walk, they were forced back to the mines to work, where because the four men 'could not perform our work to the satisfaction of the mine foreman, we were reported to the guards at the mine who gave us a severe beating.' Stecklein's account can be found at www.mansell.com/pow_resources/camplists/fukuoka/Fuku_17/stecklein.htm

89. Eighty-eight per cent of the men in camp had contracted malaria while they were in the tropics, and along with the effects of this disease, fevers from dengue fever endemic to Kyushu kept the hospital full. No X-ray facilities were available and drugs were limited, so death was a frequent visitor. The other killer at Omuta was pneumonia, with the Australians and Dutch showing the highest morbidity. Dr Hewlett writes of Robert Holman's POW group, 'It should be noted that the second Australian detail that arrived in January 1945, showed the highest morbidity and mortality of any group in this camp. They arrived from the tropics in wintertime.' The pneumonia was caused by the camp's starvation diet, persistent upper respiratory irritations as a result of gases and dust in the mine, continuous exposure to extremes of temperature in the mine ranging from 0 to 40 degrees Celcius, and lack of adequate heating in the camp buildings.

90. At Omuta the new Australian arrivals had to quickly learn that the prisoner honesties and comradely spirit of the camps in Burma and Singapore were a thing of the past. Here they couldn't hang wet clothes on a line to dry without keeping guard over them; to not do so was to lose them quick-smart. The same went for meals and utensils in the mess hall, for this was a camp where thieving, cheating and racketeering was the way of life and the Aussies would have to use their wits to get by. Starving men traded meagre rations for a few cigarettes and a complex system of mental accounting and illegal trading in food took up much of the camp's routine. There were acknowledged bankrupts and receivers appointed to manage the gradual repayment of food and cigarette debts from the overcommitted problem cases to their creditors. Enforcers were not to be tangled with in this economy of desperados.

91. Omuta was ruled by the Mitsui bosses at the mine and IJA guards at the camp, but there was an American mafia to deal with as well. It was run by a group called the Democrats, all first-arrival POWs out of the Philippines in 1943. It

is well documented that Fukuoka Branch Camp No. 17 was one of the most infamous 'King Rat' lairs of the war, and the Democrats of Omuta made life hell for anyone who tried to cross their rackets. The head of the Democrats triumvirate was Lieutenant Edward Little of the US Navy, in charge of all messing arrangements at the camp. His accomplices were two American sergeants.

In a camp of starving men, this mafia triumvirate was always well-fed; they had their own rooms and dressed immaculately at all times. They bribed their way out of ever having to work in the mines. Anyone who was not prepared to go along with them was branded a Republican and found himself working down the mine. They judged, for instance, that the senior American officer Captain A.C. Tisdelle was a Republican, which is why he became so thin and gaunt. The Democrats had decided to 'starve the bastard to death', according to the account given by G.P. Adams in his memoir, *No Time for Geishas*.

The mafia enforced its repellent regime by dobbing in POWs for brutal punishment by the IJA guards. Lieutenant Little handed one prisoner over to the IJA for stealing twelve buns and after days of torture by the guards, the prisoner died. There is some consolation in knowing Little was arrested after the war, and was court-martialled from the navy.

92. To escape the cycle of slavery in the mines of Baron Mitsui, there developed among the Omuta prisoners a culture of self-inflicted wounds. Men would insert limbs into machinery or position themselves under heavy rocks which they'd then prise loose to fall and injure themselves. Prisoners would rub lime from the latrines into chronic ulcers to prevent these from healing, so that the doctors would have to hospitalise them or place them on light duties.

Someone called the Bone Crusher could be hired to break an arm or a leg for an exhausted POW, and the camp doctors became adept at recognising his work. The Mitsui officials must have got wind of this gruesome ruse, for Dr Hewlett's report says that as a general rule, 'if a prisoner suffered an injury in the mine, some physical punishment was administered underground before he was brought to the surface. This punishment was handled by the civilian Japanese overmen.'

The daily reality of Omuta was that the prisoners were in the grip of acute anxiety, sustained by the IJA's horrific regime and the perpetually dangerous conditions of the decrepit Mitsui mine. Hardly a day passed when someone wasn't being cruelly tortured at the guard-house gates, screams from the *aeso* being the haunting theme of Fukuoka Branch Camp No. 17. And however much gaunt prisoners sent up prayers for deliverance from their daily injustice, or · schemed of ways to escape individual tragedies, there was really no recourse, for the rule of camp commandant Captain Fukuhara was absolute.

There are many recorded incidents of the sadism of Captain Asao Fukuhara, typical of the inhumane officer mentality recorded by the survivors of the IJA prisoner-of-war camps. Roy Whitecross had carried a trivial scrap of blanket with him all the way from Burma to Omuta. Trying to dispose of it in a camp trash-bin resulted in him being taken to Fukuhara's office to account for the rag. Whitecross describes Fukuhara as a small man, 'hardly over five feet tall, with a dapper appearance marred by an almost total lack of neck ... his face was round and slightly pig-like, with small beady, black eyes. He was typical of the military officer caste, monstrously blown up with arrogance and conceit.' Whitecross soon discovered he was in a no-win situation, and that Fukuhara had predetermined to punish him with a vengeance. The blanket was deemed to be IJA property and therefore not something a prisoner could dispose of. After a cursory interrogation, the diminutive captain began screaming and kicking out at his victim with his polished riding boots. Next Fukuhara picked up a heavy leather belt and began flogging the prisoner:

I was kneeling, and he stood over me on my left side and struck every blow across my head, so that the belt curled and whipped into my eyes. It was a deliberate, sadistic attempt to blind me. I knew that if I attempted to shield my face it would only lead to more torture. How many times the belt whipped into my face and my eyes I have no idea. Suddenly, a vicious kick sent me sprawling onto my back, and as Fukuhara stood over me, I realised that he was again lashing at my unprotected face. Instinct this time made me shelter my face.

With the depravity of this whipping finally concluded, the diminutive camp commandant had Whitecross taken to the dreaded cells of the *aeso*. Outside the guard-house, he was required to stand at attention with blood oozing from his face and shins, in temperatures not much above freezing, with his right eye blinded and the right side of his head skinless and swollen. Ordered to strip of all clothing except trousers and shoes, if Whitecross tried to move his arms for warmth, he was immediately threatened by the IJA guards. After a while he ceased his violent shivers and just turned blue.

Roy Whitecross's vigil was broken when a guard coming in from his post put his rifle in the guard-house rack and collected a heavy sword. 'He motioned me down to the end of a passage, and after making me kneel proceeded to go through the motions of decapitating me. Several times I felt the cold steel on the back of my neck … This was another instance of Japanese mentality. Every opportunity was seized to try to inflict cruelty, mental or physical.' Eventually the guard tired of his game and returned the prisoner to his ten-hour vigil outside the *aeso*. That night he was ordered into a narrow cell with a latrine manhole at the end, through which an icy wind was blowing. Sleep was impossible on the frigid floor of the cell. Several hours before dawn, he was sent to work at the mine but was returned to his guard-house cell at night. This was to be the pattern for the next nine days, working in the perdition of the coal-dump, only to return to the sleepless frigid nights and starvation rations of the guard-house cell.

93. The air-raid shelters at Omuta were not for the claustrophobic. In *No Time for Geishas*, Lieutenant Geoffrey Adams of the British 18th Division described conditions inside them:

*They had been intended for five hundred men, the original US contingent;
now the entire camp strength of some two thousand was forced into them,
with much beating and screaming from the guards, and the doors locked.
It was frightful inside; they were a mere three feet below ground level, and
consisted of thin wooden boards packed round with spoil from the coal mine,
so they offered scant protection from HE bombs. The headroom was only
five foot six inches; and the crush was such that those who fainted were held
upright by the press of people round them. We set up organized shouting, as
we had on Hioki Maru; but without effect. We were not allowed out until the
'All Clear' had sounded.*

94. The men were continually hungry and dietary deficiency was the main cause
    of death at the camp. Shortage of food was understandable in Japan's war
    conditions, but what wasn't acceptable was the post-war proof that since 1944
    the IJA had been withholding Red Cross food and medical supplies, gifts from
    the American people, in nearby Omuta warehouses.

    Dr Hewlett's report identifies epidemics of diarrhoea and acute enteritis
    as arising from the serving of whale blubber and questionable soups said to be
    of fish or shellfish. The prisoners called these outbreaks 'Hirohito's curse' or
    '*benjo* boogie'. *Benjo* is Japanese for toilet, a word all IJA prisoners learnt as soon
    as ubiquitous diarrhoea and occasional dysentery entered their daily lives.

95. In *The Japanese Thrust*, Lionel Wigmore records that in June 1945, Omuta and
    its surrounding areas were subjected to regular bombings by Allied aircraft.
    Then in July and August, 'Allied aircraft were over Japan in force every day.
    Much of the off-shift time was spent in air-raid shelters where proper rest was
    impossible; in July an incendiary raid destroyed many of the camp huts.' On
    9 August one of the camp's hospital orderlies counted 730 multi-engined Allied
    planes in the skies above Omuta.

96. Fukuoka Branch Camp No. 17 sat on Omuta's foreshore, built on land reclaimed by tippings from the coal mine. Across the harbour lay a many-bayed peninsula, in one of which, less than forty miles distant, was the city of Nagasaki. Early on the morning of 9 August 1945, the B29 Superfortress *Bockscar*, piloted by Major Charles Sweeney, USAF, took off from Tinian in the Northern Mariana Islands. On board was the plutonium bomb Fat Man. The destination of *Bockscar* was the arsenal town of Kokura, next door to the port of Moji where the *Awa Maru* had disgorged its human cargo seven months earlier. On 6 August, Kokura had been the secondary target for the first atomic bomb, but the skies over Hiroshima were clear that day, so Kokura escaped unscathed. Now fate was favouring Kokura once more, for *Bockscar* made three runs over its target, but each time cloud cover denied the visual sighting required by the bombardier. On board the B29 fuel was running low, so the decision was made to make for the secondary target of Nagasaki. If that too proved to be cloud-covered, they would fly on to Okinawa and jettison the bomb at sea, for their cargo was too deadly to risk landing with it.

   On arrival over Nagasaki, the clouds were still a problem and *Bockscar* circled around in a last-ditch attempt to drop its deadly cargo. On the ground, no air-raid sirens were sounded for it was assumed the circling plane was only on reconnaissance. At the last minute, bombardier Kermit Beahan made a visual sighting through the clouds. He was looking at Urakami, Nagasaki's industrial valley, location of Mitsubishi's steel, arms and ordnance factories. Fat Man descended. Five hundred metres above ground, the bomb exploded with the force of 21 kilotons of TNT, generating a searing heat of 7,000 degrees Fahrenheit and winds of well over 600 kilometres per hour. Some 40,000 people were transformed to ash in a matter of seconds. Before the year was out, the bomb's death toll would be double that number, as burns and radiation sickness took their toll.

97. In his address to the American people following the bombing of Hiroshima, President Truman described the terrible weapon he had unleashed:

It is the harnessing of the basic power of the universe. The force from which the sun draws its power has been loosed against those who brought war to the Far East ... We are now prepared to obliterate more rapidly and completely every productive enterprise the Japanese have above ground in any city. We shall destroy their docks, their factories, and their communications. Let there be no mistake; we shall completely destroy Japan's power to make war. (Quoted in R.B. Frank, Downfall, p. 269)

The IJA and their Emperor had rejected the Allied demand for unconditional surrender issued in the form of the Potsdam Declaration of 26 July 1945. The Potsdam Declaration promised Japan prompt and utter destruction if it refused to comply, and listed what it should expect after surrender: an end to militarism in Japan, Japanese sovereignty would extend only to its home islands, Allied occupation of Japan would proceed, as would punishment of war criminals, including those who had 'visited cruelties upon our prisoners'.

The writing was on the wall for Japan's warmongers: accede to the Potsdam terms and their savage game would be up. Thus they chose, regardless of the cost to their people, to pursue a fight to the finish. The name of the IJA's Armageddon strategy was *Ketsu Go*, Operation Decisive, and it was founded on the belief that America would be so shocked by the scale of human loss accrued in the act of invading Japan that terms much better than 'unconditional' could then be brokered for a cease-fire.

But the destruction of Hiroshima and Nagasaki, coupled with Russia's land-grabbing declaration of war on Japan on 8 August, decimated Hirohito's hand. It was clear the game was now up. On 14 August, Hirohito addressed the Japanese people by radio for the first time, telling them in a roundabout sort of way that they'd just lost the war. The words of this speech set in motion a mindset of denial that has plagued Japan's relations with its Asian neighbours ever since. In his first national address, Hirohito told his subjects the war had been all about bringing peace and stability to Asia, and it had never been his intention to infringe on other people's sovereignty or invade their territory. It has been noted many times that the word 'surrender' is notably absent from the Emperor's 'endure the unendurable' speech. It was left to the Japanese representatives who stood on the deck of USS *Missouri* in Tokyo Bay on 2 September, to sign their names under the words 'unconditional surrender'.

98. Roy Whitecross found there was a sudden change of POW attitude towards the Japanese once the peace was declared. Getting their own back on their tormentors had dominated many a POW discussion over the last three and a half years, but now it was all over, there were few retributions. Roy puts this down to men now occupying their minds with the joys of freedom and the end of years of starvation and unspeakable war crimes. But sadly that was not all he concludes.

> *The Japs were beyond adequate punishment, for what punishment could be meted out to a people who had treated us as they had? ... We had learned to hate with such a hatred that there could be no fitting punishment for the acts that had bred this hatred ... All we wanted was to get away from them, to try to forget them, and in the security and love of our homes try to recover, physically and mentally.*

And Primo Levi speaks for all severely brutalised POWs when in *The Truce* he describes the shame on the faces of the young Russian soldiers who are the first to arrive at Auschwitz after the Germans abandoned it.

> *They did not greet us, nor did they smile; they seemed oppressed not only by compassion but by a confused restraint ... It was that shame we knew so well, the shame ... that the just man experiences at another man's crime; the feeling of guilt that such a crime should exist ... and that his will for good should have proved too weak or null, and should not have availed in defence.*

99. Adding those who died in the instant the atomic bombs exploded over Hiroshima and Nagasaki with those who would die from burns and radiation sickness in

the two cities before the year was out, it is estimated the two atomic bombs killed around 200,000 people. It is quite chilling to know that President Truman's intention was to keep dropping atomic bombs on selected targets in Japan until the Emperor and the IJA succumbed, the President resolutely stating as such in a White House press release sixteen hours after the Hiroshima explosion. The toll of death and destruction from such an onslaught is quite appalling to contemplate.

But Truman was a veteran of World War I and knew first hand that ground combat was every bit as deadly as dropping bombs from the sky. The course of action open to him, as the alternative to unleashing atomic weaponry, was Operation Olympic, under which the invasion of Japan would have swung into action in November 1945. The second phase of the invasion was Operation Coronet, which was to strike Tokyo's Kanto Plain on 1 March 1946. Had Operation Olympic gone ahead, Robert Holman's nightmare would have come true, for southern Kyushu was its designated invasion point, and what was left of Omuta would have faced a white-hot battle zone. Available evidence shows the IJA's eradication of POWs would have occurred as soon as Allied landings commenced.

American estimates for Operations Olympic and Coronet were for somewhere between 400,000 and 800,000 of their own servicemen to perish in the process. The same estimates figured between five and ten million Japanese would die, with higher figures arising if the civilian population carried through with the IJA's demand that civilians turn themselves into *kamikaze* cannon-fodder.

There is little doubt that with Allied control over the skies and seas of Japan complete, the US invasion force would have eventually prevailed, and that the prolonged subjugation process would have resulted in utmost damage to Japan and its populace. Even if, as the US Navy was proposing, an alternative strategy of blockade and bombardment was pursued, the results would have been dire. In spite of all these reckonings, Hirohito and the IJA remained adamant that unless safe-guarding of the imperial institution was part of the surrender terms, they would fight to the very end. These men were prepared to turn Japan into a massive ash-pit rather than give up their system of power.

287

In wider consideration of Truman's decision to drop the atomic bombs, there is another element often overlooked: the plight of the Asian populations trapped within Japan's military perimeter. As American historian Richard Frank points out, 'between a quarter of a million and four hundred thousand Asians, overwhelmingly non-combatants, were dying each month the war continued. Thus the challenge whether an assessment of Truman's decision can highlight only the deaths of noncombatant civilians in the aggressor nation while ignoring much larger death tolls among noncombatant civilians in the victim nations.'

There is a further group of humans who speak strongly in favour of Truman's decision. At war's end, over 120,000 barely-surviving POWs and internees remained under IJA guard in the camps of Asia-Pacific. Because of the Allied strategy of leap-frogging up through the islands towards Japan, the great majority of these camps remained unliberated and undetected. In these occupied territories, more than half a million IJA troops were still at battle stations, their commanders were as staunchly vicious as ever, and in the shortening of days, they were plotting their own desperate resolutions.

Back in 1944, the IJA had circulated orders to do away with POWs when and if Allied forces approached their locations, and camp commandants were free to ponder a variety of extermination options for their wards. POW accounts are virtually unanimous in their reportage that as the war's end drew nearer, IJA guards delighted in giving prisoners gestures of their impending execution. At POW Camp 10-A in Palawan in the Philippines, this extermination order was put into practice. On 14 December 1944, with the Americans advancing through the Philippines, the IJA contingent at Palawan packed their surviving prisoners into the camp's air-raid shelters, about 150 men in all. The shelters were narrow, covered trenches, like those described at the Omuta camp. Under the orders of Lieutenant Yoshikazu Sato, the IJA soldiers then poured gasoline into the trenches and set fire to the men inside. Prisoners who managed to burst from the conflagration were machine-gunned, bayoneted and clubbed as they emerged.

As the Allies approached North Borneo, the local IJA decided to demolish the POW camp that had serviced the construction of their Sandakan airstrip. In the first half of 1945, the IJA forced British and Australian prisoners into death-marches from their coastal Sandakan camp, through jungle swamps and mountain passes to a diseased camp at Ranau, 250 kilometres inland. Captain Susumi Hoshijima presided over this extended slaughter parade. Here the IJA's final solution was a cocktail of drawn-out starvation, the summary execution of exhausted stragglers by bayonet, sword, bullet and club, and the encouragement of pitiless disease. Over 1,300 Australians and 640 British prisoners were done to death in this way. By the end of the war, the surviving POWs at Ranau numbered only forty souls. Twelve days after the Emperor's radio broadcast advising Japan of its capitulation, the IJA executed these last survivors of the Sandakan death marches. Mention of the Sandakan atrocity should never omit the memory of some 4,000 Indonesian slave labourers who also lost their lives.

Thus Robert Holman is not alone in his endorsement of Truman's way. The majority of surviving POWs owed their lives to it and spoke of the American deliverance as their saving grace. In the final analysis, for them it was Emperor Hirohito and the Imperial Japanese Army who brought those dreadful weapons down on the people of Hiroshima and Nagasaki.

Bibliography

Adams, G.P., *No Time for Geishas*, Corgi, London, 1973.

Arneil, S., *One Man's War*, Sun Papermac, Melbourne, 1982.

Australian Dictionary of Biography, Melbourne University Press, Melbourne, 1993.

Bix, H.P., *Hirohito and the Making of Modern Japan*, HarperCollins,
New York, 2000.

Charlton, P., *War Against Japan 1941–1942*, Time-Life Books, Sydney, 1988.

Clarke, H.V., *Last Stop Nagasaki!*, George Allen & Unwin, Sydney, 1983.

Daws, G., *Prisoners of the Japanese*, William Morrow, New York, 1994.

Day, D., *The Politics of War*, HarperCollins Publishers, Sydney, 2003.

Dunlop, E.E., *The War Diaries of Weary Dunlop*, Penguin Books,
Ringwood, Vic., 1990.

Frank, R.B., *Downfall: The End of the Imperial Japanese Empire*,
Random House, New York, 1999.

Gibbs, J.M., *Prisoner of War Camps in Japan*, Liaison and Research Branch, American
Prisoners of War Information Bureau, Washington, 1946.

Hall, L., *The Blue Haze*, Kangaroo Press, Kenthurst, NSW, 1996.

Hardie, Dr R., *The Burma-Siam Railway: The Secret Diary of Dr Robert
Hardie*, Collins, Sydney, 1983.

Hewlett, T.H., Dai Ju Nana Bunsho (Camp #17) Nightmare Revisited, 1978,
www.mansell.com/pow_resources/camplists/fukuoka/Fuku_17/hewlett_report.html

Levi, P., *If This Is a Man*, Abacus, London, 1987.

_____, *The Truce*, Abacus, London, 1987.

Lomax, E., *The Railway Man*, Vintage, London, 1995.

MacArthur, B., *Surviving the Sword*, Random House, New York, 2005.

Miller, R., Unpublished notes from interview, Sydney, 4 December 2007.

Owen, F., *The Fall of Singapore*, Pan Books, London, 1960.

BIBLIOGRAPHY

Parkins, R., *Ray Parkin's Wartime Trilogy*, Melbourne University Press, Melbourne, 1999.

Peek, D.I., *One Fourteenth of an Elephant*, Pan Macmillan, Sydney, 2003.

Richards, R., Unpublished notes from interview, Sydney, 10 October 2007.

_____, *A Doctor's War*, HarperCollins, Sydney, 2006.

Richards, R. & McEwan, M., *The Survival Factor*, Kangaroo Press, Kenthurst, NSW, 1989.

Rivett, R., *Behind Bamboo*, Angus & Robertson, London, 1946.

Watson, C., Tears of Gratitude, Unpublished memoirs, Sydney, 1996.

Whitecross, R.H., *Slaves of the Son of Heaven*, Dymock's Book Arcade, Sydney, 1952.

Wigmore, L., *The Japanese Thrust*, Australian War Memorial, Canberra, 1957.

Editor's Acknowledgements

I salute Murdoch Books for seeing this project through; to Hazel Flynn for its conception, Juliet Rogers, Kay Scarlett and Colette Vella for making it happen, and Karen Ward for her wordsmithing skills.

To Robert's daughter, Annette Rayner, and to his niece Robyn Moss and her husband Peter, deep gratitude and respect. Multiple thanks to the University of Wollongong Archives, to Robert Holman's brother-in-law, John Downton, for his insights, and to Graham and Gwenneth Wishart for their hospitality in Gerringong.

Dr Rowley Richards and Roy Whitecross, veterans of many of the events recorded in this book and authors of definitive books on the Railway of Death, are living monuments to the Australian spirit. It was a singular honour to have sat by their sides and talked through POW issues of the Pacific War.

My mother-in-law, Loelie Wynberg, and my father, Sir Ian Thomson, both died while this book was being written, but not before giving extensive advice on its subject matter. He was a veteran of the Pacific War's Bougainville campaign; she spent her youth in IJA prison camps in Java. As ever, I pay homage to them both.

Index

The initials 'RH' refer to Robert Holman. The letter 'n' after a page number indicates a note.

First published in 2009 by Pier 9, an imprint of Murdoch Books Pty Limited

Murdoch Books Australia
Pier 8/9,
23 Hickson Road
Millers Point NSW 2000
Phone: +61 (0) 2 8220 2000
Fax: +61 (0) 2 8220 2558
www.murdochbooks.com.au

Murdoch Books UK Limited
Erico House, 6th Floor
93–99 Upper Richmond Road
Putney, London SW15 2TG
Phone: +44 (0) 20 8785 5995
Fax: +44 (0) 20 8785 5985
www.murdochbooks.co.uk

Chief Executive: Juliet Rogers
Publishing Director: Kay Scarlett

Commissioning Editors: Hazel Flynn and Colette Vella
Editor: Karen Ward
Design: Katy Wall
Production: Alexandra Gonzalez

Text copyright © Robert Holman and Peter Thomson 2009
The moral right of the authors has been asserted.
Design copyright © Murdoch Books Pty Limited 2009

National Library of Australia Cataloguing-in-Publication Data
    Author: Holman, Robert
    Title: On paths of ash : the extraordinary story of an Australian prisoner of war /
        Robert Holman ; edited by Peter Thomson.
    ISBN: 9781741962314 (pbk.)
    Notes: Bibliography; Index.
    Subjects: Holman, Robert. Holman, Jack. Changi (Concentration camp).
        Burma-Siam Railroad--History. World War, 1939-1945--Prisoners and prisons,
        Japanese. World War, 1939-1945--Personal narratives, Australian. World War,
        1939-1945--Conscript labor--Japan. Prisoners of war--Australia--Biography.
        Prisoners of war--Thailand--Biography. Prisoners of war--Burma--Biography.
        Prisoners of war--Japan--Biography. Prisoners of war--Singapore--Changi
        Nagasaki-shi (Japan)--History--Bombardment, 1945
        Other Authors/Contributors: Thomson, Peter.
    Dewey Number: 940.547252

Printed on FSC-accredited paper by Hangtai in 2009. Printed in China.